THE CROWDED HOURS

HOURS

The Story of Sos Cohen

Anthony Richardson

SAPERE
BOOKS

THE CROWDED
HOURS

Published by Sapere Books.

20 Windermere Drive, Leeds, England, LS17 7UZ,
United Kingdom

saperebooks.com

ISBN: 978-1-80055-711-6.

TABLE OF CONTENTS

FOREWORD

I don't suppose it has fallen to the lot of many Commanders-in-Chief to have on their staff a relatively junior officer wearing on his chest the ribbon of a medal awarded for a campaign that took place before he (the Commander-in-Chief) was born! But so it was with Sos Cohen.

It was stretching pretty far the terms of reference of a liaison officer at the Admiralty, to have him constantly flying on operational sorties. But it paid off handsomely. One would say, for instance, 'Sos, I'm not all that happy about the training of air gunners in such and such a squadron.' Sos's idea of checking on that was to sit in the tail turret of a Liberator for about fourteen hours in mid-winter over the North Atlantic on a convoy escort.

He was an inspiration to all of us, in the Headquarters and in the squadrons. One just could not keep him out of the air.

I have never put up a recommendation for a D.F.C. that I thought more well deserved than for old Sos in his seventieth year. A wonderful culmination to a life of daring adventure which this book describes so well.

John Slessor

'The thirst for adventure is the vent which Destiny offers; a war, a crusade, a gold mine, a new country, speak to the imagination and offer swing and play to the confined powers.' — Emerson

TO
V. M. C.
Mrs Sos

PRELUDE: 1944

There was something wrong. Sos was quite certain that there must be something wrong, because the last burst of 'flak' had been so close to the Halifax that it had shaken the aircraft and had seemed to leave it shuddering.

Two thousand feet below, he could see from his gunner's turret the two fierce red glowing patches of burning ships of the enemy convoy which they had just attacked. Above, the quarter-moon was bright. It was three hours back to base and the Halifax was behaving badly.

It was strange how familiar anyone could become with a particular aeroplane. He supposed it was the same with the comradeship that existed to such an intense degree amongst air-crews. The ever-present menace of disaster and death enhanced each moment and broke down barriers of reserve so that friendship blossomed out of acquaintanceship on the instant.

That's how it had been with Henry, his pilot, almost from the first. Henry flew the Halifax perfectly so that was why Sos now knew something was wrong. He had the feeling that the aircraft was crippled, but Henry would know what to do. Henry knew everything about aeroplanes, just the same as the rest of the crew of course, but Henry was outstanding.

He was tall and slender and dark-haired and his eyes were soft and gentle. He had moreover a slight lisp, which made it all the more incongruous that such a very gallant young man should have such a fragile air.

As soon as Sos had entered the Mess ten days ago he had encountered Henry. It had been a long drive down from

Admiralty, where Sos was the R.A.F. Coastal Command Liaison Officer; and he had wanted a drink. He had been fumbling at a bell-push when Henry had encountered him.

'It's no good pressing the tit in this joint,' Henry had said. 'They dropped some bombs on us last night and the current's off. You have to put your face round the Expense bar next door to the gentlemen's toilet. Then you shout.'

He'd spoken as if he were giving angelic advice to a Sunday class.

'Let me do it for you,' he said. 'What might it be?'

'Whisky with a little water.'

He'd returned and they drank.

Henry had been very much at ease, because he enjoyed with a most natural spontaneity playing host to any stranger visiting his Mess, which he treated with the familiarity and respect with which he would have treated his own home.

Sos for his part had not been so unembarrassed. For all his nigh seventy years and for all his encounters with life and evasions of death, he was essentially a diffident man. He had come to check up on the operational activities of Henry's station.

It had been the same old infallible argument at his headquarters.

'You ask me why Coastal Command aren't getting the results down there, sir. How can I answer you, if I'm not allowed to go and see?'

'Seeing' meant flying with the Squadron against the enemy.

'All right, Sos, off you go.' So he had gone.

Then he had been down amongst the lads again and this particular young warrior had taken stock of him, eyeing mildly the ribbons on the stranger's chest: the ribbons of the Matabele War, the Boer War, the First World War of 1914-18, the Order of the D.S.O., and the Military Cross. Henry had also noticed the half-wing brevet of an observer.

That had always been the way. First they wondered how Sos could be serving in any kind of active combatant force in the middle of the world's most devastating war, and then they had puzzled their brains to discover why he was allowed to fly. It was the sort of thing that didn't add up.

That was what had always made the first contact a little delicate, adding to that a distinct apprehension that anyone should come to regard his curiosity regarding their work as something connected with the foul and fearful act of 'snooping'. He had known more than one pilot who referred to members of high authority in Adastral House as 'Air Ministry Narks'.

But he had had no difficulty anywhere, so far. Nor had it been possible for him to see himself through the eyes of others. Once an inoffensively curious youngster had asked what he'd got his D.S.O. and M.C. for.

'I really don't know,' Sos had said. And that had been the truth.

Now it was his fourth trip with Henry and his Halifax, and for himself his sixty-ninth sortie in all. It was only a few more weeks to his seventieth birthday and now he was beginning to wonder if he'd ever reach it, because the inner starboard engine of the aeroplane was on fire.

He could see the vicious red glow distinctly from in here he was and the thick oily smoke began to roll past the perspex of his turret. He knew perfectly well that a few seconds could see the whole aircraft on fire, turning the machine into a raging furnace. There would never be a chance to get out. The fire would sweep, at the pace they were going, from the nose to the tail like a lightning flash.

The smoke thickened so that the source of it now became a dull blur of red, as the sun through a November fog. He wondered in an oddly detached way if there were any enemy night-fighters in the vicinity. Illuminated as it was, the Halifax would be a sitting target.

He got through on the 'inter-com':

'Air Gunner to Captain... Sos here, Henry... your inner starboard engine's on fire.'

Henry's voice crackled back. It sounded a little high-pitched.

'Okay. I know.'

Sos wondered if the rest of the crew knew. Somehow it seemed unreal that calamity should come to these people. There had been a sort of feeling of immunity about them as if they, so complete, efficient and consolidated as a team, were above such a matter as being hit by enemy gunfire and set alight, above the mere sickening routine of mutilation and maiming; above — death.

Then he wondered if it had always been so; that each and every man thought: 'I shall get through. The others may be hit, but I'll get through. They'll never get me.' So it had been with him when he'd faced the Matabele at the age of seventeen in the African bush; when he'd outwitted the Boers on the borders of Portuguese East; when he'd led his natives against the Germans in German East Africa and almost even now with death's hot breath upon his forehead. So that at the very end, perhaps, death came as an outrageous personal affront, calling the bluff at last.

There was nothing at all he could do about it. The only person who had the authority, and the means, was the captain of the aircraft. Without a doubt Henry had already 'feathered' the propeller of the stricken engine and was pumping anti-fire solution into it. Thereafter, all that remained was to wait and see.

It was very unpleasant, to say the least of it — the inactivity, the sense of frustration, the feeling of complete inadequacy to the occasion. The situation might last almost indefinitely, or the end might come so suddenly that Henry wouldn't have the merest chance of giving an order to bale out. Even if they got clear there was the sea below, hungry and waiting and cold.

It was queer how the mind went back in an emergency. Or perhaps it was what the psychological boffins called a defence-mechanism, which was just another way of saying a chap was taking refuge in certain thoughts to prevent him facing an unpleasant reality.

Henry was on the 'inter-com' again:

'Captain to Air Gunner... Sos! Any improvement?'

'I can't see properly. There's too much smoke.'

'Let me know if it gets worse.'

'Okay.'

The glow behind the fog of smoke was still visible. Three hours to base. Three hours out of nearly three-quarters of a century of living. So long a life. Or so short?

What was an hour more or less to anyone who'd seen so much, whose mind could go back so long ago; to the great square house in Tankerville Terrace, Tankerville House in that year of grace 1883; and himself as a little boy in a sailor-suit and they'd put little white silk socks on him to send him to school at Singleton House. They had, you know. White sissy silk socks that were enough to damn anyone right from the start. Tankerville House, his home and his family's home at Newcastle-on-Tyne, long, long ago ...

1883–1892

CHAPTER ONE: A VERY SPECIAL DAY

It was going to be a very special day. It was not quite a question of favourable omens. The arrangements had already been made and were now being carried out. Everyone in Tankerville House knew all about it. Cook knew — well, without her and her art where would they have been anyway? The five maids knew and even the children were almost in the know right from the start; Blanche and Rowena, Emily Gertrude who was very soon going to put her hair up, and Beatrice and Henrietta. Nor on this occasion were the boys far behind though they were never in such direct communication with the Olympians — which was what Rowena called the grownups — as the elder sisters. There were the six brothers, Mordaunt, Edward, John Andrew, Caesar Decimus, Arthur Saville and 'Sos' — Lionel Frederick William. And all of them lived in their own especial section of the grand, gaunt house.

The Olympians, who were really a race apart though they lived under the same roof, had apartments that were practically private. There was Mamma's room, which only the girls knew with any degree of familiarity. There, before an occasion when there were guests to dinner and when the children would be allowed down in the dining room to sip a little watered claret, Rowena and the rest would parade before Mamma and her maid Susan, and then under the gaslight that gleamed and babbled behind its natty little bead-curtain shade, bows would be retied, sashes corrected and a brooch here and there discreetly adjusted.

The boys seldom went to Mamma's room, though she went at nights to theirs, calling on each in turn, rustling into the half-light of their rooms and bending over each bed with a faint tinkling of jet and the faintest hint of a delicate and elusive perfume. Then like a queen in the midst of her subjects — which indeed she was! — she would sweep out again, having maybe gently admonished some sleepy erring soul over the errors of the day; bringing for instance to the notice of Lionel Frederick William the undesirability of playing marbles with 'blood-alleys.'

An occasion such as this would be a heart-rending one for Sos, who now, at the age of eight, was entitled to threepence a week pocket money and laid out his investments with considerable care. 'Blood-alleys' had latterly assumed a priority of importance.

'But, Mamma, there's no *harm* in playing marbles.'

'Harm!' Mamma's voice rang out of the scented darkness perhaps a little more sternly than might have been imagined. 'Only common little boys play with marbles.'

Heigh-ho! And that had been that.

Sometimes, however, a glimpse might be caught of Papa's dressing-room with its beautiful razor cases and shining, polished chest of drawers with the spotless linen coverlets, and the bright tall mirror that stood on its own, so that Papa could cast a critical eye over his immaculate, handsome self, and straighten a cravat and shoot a cuff. In the year 1883 the senior partner of the shipping company of Andrew Myer and J. F. Cohen, of Newcastle-on-Tyne, was a dashing figure.

But Grandpapa's room was known to all. It was a sort of communal and unconventional Holy of Holies, presided over by this patriarch with the fine white beard overflowing onto the chest of his night-shirt.

Grandpapa held his court every evening by his bedroom fireside. Sos thought Grandpapa was very Godlike, seated on his throne, wrapped in his royal red dressing gown, with his bare and marvellously thin smooth ankles showing over those long lean leather slippers, which were sometimes removed and their soles applied to the bottoms of Caesar Decimus, John Andrew, Lionel Frederick William and the others. But by and large Grandpapa was benevolence and kindliness personified.

He could produce, like a conjuror, in a quite beautifully casual fashion, a bull's-eye from nowhere, or a ginger nut or a ribbon for one of the girls. There at his knee Sos learnt many things, heard many stories of great men and true women, and in time it seemed to sink into his mind that one of the great principles of Grandpapa's philosophy was that the two foremost allied enemies of man were fear and pain, which could only produce cowards; and that, like cowards, those two allies must be treated with the contempt they deserved. Because in the age-old, dark and deep traditions of the race, the shield and buckler and spear had only been held by men of courage, who had sometimes through the long centuries had to stand alone and assailed, with every man's hand against them. So Sos grew to love Grandpapa and confided in him a great deal.

'Tell them to take away the socks,' he said to Grandpapa. 'Proper boys don't wear white silk socks.'

'I mustn't interfere, Lionel. Mamma knows best.'

'Mamma doesn't have to go to Singleton House. Beastly socks.'

'Not to swear,' admonished Grandpapa.

'Beastly isn't swearing, Grandpapa. Bertie said so.'

'And who may Bertie be?'

'Susan's young man. She's walking out with him.'

'Good gracious me,' said Grandpapa. 'Whatever next! I don't think I should take Bertie as an authority. You're not encouraged, you know, to become over-familiar with the servants.'

'Some of them are pretty nice.'

'All very well in their place,' said Grandpapa.

'There's another thing. When Mrs Montefiore called last week and we went down to the drawing-room, she called me Lennie in front of everybody. That's awful, Grandpapa. It's a girl's name. It might stick. Do something to stop it all. Please, Grandpapa.'

'But they call you "Sos" at school. I can't think why, but anyway you don't seem to object to that.'

'That's different,' said Lionel Frederick William and with some pride. '"Sos" is short for sausage. I'm supposed to look like one.'

Then, of course, there were the other two rooms of first-rate importance, the kitchen and the library, related together since the presence in one could lead to another of those slippered interviews with Grandpapa or Papa in the other.

The library was presided over by the bust of Josephus on the top of the largest and noblest cabinet, while the kitchen was dominated by the bust of Cook. Indeed she carried all before her and had five maids as consorts, so that she moved majestically and with infinite dignity from one operational position to another, from her range and hob to her pastry-board, moving like a great galleon of the line with her escorting frigates. In the background two pretty housemaids flittered like moths.

There were two things in the kitchen, besides Cook's presence, that were utterly entrancing. Sos was never tired of them. One was the clockwork spit in front of the open range, the other was Cook's girdle-cakes. It was a most impressive spectacle to watch the great joint roasting as it slowly turned. It spluttered and spat, while the rich fat and gravy dropped steadily into the drip-pan beneath. One of the lesser maids basted the meat at regular intervals, and now and again Cook would bear down from the newly scrubbed vegetable table with its bowls and dishes of greenstuff and potatoes, and take a turn with the basting ladle, just to show who really was mistress of the situation. But that was not the time to suggest girdle-cakes.

At this solemn hour, with a splendid luncheon party threatening like a thunder-cloud on the horizon of noon, little boys could scarcely be tolerated to be seen or heard. It was enough then to lurk in some cranny, peering perhaps round the corner of the dresser where the blue and white crockery was ranged along its shelves and the great soup tureen stood on the counter. Then it was possible, with infinite care and caution, and with an assumption of sublime indifference, to edge step by casual step along the length of the dresser until a strategical position was achieved, whereby the whole field of operations could be seen and dimly comprehended. Even then the observer might be shoo-ed away.

'Master Lennie... Master Jack ... I can't have you here now. You've no business in my kitchen and well you know it. Often enough you've been told. Now, go along with you. Do you want me to tell on you?'

She never had told and they knew she never would. Only, of course, sometimes Mamma dropped in, to give orders and to inspect what the tradesmen had brought. Then there would be ructions and another visit to the library.

In the library, even the books with their supercilious shiny backs and their immaculate bindings had an antagonistic air, as if, dumb but all-knowing witnesses of what must inevitably occur, they were expressing silent but contemptuous criticism.

For here would Papa stand waiting, assuring the current miscreant that what was about to happen would be more painful to him than the recipient. Only here was that special chair — had it ever been used for aught else? — over which a small figure must bend to a satisfactory strain of the seat of his sailor-suit, to await the first telling, stinging swipe of Papa's long lean shoe. And then, of course, the rest to follow; one, two, three, four, five — *stop!* But never a flinching or a tear in the eye and walk very steadily, please, as if nothing had happened, to the door and shut it without a tremor. And no rubbing till outside and out of sight.

But all this was well worth the risk for a girdle cake or two and certainly if Bessie Taylor should call.

Bessie Taylor came from Huddleston and she was very beautiful. She was tall and strongly built and though her bare arms were round, they had the look of a man's strength. She walked with a fine springy step and a straight back. Her hair was as dark as the night and her eyes as bright as its stars. Her features were fine with a generous smiling mouth and a patrician aquiline nose. She understood little boys very well. She was a fish-wife and every day she brought the fresh fish in a creel all the way up to Tankerville House from her husband's coble.

Bessie and Sos were very great friends. His admiration of her was complete. It never occurred to him that she could mother him. Rather they shared between them secrets of the sea, of stolen nights, fishing when the family were at the seaside and Bessie was near by; of bread and jam eaten surreptitiously between meals, of cups of milk with a dash of sugar, and glasses of home-made lemonade.

Then was the time to catch Cook, when Bessie had called and the former was in an expansive mood and about to make a cup of tea for the two of them. There they would sit, opposite one another, across the kitchen table, while the copper kettle simmered and sighed on the boiling-plate of the range. The wicker fish creel would often be between them on the tiled floor and just as often the fish, so fresh were they, would be still alive, flipping a tail or quivering down their silvery sides.

Then, when the kettle was on the boil, Cook would make the girdle-cakes. It appeared to be a very simple operation, but it was not as easy as it looked, because Sos had tried one day and burnt his fingers and made such a mess on the stove that Cook hadn't allowed him in her kitchen for nearly a month — a century of banishment. First of all, in a bowl, she made the mixture which was very much in the nature of batter, while the hot-plate was heating over the stove-hole. When everything was ready she would pour a tablespoonful or so on to the hot metal and within seconds the miracle would take place. The mixture would cook into a pancake-like disc of pale yellow with a delicate tinting of brown spots. Light as thistledown, eaten straight from the stove and smothered in butter, it was a delicacy fit to put before the Queen herself.

So much then for Tankerville House, which always seemed to Sos to have withdrawn from the teeming town around it. The high wall which surrounded the garden seemed to emphasize this atmosphere of splendid isolation. The house was a law, an entity, unto itself. Within it the family, self-complete, self-centred, lived its own especial life, ordered and excellent, disciplined and directed by the authority of Mamma, while in the background Grandpapa kept watch, benevolent and all-seeing like a prophet of old. Only Papa, vivacious, handsome and all of a dandy, displayed any of that worldliness that must permeate any ship-owner's office or the quays and clubs and meeting-places where the men who go down to the deep in ships take pleasure in meeting.

It was, therefore, to Sos a great joy at times to leave Tankerville House and everyone within that little kingdom behind him and to steal out through the big iron gates and let them swing to with an ominous clang as if he had shut out one kind of life at the back of him and was venturing forth upon another. And always when such a mood was upon him — and it was not seldom — his footsteps led in the same direction. He would go through the busy streets, sometimes taking a horse-tram, sometimes walking; a small sturdy figure, independent and self-reliant, pausing sometimes, if his pocket permitted, to buy for a penny from a street vendor one hard-boiled egg and a biscuit to go with it, or dropping into Lockhart's and for the same price buying a cup of cocoa and a slice of bread and butter. But his destination was always the same. Tyneside and the docks.

He knew his way about with the experience of long familiarity and with the knowledge that comes of adventuring alone. Once in days past Uncle Joe, scarcely known to the children, had volunteered to show Sos around and he had been overjoyed at the invitation. Only when they arrived where some of their own ships had been berthed, there had arisen a slight contretemps which Sos had found vastly disturbing, quite possibly to Uncle Joe's amusement. As they had reached the otherwise deserted deck an elegant lady had appeared from behind the deck house and with a squeal of delight had tripped daintily across and flung her arms around the Uncle's neck. They had embraced as long-lost friends — or something more.

Sos had felt very uncomfortable, aware in some dim, deep way of something vaguely unchaste and repellent, of something being done which should not have been done, of something which existed but which was forbidden. Of something, indeed, which merited a visit to the library with Grandpapa waiting, with his hands behind him, by the fireplace.

He had not been reassured when, the presumably illicit proceedings concluded, his Uncle had rounded on him, with: 'If you tell your aunt anything you've seen, I'll wring your neck for you.'

Sos had been quite convinced that the threat would have been carried out. Thereafter he made his excursions alone.

He knew what to look for and where to look for it. There were cargo ships newly in and 'tramps' at the quayside. Here they would be loading coal, here the cranes would be swinging the cargo out of the holds. There were cases and barrels and boxes blazoned with the wonderful names of foreign lands. There was the smell of tar and the muddy tang of the river. There were noble ships with their top-hamper enamelled white and there were 'coasters' with the red rust staining their sides. But best of all he liked the deep-sea ships.

He had been aboard one once, led by the hand of a dark-faced scoundrel with gold rings in his ears and a jagged scar across his face. The word 'Bilbao' had been across the bows of the ship, beneath her undecipherable name. He had been led to the foc's'le and given a great mug of steaming tea and a very small man with very bowed legs and smelling of garlic had told him in broken English, accompanied with the most appalling grimaces and gesticulations, of all manner of terrible things that happened at sea and in the lands beyond the sea. He talked of shipwreck and mutiny and of ghostships that sailed on their own through the night; of islands which studded a pearly sea of tropic warm water, where the spices of the land could be savoured a hundred score ship's lengths out; of fabulous monsters that only came to the surface when the moon was at the full and of how they lay glittering as the waves rippled along their phosphorescent sides; of coves with yellow sand and caverns beyond with oaken iron-bound chests filled to overflowing with golden Spanish doubloons and dazzling gems and ropes of pearls. He was late home that afternoon.

He never saw either of those friends again, but he never ceased to look for them, because there were many other things he wanted to know. But every time he first caught sight, between the buildings and the warehouses along the wharves, of mast and spar and funnel, his heart turned within him, longing for a sight of a distant tropic isle or some fierce land beneath a burning sun, where the palace domes were of gleaming gold and where the walls shone like ivory and none of the buildings were made of blackened brick like Tankerville House — though he loved his home and everyone in it — and where the self-same sun that now strove to pierce the dank mist that crept down-tide of the River Tyne might blaze in a sky that framed an Eldorado.

But today was a day of days.

Cook had been hard at it for hours, plunging her hands deep in great bowls of dough, rolling out pastry for pies and tarts and titbits. She had made mounds of mincemeat and spiced meat. She had used pounds of jam and gallons of milk. There were game pies and steak and kidney pies. There were jellies and fruit salads. There were hams and sardines and basket after basket of assorted fruits, oranges and apples and bananas and pears. And now it was all in two vast hampers, strapped down and ready to be lifted into the horse-drawn brake as soon as it arrived. For this was a midsummer's day and everyone was off for a magnificent picnic party on St. Mary's Island in Whitley Bay that lay just off Cullercoats.

The Company's ships' captains were coming as guests. Sos wondered if Captain Crawley would be there. He thought a great deal of the Captain, because he had the very rare knack of talking to small boys — and girls for that matter — on their own level without any condescension, and, more important still, without himself becoming embarrassed. He had, moreover, a remarkable sense of the proper gift at the apt time and of producing the unexpected. He could give, without looking foolish, a perfect present that would be valued above price. He had once handed Sos a combination knife, containing two blades, a corkscrew, a screwdriver, an awl and a hook for taking stones out of horses' hooves. He had produced it out of his pocket, remarking that he had no further use for it, as the only thing of interest to him had been the corkscrew, and that was broken, and as the whole contraption took up a lot of room in his pocket — well, it would be a kindness if Sos would relieve him of it. He was that kind of man and he ranked next to Grandpapa in Sos's mind amongst the Olympians.

The family went off by brake and a great show it was, with Papa seated on the box by Mamma, with her new parasol and bonnet. Grandpapa stayed in the middle of the brake, to keep an eye upon the children, especially upon Caesar Decimus, who generally got so excited that he was sick, but they reached Whitley without accident and leaving the brake at an inn and instructing the coachman to stable the horses, climbed down and took the two great hampers out of the boot.

The sea captains were there to welcome them and took charge of the hampers. Then they all set off to walk across the narrow isthmus connecting St Mary's Island to the mainland. They had judged their time precisely and in many places the spit of sand was above the water level of low tide and as dry as might be. The sun was brilliant, though the air was heavy and far out on the horizon beyond the island a dark layer of sombre mist-like cloud lay at the lower rim of the translucent blue sky. But fine as the day was, and though the water was warm round his ankles and the wet sand trickled deliciously between his toes, the day seemed already spoilt to Sos, because Captain Crawley wasn't there.

The Captains and the family went on ahead, all chatting and nodding and Mamma being very gracious. Grandpapa walked between two of the older men and seemed absorbed in their conversation, and moving from couple to couple as the little train of people crossed the sandy isthmus, went that debonair Uncle Joe who had threatened to break his nephew's neck. Sos kept his distance.

Some of the children ran on ahead, and others lagged behind and nobody took much notice of them, because there was precious little harm they could get up to here. But Sos kept to himself, trudging solemnly along, because Captain Crawley wasn't one of the party. Sos had sense enough not to ask why, because he knew it was no concern of his, but the heat seemed to have gone out of the sun and the wooden spade which he'd brought with him to build a fort seemed a heavy useless thing; he wished he'd left it behind. Anyway no one had been allowed to bring buckets because last time Mordaunt and Jack had made a great collection of marine creatures, such as little crabs, a shrimp or two, some mussels found in a drainpipe, and several small dabs. They had carried their precious assortment back home and housed them in the hot-house under the geranium shelf, by the heating pipe. Then they'd forgotten them and a week or two later when Mamma went in to examine the cuttings, the smell was so excruciating she'd nearly fainted.

But as they reached the dry sand of the island shore, Sos saw Captain Crawley. He didn't see him at first because all the grownup people were in the way, but when he did his joy was so great that he could have shouted out loud. And what was more Captain Crawley wasn't alone. He had the most marvellous person with him. A young black boy.

He was as black as anyone Sos had ever seen, even down at the docks. His skin was a velvety chocolate-black and as smooth as satin. The pupils of his eyes were black, but the whites were whiter than white itself, being tinged with the palest and most beautiful and delicate tint of blue. His head was covered with a mass of minute curls, all twined together. Sos realized at once that he must be at least five years older than himself. The other was twice his height, though Sos had half again the muscle in his arms and legs. Even as he watched, the black boy rolled his eyes and grinned up at Captain Crawley whose hand was on his shoulder. The way his teeth flashed made Sos gasp. This was, indeed, Captain Crawley's great conjuring trick for the day. Then they were being introduced.

Sos said 'Good morning' rather shyly to Captain Crawley and his hero beamed down on him and said: 'How are you, Mister? All clear aft?'

That was pretty good, because that was the way a skipper talked to his mate; though there was a whiff of rum from Captain Crawley's lips.

'Very well, thank you,' said Sos.

'This is Martin,' said Captain Crawley. 'I've brought him all the way from Africa to see you. He's my cabin-boy and a protégé of mine.'

Uncle Joe gave a highly affected cough and a funny sort of snigger, so that the beaming smile went suddenly off Captain Crawley's face and his eyes looked quite fierce when he stared at Sos's Uncle. In fact the glint in his eye seemed to pick out Uncle Joe from the rest of the happy group.

'A protégé, sir,' said Captain Crawley. 'And he is the second son of a chieftain. A race of fighting men, sir, who have their own code of honour and a valley where those who break that code are thrown to their death. Men and women, sir — to their death.'

Then he turned to Sos.

'I leave him in your care.'

Sos smiled at the black boy, and Martin smiled. They put out their hands and then thinking they'd made a mistake withdrew them, so that Captain Crawley clapped them both on their backs and said:

'Shake like gentlemen.'

They shook hands, and Martin said to Captain Crawley: 'Thank you, Massa.' He spoke very clear English, but seemed a little downcast in front of the white boy and kept his eyes lowered.

'I have brought him home for schooling and he's worked his passage fair,' said Captain Crawley. 'The missionaries taught him his English and well enough they did it, but we can do better over here.'

'You can overstep the mark with the native,' said Uncle Joe, but nobody seemed to take much notice of him, and Captain Crawley doffed his hat and offered Mamma his arm to help her over a patch of small pools. Then they chose a site for lunch and sat down for the meal.

It seemed to Sos that food had seldom tasted so good before. Martin sat on the sand beside him and ate slowly and thoughtfully as if he were digesting Sos's words as well as his meal. Sos spoke freely and joyfully of his family and his home. He was delighted with Captain Crawley and the surprise he had sprung. He talked about Tankerville House and how many rooms it had and pointed out members of the family.

Martin took it all in but when Sos wanted to enlarge Martin's acquaintance with the family he grew shy once more and made excuses, and Sos, not understanding why there should be any difference between black and white, was still sensitive enough to know it would wound somebody, somewhere, and so desisted.

Once he caught sight of Uncle Joe talking to Grandpapa and quite clearly about Martin, and he seemed to be getting quite hot under the collar about it, but Grandpapa was helping himself to whisky and didn't seem to care, while Mamma was sitting bolt upright behind one of the hampers. With the meal coming to an end, the sea captains had drawn together as if by mutual consent and were lolling on the sand, supping rum and smoking cigars. The girls had gone off paddling.

'Where do you live?' said Sos.

'Africa,' said Martin.

'That's a long way off.'

'Massa — my master — brought me over. He is a good man. Does your Papa beat you?' said Sos.

'No,' said Martin. 'No one beats a chief or a chief's sons. They may kill them, but not touch them like that.'

'My Papa beats me,' said Sos. 'So does Grandpapa. They use a slipper. That's when I've been up to no good.'

Martin shook his head: 'Nobody must ever beat a white man,' he said. 'None of my people would ever lay hands upon a white man unless he showed fear.'

There was a lot of laughter and loud talking now from the sea captains but their wives, who were also guests, had gathered round Mamma who was now seated on her hamper and holding court. Indeed, it was just like being in Tankerville

House again, when the gentlemen were left to their dessert, but now it was in the open air. Far away there was a rumbling sound and for a little time the sun darkened, then it was very bright and hot again.

'I'm going to build a fort out of the sand,' said Sos. 'I've brought my spade. You can help me if you like.'

He drew a line in the sand with his forefinger.

'I shall do it like this,' he said. 'I know quite a lot about forts.'

He completed the line into a circle.

'That will be the moat. And then inside there will be a glissade.' He was very proud of the word. 'That's a long slope that people have to crawl up without any protection if they get across the moat. Then you shoot them down easily. Jolly good fun I should think.'

'Do people live inside your fort?'

'Of course they do. And there's a powder magazine.'

'My people live in a kraal.'

The slender finger traced another circle in the sand.

'That's a mud wall.'

'Pooh!' said Sos. 'I don't think much of that. One shot through that and you'd all be blown up.'

'It doesn't happen that way in Africa.'

'I know a bit about Africa myself,' said Sos. No chieftain's son was going to have it all his own way. 'I met Mr Stanley. He's the man who discovered Doctor Livingstone. You know all about that?'

'No,' said Martin, truthfully.

'Well, I never,' said Sos. 'Nobody's been talking about anything else. I was in a display they gave Mr Stanley when he visited Newcastle. There were quite a lot of young children with us, too. Mr Stanley shook me by the hand and then he talked about Africa. It's funny you didn't meet him out there.'

'It's a very big place,' said Martin. 'And there are millions and millions of black men and very few white men. They came out to my country, so my people know, a long time ago and they farmed the land and bred cattle. It's very important to breed good cattle. My people live by cattle. You can buy a wife for twenty oxen, but they must be good. Then sometimes the lions get them.'

That was a little confusing. Did the lions get the wives or the oxen? Both, at times, it seemed. But — lions!

'Have you ever seen one?'

'Many times,' said Martin. 'And at night they come near the kraal and roar. If there is danger we light fires and beat drums to drive them off, but in the daytime we hunt them.'

'You shoot them?'

'Only a few of us have guns. They are very scarce. But we have shields made of hide and stabbing spears —'

'Go on,' said Sos. 'Go on. Has one ever bitten you?'

'My father was a great hunter,' said Martin. 'And his father before him —'

He sat bolt upright on the sand, his legs crossed, his arms locked around him, and Martin spoke of his native land as only one may speak who is homesick and longs for his own kin again. He spoke, too, of lions and elephants and the wildebeest and the springbok. Sometimes luck held and you got quite close to them. There were giraffes, and ostriches, which were great birds which could kill you with one blow of their foot. There were rhinoceros in the bush and hippopotamus in the wide rivers, which teemed with tiger fish. And there were crocodiles, lying like inert logs in the shallows, till you drew near and they snapped your leg off. He talked of the burning days and the glittering tropic nights, of the routines and decencies of native life, of marauders and cattle thieves, and the warriors who went out to avenge the loss. He spoke, too, of a yellow metal the white men were finding and how excited it made them. It was time to go home when he had finished, and then Sos knew that Martin had really only just begun.

'I didn't see you come across here when we came,' said Sos. The brake had arrived from the mainland, crossing by the spit of sand on the turn of the tide. Mamma was marshalling the children together and Sos wanted to find a place for his new and remarkable friend beside him.

'I came with Massa,' said Martin. 'He and four other captains sailed across in a whaler.'

'You sailed across?'

'Yes.'

'You'll sail back?'

'Of course.'

'I'll come with you,' said Sos.

This would indeed be a fitting end to this day of all days. Martin might have sailed all the way from Port Natal, but he would show him that he knew something of what it meant to be a sailor too. Indeed, hadn't Captain Crawley that very morning greeted him as he might have done a shipmate?

'It will be rough,' said Martin. 'You may get wet. Then you will perhaps get into trouble.'

'Pooh!' said Sos, and knowing the lingo. 'It's as calm as a mill-pond.'

It was very calm, the sea with an oily shining surface and with a rising ground-swell. Only far out on the horizon that purplish bank of mist which had been there all day seemed to be tinged a little darker as if there were a sore, inflamed membrane between sea and sky. And again there was a faint rumbling.

There was no difficulty in evading a lift in the brake. The party had been a complete and continued success, and everybody was so occupied with congratulating everyone else and thanking Mamma that no one thought of checking up on the vacant seats. Sos's absence was not observed.

The whaler lay beached a little way round a turn of the shore. A deck-hand in blue jersey and sea-boots had already pushed her down into deeper water so that she was half afloat, gently rolling in the swell. Her brown standing lug-sail lay crumpled in the well and her single halyard slapped against the swaying mast. Lying alongside and tied to her stern was a small canoe.

Two minutes later Captain Crawley and three other fellow Masters appeared. They were in high spirits and one of their number seemed to have some difficulty in making his way through the loose dry sand. It seemed to be clogging his feet, so that his companions had to help him along. As they approached Sos could hear him, expostulating to the effect that he was all right and didn't need no slab of a drunken seaman to get him home. They all seemed to take that as a very good joke, especially when he fell on his face in the shallow water around the whaler's stern, but he managed to clamber over the counter and subside into the stern-sheets. When he started to swear Captain Crawley reprimanded him.

'Mind your tongue, Tom. The boss's lad is alongside.'

They climbed aboard and the deck-hand poled them out, with the little canoe trailing astern and bobbing in the water. When they were half a dozen lengths out the deck-hand put the whaler about and up to wind.

'Do you want a reef?' he said and he cast his eye seawards.

'Blast all reefs,' said Tom, from somewhere under the after-thwart. 'Do you think we're going round Cape Horn? It's less than a mile across to the mainland.'

He spoke with the intonation of the 'Geordie'.

Captain Crawley patted Sos on the shoulder.

'Glad to have you along with us. The first time you've put to sea with me. We'll make a sailor of him yet, won't we, Martin? Now you two lads sit yourselves here on the weather side. All right, Harry, hoist away. Let's go before the storm catches us.'

A spot of rain fell heavily into the boat, as the red-ochred sail went rattling up the mast. Captain Crawley put the sheet through a fairlead and put up his helm. On the instant the sail filled, the whaler quivered like a young mare feeling the turf beneath her feet and they were away.

The sudden change from the pitching, wallowing boat, that rolled from side to side, to this sail-taut, intense and alerted creature that bared its breast to the waves, cleaved them and sped on with ever increasing yet soundless speed was one of the most marvellous things Sos had ever experienced. He gripped Martin's lean dark arm with excitement, forgetting on the moment that he was betraying his lack of vaunted experience. But Martin smiled at him and his lips curled back over his white teeth, and they both laughed again as a shower of spray burst over the bow and clattered about them. Tom in the stern-sheets was searching for a bailer. Under his tan he looked green.

Captain Crawley was glancing astern. Harry by his side was also staring in the same direction. The whaler seemed to be gathering still greater speed every moment.

'It's grand,' shouted Sos.

He was disappointed that Captain Crawley didn't acknowledge the compliment, but he seemed a trifle preoccupied.

'Thunder squall,' he said. 'You were right about that reef. Get off my feet, Tom, you tipsy fool.'

The whaler shuddered as a puff hit her and she yawed across the seas till Captain Crawley clawed his helm right over. Sos looked out astern and he could see their wake, white and bubbling and spread out like a fan. The sun suddenly went in and there was a small whistling noise as the wind caught the shrouds and Captain Crawley's cap blew off, so that Martin must retrieve it. Captain Crawley crammed it on his head without a word of thanks and still he kept his eyes astern.

Now Sos could see on the far horizon, under the deep purple of a low range of cloud, a line of white and beneath another deeper line of black under the very edge of the sky. A gull wheeled overhead crying like a lost soul.

'Stand by,' said Captain Crawley. 'There's a bit of a blow a-coming. Stand by in case she jibes. Get clear of my feet, Tom Carter, you.'

Even Sos with all his inexperience could see the squall coming. The water went as black as ink and the tops of the waves became, all of a sudden, whipped white, the spray flying before with the wind. Then the thunder-gust was upon them.

It struck the whaler with a mighty buffet, and as it struck it veered. The standing lug flapped madly. The whaler drove her stem into the trough and then as she jibed all standing, the following sea pooped her and the water fell into the stern-sheets down Tom Carter's neck. He struggled to his tipsy feet, fell and clutched at Captain Crawley. As the lug-sail went over, the yard crashed against the mast which stood, the whaler yawed, broached to, and full to the gunwales, capsized.

She threw Sos clear; he fell into the water and the frothy spume blew over him. He cried out as he went and as he sank he took in a great gulp of water. He could swim a little but he had never been out of his depth before and now the sea was all around him and he was alone, utterly panic-stricken and completely taken by surprise. He shouted and took another mouthful of water for his trouble and a playful sea tossed him to its crest and then sucked him down into its glassy valley.

He was lost, he was drowning, he was going to die. It was the first taste of terror and despair that he had known. One moment he had been in the company of his trusted comrades, confident and at the very height of his excited entrancement, the next he was deserted and doomed. The fear of death was a terrible torment and then he felt the grip of arms from behind. A pair of arms went around him and two hands were locked on his chest, and a voice shouted in his ear:

'Lie back. Keep your mouth closed. I've got you.'

He lay back and found that his legs would float quite easily and that he was supported. Then he felt a kicking beneath him and knew that he was being propelled along. With dim surprise he saw the sky blue above him and noted in an oddly detached way that the sun was coming out again.

'Now turn round.'

He wriggled round and found Martin's dark face beneath him. The African lad was floating easily on his back. There was the shape of something like a boat beyond him. It was the canoe. Sos clutched at the gunwale and with Martin propelling him upwards with a vigorous thrust on his backside, clambered in.

The frail little craft, still fastened to the whaler, rocked violently and then Martin was beside him.

They crouched on the floor boards and Martin put an arm round Sos and in the strangest way began to stroke him as if he were some lost pet that had been found.

'That's all right,' he kept on saying. 'That's all right.'

Sos clung to him, because he was still terrified almost out of his wits, and when the canoe lurched, tipping its nose up to the sky and then dipping it down into the green, he cried out on the first occasion, but Martin's arms comforted him and his confidence returned, so that in a little time he struggled free and took in what was going on.

The squall had passed. Already the sea was subsiding. The whaler lay on her beam, her sail spread out on the water like a square patch of rust. The heat was coming back into the sun.

Harry the deck-hand was holding on to the tip of the horizontal mast and forcing the luff-rings down, having cast off the main halyard from the peak. Captain Crawley with Tom Carter by his side and with the other two sea captains at either hand, was half-perched on the starboard gunwale, swinging in unison to right the whaler. As she rolled over on to an even keel, her gunwales awash, Harry stowed the sail.

They started to bale then, ladling the water out, working from outside the boat. In a little time it rose half a foot and Martin slipped into the sea again and swam to her and because he was the lightest, climbed aboard. After that, the baling became easier, but it was an hour before she was on an even keel and still longer till she was under way, with a tattered sail.

Sos sat in the canoe and was towed along and Martin sat on the counter of the whaler and grinned at him. Captain Crawley had lost his cap and his grey hair was plastered over his forehead, nor would he speak to Tom Carter, whom he judged to be responsible for the accident.

'I'll have no words from you, Tom Carter,' he said. 'There'll be enough when we get ashore.'

There were.

Papa was there with Uncle Joe, and so was Grandpapa. There were a group of longshoremen around them and they cheered when the whaler grounded and her stem crunched on the beach, because by and large, it had been a very near thing well handled and no lives lost. But Papa was shaking with fury, and Uncle Joe was literally hopping mad. He couldn't keep still. Grandpapa stood just behind them and he was very white, his lips almost bloodless, while the breeze plucked at his long white beard.

The anguish of the last hour had driven Papa to a point of bitter frenzy. He shook his fist in Captain Crawley's face as he floundered ashore. He cursed him for a drunken sailor who hadn't the right to hold a master's ticket, who risked his crew on a foolhardy errand, who'd imperilled a young boy's life.

Captain Crawley took it all very quietly, because he was a fine man and knew what Papa must have suffered, and he clapped his hand over Tom Carter's mouth, who, almost in tears, was trying in his rough way to confess whose fault it was. A look passed between Captain Crawley and Grandpapa as of two men who understood one another, and Grandpapa laid a hand on his son's arm and restrained him, so that the Captain and the rest of them set about beaching the boat.

Then Papa turned on Sos and upbraided him. Who had given him permission to go in the boat? Was it an honourable thing to steal away alone when he should have gone in the brake? Did he realise what trouble he had caused? He shook Sos till his teeth rattled. Sos didn't cry, but stood his ground, a little aggressive, his short legs apart and his hands clenched behind his back. This sort of thing didn't frighten him. He was always in trouble and was quite accustomed to it and to the inevitable consequences.

'I'm sorry, Papa,' he said. 'I meant no harm.'

'Wretched child!' said Grandpapa.

That hurt, because even in his most awe-inspiring moments, Grandpapa was always compassionate. The hot tears burnt at the back of Sos's eyes because he knew he had done wrong and brought distress to them all, though he couldn't quite see how he was to blame for the sudden change of the weather and for Tom Carter's drinking and the boat upsetting. But the Olympians were always unpredictable and the fact remained that the centre of this somewhat unedifying scene was himself.

'I am very sorry, Grandpapa,' said Sos and his voice shook a little. 'I didn't think there would be all this trouble.' And he blinked his eyes rapidly, which was a way he'd learnt to keep them dry.

'I'll see you later in the library,' said Grandpapa, and he cleared his throat in a very brusque sort of way as if he were trying to sound fiercer than he felt.

Martin stood on the edge of the crowd and he seemed a little confused with all that was going on. He looked from one white face to another, but he couldn't make much sense of it all. Vaguely, he knew that hard words had been said to his master and knew that they had hurt, because he'd seen the look on Captain Crawley's face, as he'd turned away from the rebuke. His new young friend, too, seemed to be in trouble. He couldn't understand why. There had been an accident but no lives had been lost. In fact it hadn't been a serious accident at all. It was nothing to fall into this English sea where there were not even sharks. It was a very different matter to capsize a canoe on the Limpopo River. There were the 'crocs'. But one of the white men was staring at him and he wondered why.

'There's that little black blackguard,' said Uncle Joe. 'If it hadn't been for him! I told you so! That's who led young Lionel astray.'

Sos was so aghast that at first he couldn't believe his ears. It was his first real taste of the infamy of human injustice.

Uncle Joe crossed over to Martin and his face was full of contempt and fury, making him look vindictive and ugly.

'You keep to your own kind in future,' said Uncle Joe. 'You can't touch tar without getting dirty.'

'No,' said Sos and his voice was high and squeaky, as if it belonged to someone he didn't know.

'You mustn't say that,' said Sos.

'You keep quiet,' said his uncle.

'He saved my life,' said Sos. 'Martin saved my life. I'd be dead if it wasn't for Martin.'

'Fiddlesticks,' said his uncle. 'Don't talk such rubbish to me. We could see everything that happened from here, couldn't we? Now, pack off, you little black brute, and don't let's ever set eyes on you again.'

Martin slunk back as if he had been struck. He walked slowly backwards step by step, keeping his eyes all the time on Sos's uncle as if he were a wild animal who might spring upon him and rend him at any moment. When at last he reached Captain Crawley by the whaler, which was now properly beached, he turned and hid his face in the flap of the white man's blue serge reefer jacket. Captain Crawley's great hand seemed nearly to cover the black boy's head.

Later, Sos kept his appointment in the library and saw Grandpapa and Papa. But he never saw Martin again.

CHAPTER TWO: A DOZEN DIAMONDS AND THE QUEEN'S SHILLING

Six years later the entire family, with Grandpapa and Papa dead, moved South, to London. They took up residence at Highbury New Park.

The house at New Park wasn't anything like Tankerville House. It was a very suitable residence for people of position, but to Sos it was like associating with an upstart after long familiarity with a personality of degree. Indeed, the personality might have been a little overpowering at times, but there had been a sort of stolid provincial integrity about it. The Highbury house, with its town airs, seemed to one who had lived all his fourteen years with the country cousin a little pert, over-fastidious, too critical.

He suffered, too, at times, a quite desperate nostalgia for Tyneside and its ships. True enough, when the move had taken place he had begged to be allowed to travel by sea and after a great deal of confabulation, and probably as the result of exasperation at a member of the family who could never fall into line like the others, the request had been granted. But that had been a small compensation for the hours stolen away in former days, for the stories heard and the wild tales told over a fine enamel mug of steaming sweet tea, taken seated on a locker in a fo'c'sle.

Moreover, he hadn't the time. They had put him to work with Lewison's of Charterhouse Square, Aldersgate, General Merchants. Sos wondered if there ever had been merchants who were so general. They dealt in an astonishing range of commodities, and oddly enough the self-same commodities aroused in Sos once more that inexplicable longing to pass beyond the confines of a small island, where nothing of importance ever seemed to happen.

The firm of Lewison's dealt in ostrich feathers from Africa and bristles from Russia. There were diamonds in little folded slips of white paper, and human hair from China. In the end Sos discovered that the latter was used for stuffing sofa cushions and it seemed to him, with his increasingly Imperial views of 1889, that it was very meet and right that the hair from a Chinaman's head should serve a more useful purpose for the extremity of an Englishman. He mentioned this to Joseph, of the gigantic moustache, who was his immediate boss but Joseph rather evaded the issue, wondering perhaps if, in some remote and subtle fashion, he too was being mocked.

But besides diamonds and hair, they traded in tortoise-shell and ivory, copper and quicksilver and quinine. The reading of the catalogue which it was part of Sos's duty to price — in so far as he put down the figures as Joseph dictated them in the Board of Trade's Cutler Street warehouse — should have aroused visions of Aladdin's Cave or the treasure of the Forty Thieves, but in reality his place of work was dark and dusty and silent.

He worked regularly each day on the top-floor office in Charterhouse Square. He stood behind his table and waited for the buyers to come in. Under the table on a little shelf was a very special pistol that was kept loaded. It had never, in all Joseph's memory, been used and Joseph admitted that he really didn't know what would come out of the spout, if anyone pressed the trigger. Nevertheless, there might come a time, because nobody ever knew, and anyway it gave a fellow confidence. Many of the American customers paid in thousand-pound notes.

There was a reason too, of course, for having the office right at the top of the building. If anybody started what is now known as a smash and grab, there was double the chance of catching the raiders on the way down the stairs, that there ever would have been if the ground floor had been used. Joseph had thought it all out.

Joseph was what is known as a 'keen' man. He was in his early forties and had been with the firm since his youth. There was no question as to his integrity and capability. He knew his job.

He knew his job so well, that like so many keen men in the City of London, he knew little else. Once a fortnight, he would go to a music hall or a musical comedy, prompted no doubt more by a sense of duty than any undue anticipation of pleasure. Maybe he was justified, for later Mr. Lewisohn, the firm's American associate, married Miss Edna May direct from *The Belle of New York*. Once a year he took a fortnight's holiday and went with his wife to Margate or Ramsgate. There he sat on a donkey and had his photograph taken and sometimes he paddled. On one occasion he hired and put on a bathing suit, with narrow horizontal stripes, and a buttoned neck-vent, and with legs that reached down just over his knees; but he felt he looked ridiculous because the thing reminded him of his wife's combinations, so he didn't do it again.

His real life was in Charterhouse Square. There, adorned with his tremendous moustache, a three-inch collar and a coif across the smooth hair plastered above his forehead, he was authority incarnate. He knew the price of every commodity the firm handled; and there was no knowing what they might decide upon next. One day it might be industrial 'boart', the next Edam cheeses from Holland. Even on the cheeses he could pass sound judgment, though the concentrated odour of several thousand of these delicacies in the warehouse nearly suffocated Sos.

The important day of the week was the day on which the diamonds were posted to America. Then with the fearsome pistol in his pocket Sos would follow Joseph down the pavement, a devoted bodyguard, who in the event of a felonious assault would probably have shot his charge between the shoulder blades in the excitement of the moment. Other days were spent in the Cutler Street warehouse. There Joseph decided, catalogue in hand, the market value of ostrich features, tortoise-shell and ivory, which Sos annotated.

Joseph was kindliness itself to Sos and he explained his way of life. The Beginning and End-all of life was Business; and the reason for that was because that was where the money lay. Wherever the money might lie seemed to Sos as illusory as the crock of gold at the rainbow's end. Because here, indeed, was no scintillating, many-coloured path to enhance the search, but only the deadly monotonous routine, plodding on month to month for the security of a pittance.

'All these things,' he said to Joseph, 'wouldn't you like to go where they come from?'

'What's that?' said Joseph. He was checking a ledger and was not over-pleased at the interruption.

'There's things in this building,' said Sos, 'which come from all over the world. I can't think of anywhere, where we don't get things from. Wouldn't you like to go to some of those places?'

'I'm quite happy with my fortnight,' said Joseph and heaved at the ends of his moustache. 'It doesn't do to expect too much,' he added.

'I didn't mean that,' said Sos. 'But I'd like to travel about, wouldn't you? I'd like to see things. I'd like to *do* things.'

'Then you'd better get on with these figures,' said Joseph. 'Application, that's what you want to cultivate. And then you may get there.'

And again the act of Getting There seemed to Sos very much on a par with the crock of gold.

The morning he crossed Trafalgar Square hadn't begun propitiously. Words had been bandied across the Highbury breakfast table. Rowena had remarked in all innocence, having received a letter from the North, that she wondered how Newcastle was getting on. Nobody but Sos took much notice of a sentiment which so closely bordered on the inane.

'I wish we were back,' Sos said.

He made the statement, scarcely realizing he'd voiced his views aloud.

'And why, may I ask?' Uncle Joe, who was visiting, took up the challenge at once. He had long ago decided that with one member of the family, at any rate, it was necessary to nip criticism in the bud.

'I'm sorry,' said Sos, and knew at once he'd said the wrong thing, apologizing where no apology was due, revealing in his folly the guilty longings of his heart.

'It might occur to you sometimes,' said his uncle, 'that this household isn't run entirely for your benefit. There are other members of the family besides yourself, and nobody else has complained.'

'I wasn't complaining,' mumbled Sos.

'You'll be late for your bus,' said Mamma with characteristic tact. 'Now run along.'

Sos had fled from the room, snatched his bowler from the hatstand in the hall, and slammed the door. He was late reaching the office and Joseph's comments were terse and to the point.

'Day-dreaming again,' he said. 'That's what it is. Your mind's not on your work. What we need here are keen men.'

It was not like Joseph to play the scold, but maybe like Uncle Joe his liver was a little out of sorts or maybe providence herself was now taking a hand. Joseph sent Sos on an errand to a West End hotel with a little wooden box containing a dozen uncut diamonds. For two pins, Sos told himself, he'd have pitched the lot in the gutter. Then on his way back he crossed Trafalgar Square.

The Recruiting Colour Sergeant was standing by the column. His chest glittered with medals and their ribbons and his shoulder sash was scarlet. His moustache was waxed to two points as sharp as skewers and he carried a box-wood pacing-stick under his arm. He was talking to a young man whose nose scarcely reached the top button of the Colour Sergeant's uniform.

Sos stopped dead in his tracks. Forgotten were Joseph and Uncle Joe, the Aldersgate office and the Highbury house. Here before him was the very embodiment of his half-formed, secret desire. Those medals had not been won on a barrack square but on a field of battle in some far-flung, foreign clime. Those marble-like, glassy eyes had stared death calmly in the face. That furious moustache had bristled in the very face of the enemy. Those thin long legs, braced no doubt with muscles of wire and steel, had never wasted their energy in climbing the dusty stone steps to an office perched beneath a warehouse roof; they had carried their owner into the very thick of the fight. Beneath that brilliant red jacket beat a heart as stout as any in England. Beneath that immaculate peak cap of the Royal Marine Light Infantry moved a brain which must retain the memory of many a distant land.

The conversation with the young man was finishing. The latter lounged away with his hands in his pockets, with an obviously assumed nonchalance. Sos stepped forward.

'Well, me lad, and what can I do for you?'

'I want to enlist,' said Sos.

'That's what I like to hear,' said the Colour Sergeant. 'Now you come alonger me and we'll talk this over.'

He led the way in the direction of Chandos Street. A minute later he was ordering drinks at a bar.

'A pint of porter for me, Miss,' said the Colour Sergeant, 'and what about you, young feller-me-lad?'

'I'm not thirsty, thank you,' said Sos.

'In the Royal Marines you don't drink because you're thirsty,' said the Colour Sergeant. 'Give him a half o' mild.'

'I'd rather have a lemonade,' said Sos.

'Make it a shandy,' said the Colour Sergeant. 'Half and half. Got to bring them up in the right way. What's your age, boy?'

'Sixteen,' said Sos, adding a year.

'A likely enough lad,' said the Colour Sergeant, 'for the Queen's shilling. And here it is, me boy.'

He slapped the coin down on the counter. Sos picked it up and pocketed it. Of all indifferently small actions it seemed to be the most portentous he had ever made.

The Colour Sergeant raised his tankard.

'Drink hearty,' he said.

'Thank you,' said Sos and sipped and choked.

'We'll make a man of you yet,' said the Colour Sergeant, and slapped him on the back, so that he spluttered again.

Thereafter affairs progressed very quickly, so that Sos became a little dazed. In that year of grace 1889 no Recruiting Sergeant ever allowed his fish to escape when once he'd been hooked, however lightly. They went down Whitehall to the

Recruiting Office, where Sos took the oath and signed on for twelve years and two years Boy's Service. Then they wrote out a lot of details on bits of paper. At last they handed him a railway warrant and a routeing form. The next thing he knew was that he was in the train for Deal.

It was the same routine of efficiency and bustle when he reached his destination. He found his way to the barracks, reported to the guard-room and handed in his papers. A corporal set a marine to look after the newcomer and the marine, with an eye on Sos's bowler hat and stiff white collar, such as the officers wore off parade, took him across to the quartermaster's stores with a grin on his face.

They gave Sos a uniform and issued him with a complete kit, and then he was taken to the ablution-benches, stripped and given a bath. An hour from the time he had entered the depot gates he was by the bed allotted to him in his barrack block, sorting out the articles of his new equipment and with his civilian clothes packed in a brown paper parcel ready to send home. They had not been able to include the bowler hat with the other garments which they'd done up for him in the store and it now reposed on top of the parcel, which in turn rested on the stool by the side of his bed with its straw-filled palliasse.

He knew the clothes would never find their way home, because no one there must have an inkling where he might be, even to as small degree as a postmark. What ever might happen to the bowler hat, he could scarcely care. It was getting late and men were coming into the barrack-room in twos and threes. The room began to fill up. Voices sounded unnaturally loud, and they were harsh and coarse and in reference to all kinds of material for conversation, it appeared that all were bleeding.

Sos undressed and climbed into bed and turned his face into the hard canvas pillow, because a sudden surge of homesickness and panic at what he had done possessed him. But the mood passed almost at once because he told himself that if they liked to think at Highbury New Park in London town, which now seemed so far away, that he was the black sheep of the family they could jolly well think so; he would show them all he could look after himself, for wasn't he now a fully fledged recruit under instruction of a leading Corps of the Queen — the Royal Marine Light Infantry?

He was on parade the next morning before the light had been in the sky scarcely sixty minutes. He had been roughly awakened at reveille and had washed in icy water. He had struggled into his new uniform and buckled on his belt and tried to settle his cap on his head. His breakfast had been porridge and beans and luke-warm tea. He hadn't liked to ask the way to the latrines and was in discomfort. Now the drill sergeant was facing him.

He was a high-cheek-boned, clean-shaven man, with a pockmarked nose and cold grey eyes. He looked Sos up and down with obvious disgust.

'You blanco your belt every morning,' he said, '*and* clean your bleeding buttons *and* clean your bleeding boots. You keeps your cap straight and level on your 'ead and off your bleeding ears with the badge to the front and over the forehead.'

Then he took four paces back.

'Squad —'shun!'

It was ear-splitting. It seemed to Sos that he could feel the sergeant's breath like the fumes from a blast furnace pass his face.

'Stand a-a-at — Ease!... Easy.'

The squad of recruits relaxed. The drill sergeant clasped his hands behind his back, his cane under his left arm, his legs straddled.

'Every time there's a new lot of rookies into this 'ere depot,' he said in a deep voice of infinite self-pity, 'the night before I gets an 'orrible nightmare.'

He let his glance wander down the uneven ranks.

'It's 'orrible,' he repeated. 'It's simply bleeding 'orrible. I don't know 'ow I sticks it. I goes into a cold sweat right from the start, I do. There's faces that I see. Well, in a manner o' speaking they're not proper faces, they're 'orrible blobs. They aren't really human because their bodies is all skinny and scrawny and their backs are bent. As for their chests, they just ain't got none. Most of 'em is 'unch-backed. Poor beggars!'

He paused and shook his head sadly. Then his mouth opened like a coal hole.

'And I ain't properly awake yet,' he roared. 'I'm still looking at 'em! Squad, 'shun. Turning to the right by numbers. On the command "one" you turns to the right on the 'eel of the right foot and the ball of the left foot. On the command "two" — 'ere, you number four in the front rank, can't you keep your belly in? What's it going to be?'

At the end of the day Sos returned to his barrack-room to find, though the parcel of clothes was still intact, his bowler hat was gone. Beyond the intervals for the midday meal and tea, he seemed to have been on his feet all day. He was tired and not a little bewildered, baffled for the moment by his new way of living where every action was timed and every thought tabulated. He sat on his bed trying to collect himself.

The day had started with the barrack-room drill, where the men worked in two ranks, one kneeling with buckets of water and scrubbing with soft soap, while the rear rank followed, swabbing. The mess table had been similarly scrubbed and every man had been allocated a special job. It had been Sos's lot to clean the forks. Thereafter, there had been the squad drills and a brief half hour in the gymnasium. Now he supposed the day was over and time was his till 'Lights out'.

The barrack-room was filling. The old soldiers, wise in their generation, were stretched out on their beds reading, while others cleaned their equipment against a guard duty. Defaulters were getting into uniform and full pack pending their night's fatigue. Some of the younger men were getting into their 'walking out' blues and there was a great talk of 'square-pushing' and of 'tarts' and other such things of which Sos was but dimly aware. Others were in small groups discussing 'form' or picking the winners for the next day. Over all a corporal was in charge. He seemed to Sos to be as lonely as himself, being aloof from the men, The man in the next bed to Sos had propped himself up, with his back to the wall. He was a big fellow in the early thirties, with a high peak of curly hair above his forehead and brown cow-like eyes. He had been watching Sos for some time.

'Well, what do you make of it?' he said.

'It's all right,' said Sos. He was a little startled to realize that he had been under observation.

'It's all right when you get used to it. It's the first ten years is the worst. Where do you come from?'

'Newcastle,' said Sos and was conscious of his accent at once.

'I come from Pompey. Name of Noakes.'

'I'm Cohen. Lionel Cohen. Lots of people call me Sos.'

'Why?'

'Oh, it's just a name.'

'Then I'd keep that sort of information to myself,' said Marine Noakes.

He stared at Sos solemnly.

'Been up to something?' he asked.

'I'm afraid I don't understand.'

'Well, people of your sort don't usually join up in the ranks.'

'I've done nothing wrong, if that's what you mean,' said Sos.

'Bit of a mystery, that's what I call it. Not that I bears anything against you for that. But some of the others think so, too.'

He jerked his head in the direction of a group of young soldiers at the far end of the room. They were enjoying a joke, and somebody was laughing shrilly.

'They've got my hat,' said Sos suddenly. 'I say, they've got my bowler hat.'

He started to his feet. Private Noakes put out a hand and laid it on Sos's arm.

'I'd let it be,' he said, not unkindly.

'But it's my property,' said Sos. 'Look, that fellow's got it on his head. He can't do that, you know.'

'Have it your own way,' said Marine Noakes and rolled over on his side and picked up the inside sheet of the Sunday paper, which he'd been reading.

Sos set off down the barrack-room towards the group of young men at the far end. He wasn't sure what he was going to say and he was quite uncertain what he was going to do. He acted instinctively, out of impulse, but it seemed to him completely outrageous that anyone should appropriate his property without as much as by your leave. Indeed, it was more than that. They were making a mockery of his property and therefore they were mocking him.

But the problem of what to do or say was not to arise, because the situation was already out of his hands. The young marine with the bowler perched on the side of his head minced down the room, drew up immediately before Sos and bowed elaborately.

He said in a highly affected voice:

'End how du yu du?'

There was a roar of laughter from his companions, who had followed him down and had now gathered round.

'That's my hat,' said Sos.

'I should bally well think it is,' was the reply. 'Do you know my people?'

'Come off it, Ned,' said one of the older men. 'Leave the kid alone. He's all right.'

'Fraightfully bally all right I should say,' said Ned. 'I saw him when he reported. You might have thought he'd got the bleeding Crown Jewels sewed in the seat of his trousers.'

Sos felt the colour burn in his face. He'd never had any trouble at Singleton House, despite the white silk socks, because he'd come of a large family and learnt the rough and tumble. But this was different because these were men not boys and there were at least a dozen of them. Nor were they the kind of men he'd known, except in his excursions down the docks and then everybody had seemed to have known who his father was and had welcomed him with tea and tales. But these boisterous, loud-voiced young men were antagonistic in some sort of way, that was unfair and unreasonable.

'I 'ope you enjoyed your night's rest,' said Ned. 'I'm afraid the silk sheets are at the wash this week.'

There was another outburst of laughter at this sally and someone knocked the hat off Ned's head and another picked it up and sent it sailing through the air, where another caught it and kept the ball rolling. Then on an instant it came spinning in Sos's direction and he deftly caught it.

'Gimme that,' said Ned and snatched.

Sos backed swiftly and evaded his tormentor's grasp.

'Come on now,' said Ned. 'None of yer airs and graces 'ere. You're one of us now and you can forget what your dear Mamma said as she kissed you goodbye.'

'You can leave my mother out of this,' said Sos and he was panting a little, the hat clutched in his arms. He was frightened because he was entirely at the mercy of Ned and his friends, but he was also angry, with a white-hot fury because this lout with his stupid face and stupid taunts was a fool and something a little worse than a fool. But the anger was greater than the fear.

Therefore he stood his ground at the other's approach and when Ned put out his hand again he struck at him with the panic of despair. The blow caught Ned on the chest and he gave a great roar of laughter. He held Sos by the shoulders with both hands, and Sos dropped the bowler hat and hammered at Ned's breast-bone. He might just as well have been pummelling a sandbag and all the time Ned was laughing. But the laughter stopped when Sos kicked him on the shin. Because it hurt.

'So you would, would you?' said Ned. 'Nasty vindictive little geezer. Can't take a joke, eh? Well, we'll soon see about that. We teach nippers like you manners in the Royal Marines. We'd better christen him, boys.'

Sos had no idea how many hands seized hold of him, but he knew he was powerless and resistance would only add to the bruises which were doubtless already there. They carried him shoulder-high down the barrack block towards the ablution benches with their scoured bowls and white-wood duckboards, and with the urinal buckets, one each end of the bench. The basins were empty but the buckets were half-full. They turned Sos upside down, so that he was looking on to the floor and then he was immediately over the urinal bucket and looking in.

'One,' said Ned and they began to swing him.

Sos began to struggle again, for this was unspeakable.

'Two,' said Ned and they swung him again.

It was quite impossible to move a limb, because the many hands gripped him as securely as if he had been bound with ropes.

'Three,' said Ned, 'and in he goes!' and they swung him higher till his hair brushed the rim of the bucket, and the acrid smell of ammonia was in his nostrils.

'Now, what's all this?' said a voice and Sos found himself lying across one of the duckboards with the bucket at his side. There was no sign of his assailants. They had scattered. He could hear the sound of their footsteps, echoing down the stone stairs that led out of the ablutions. He sat up and rubbed the back of his head, on which in their hurry they had dropped him to the floor. The barrack-room corporal was striding towards him.

'Now what's all this?' he said.

He stood staring at Sos as if the latter had tried to set the barracks on fire. Sos scrambled to his feet and went to his bed.

'Nothing, sir,' said Sos.

The corporal's cheeks went purple, where they had been red, and his neck seemed to swell.

'Well, we don't want any more of that, anyway,' he said.

The corporal turned to Noakes.

'What's been going on here?'

'Nowt,' said Noakes.

'Who's been mucking about with that young recruit?'

'Better ask him, Corporal. He knows best.'

'Come here, you,' said the corporal.

Sos trotted up to him. Noakes returned to his paper.

'Has anybody been setting about you?' said the corporal.

'No,' said Sos.

'Then what are you doing out in the ablution benches?'

'I slipped, Corporal.'

'On the soap, I suppose.'

'Yes, Corporal.'

'Well, there ain't no bleeding soap kept out there. Each man's got his own.'

A deep subterranean rumbling sounded from behind Noakes's paper. The corporal glanced in Noakes's direction, but the sound ceased, though the edges of the paper continued to quiver.

'Now see, me lad,' said the corporal and he stood with his arms akimbo and his head on one side and he screwed up his eyes, so he looked a very wise owl indeed.

'Now see,' he said. 'If you'd been more than five minutes in the Service I'd have taken you before the Officer for conduct prejudicial to good order and 'iding the truth beside. But seeing as 'ow you're nothing more than a poor bleeding little rookie what don't know 'is nose from 'is nappies, I'll look it over this time. But another squeak outer you, young feller, and I'll 'ang, draw and quarter you alive.'

And with that he strode from the room.

Sos crossed the spotless floor to where his battered bowler lay and picked it up and carried it back to his locker. The rim of the hat had been nearly ripped off and there was a hole in the crown and a great dent in the side.

He handled it tenderly under the fan-tail gas light that buzzed in the wall between the beds, but the brim came off, so that he dropped the thing on to the parcel of clothes and sat down on the edge of the bed, because there seemed nothing else for it but to turn in.

Noakes put down his paper and surveyed him mournfully.

'You don't want to take no notice of him,' he said. 'All corporals is the same. All spit and splutter.'

He sucked his teeth expressively.

'But you'll do,' he said and went back to his reading. Ned and his followers began to return in ones and twos as Sos climbed into bed. It appeared that they had managed to dodge the corporal, but it had been draughty below in their shirt sleeves. After a little time they gathered in a little group once more and began to talk in undertones, then they went across to Sos's bed and he became afraid again. He was doubly afraid now because whatever they might do to complete their interrupted programme, he would incur the wrath of the corporal as well, whatever Noakes's views might be. He felt then very lonely and deserted, but he sat up as they approached the foot of the bed and clenched his fists beneath the blankets.

'Did the corporal have anything to say to you?' said Ned, and he laid his hand on the truckle at the foot of the bed so that he could tip Sos out at a moment's notice.

'Yes,' said Sos. 'He asked me if anyone had been setting about me.'

'So you told 'im, eh?' said Ned and he raised the truckle a few inches from the floor.

'I told him nothing,' said Sos.

'You swear on oath?' said Ned.

Noakes put down his middle page and rose slowly to his stockinged feet. Sos thought that he had never seen such a big man, now that he was standing. His shirt was open at the chest and the hair bunched out of the gap like a tawny beard. His shirt sleeves were half rolled up and his arms, too, were thick with a reddish growth. There was an intertwined snake in purple and vermilion tattooed round his left wrist.

'No one's swearing nothing on oath,' said Noakes, 'because there ain't no call for it. And this lad's all right and he's speaking the truth. And if you'll take the advice of a friend you'll drop this little bit of fooling and make yourselves scarce and take a nice walk before lights out and cool off.'

'There's no need for you to interfere,' said Ned, but he dropped the truckle.

'I ain't interfering with no one,' said Noakes. 'That's not my way and you know it. But the last bloke wot doubted *my* word — and I'm saying this lad is speaking the truth, for I've been here all the time — the last bloke was Danny O'Flaherty wot was one-time middle-weight champion of this 'ere very Company. And he ended up with a broken jaw and a mouthful of teeth.'

He raised his left forearm and Sos saw the clenched fist that looked as if it were carved out of a gnarl of oak. The intertwined serpent looked like a very ringlet of chivalry.

'And this is wot did it,' said Noakes.

He watched them as they shrugged and grinned a little sheepishly at one another and then he touched Ned on the shoulder, so that for the moment the other nearly started back.

'That's all right,' said Noakes. 'You're a good lad, Ned. It's all over and done with and we're all good boys together and we won't live a thousand years.'

They went off then at once and Sos went down under his blankets and his heart began to stop its thumping. He heard the next bed creak as Noakes rolled back on it. He turned on his side and went to sleep.

Thereafter it was all comparatively easy. No one molested him again. On the square the drill sergeant perceptibly softened as the weeks went on. He no longer seemed to look upon his protégés as creatures too inhuman to contemplate. True, he seldom praised them in any direct fashion though he compared them quite favourably with some of the lower forms of insect life.

But the range and the small arms school chiefly delighted Sos. He took to his musketry with a natural aptitude and he looked forward to every bayonet-fighting class. He came to know other lads in the depot enlisted in the terms of the Boy's service and they served as companions, but not altogether satisfactorily. Therefore he returned to Noakes.

Noakes had naturally assumed the sort of aura, though of a very different kind, that had once been Grandpapa's. He was mentor and confessor at the same time. But the things he taught were not all the sort of things that the patriarch of Tankerville House would have sanctioned, though it is very doubtful if inwardly he would have disapproved. Wise in his ancient generation, he had always known the value of a practical and worldly knowledge.

There were two leading subjects which interested Noakes and given the opportunity he would discourse upon them for hours at a time. One was square-pushing and the other was booze. He took both subjects with a kind of melancholy satisfaction in his own techniques. He was not an unduly licentious man and it is doubtful if he ever indulged to the slightest degree of excess. As Joseph had expounded on the qualities of Keen Men, who knew where the money lay, so Noakes could only feel it part of his duty to tell the rising generation what a young soldier should know.

Basically, square-pushing was the art of picking up members of the opposite sex successfully when off duty, without being snubbed in the process. Once that first step was accomplished the business took — or should take — the form of a routine. It was a kind of drill.

It was, said Noakes, for instance quite a reasonable proposition which might show dividends, being in best blue complete with swagger-stick, to journey to one of the neighbouring residential resorts when the nursemaids were taking the children out for an airing on the promenade. Once there, it was necessary to curb any temptation toward the impetuous and to make a careful reconnaissance of the field of activity. Sure enough, sooner or later, so Noakes assured Sos, a presentable piece of homework would come in view. At this point caution was necessary. Only ladies wheeling babies in prams were suitable subjects. Sos asked why.

'Don't be so daft,' said Noakes. 'Sometimes I wonder if I'll ever make anything out of you. If she's got a kid what can talk, when it gets home it'll blab, won't it? You ain't 'alf dense.'

'Well, what do you do with the baby?' said Sos. Even at that stage of his career he was quite convinced that two were company and three were not.

'Gawd strike a light,' said Noakes. 'You don't do nuffink with the bleeding baby. What you do is you goes up very politely, having walked past once or twice and had a dekko at the likely female, and you does a bit of a salute, jaunty-like and says something in a hoity-toity way, such as "Morning, Nurse, how's the baby?" Well, if she cottons on to that, you just keep company with her, keeping a weather eye open to see if the old woman's coming along.'

'What old woman?'

''Er Missis, softie. The old 'aybag that employs her. 'Cos she'll scotch it all if she catches you. Well, you take a little walk up and down and tell 'er the baby's a proper little nipper and then you ask her if she often comes out for an airing this way. If she lets on, you can reckon you have made a very nice start. So you meets her again, just the same way, and you do the same, about four times. You can't rush these things for proper results. Then, when she's got to expecting you like at those hours when you're off and what suit her, you ask her what's her night off. If she tells you that, too, you're coming along fine. Then you meets her.'

Noakes sighed and then sucked his teeth reminiscently.

'Well, you takes her out. It'll make a bit of a hole in your pay-roll but you can't help that. You take her to a music-hall or if you can get into one of them 'oly concerts what's free all the better. You can take a little drop of something in your pocket and give her a nip or two. Some like it, some don't. It mostly depends on their ages and what's gone before.'

'What's gone before?'

'Yus. Whether she's a cut-and-come-again or just a teaser. I think you ask these here silly questions just to aggravate me. Well, after a time or two, you suggests a walk. It ought to be a nice fine evening. You goes out into the country —'

'Where's the baby?'

'Oh, Gawd struth, she ain't got no baby with her, it's her night off. The baby's at 'ome, piddling in it's cot as 'appy as can be. Well, you gets her out in the country, if you'll allow me to tell you — and you find a nice seat in an 'edge with them pretty butterflies buzzing around you and you slips your arm round 'er waist and gives 'er a squeeze — and there you are.'

'Are you?' said Sos.

''Ark at him,' said his tutor. 'Suffering smoke, why don't you go and spend half an hour at a zoo looking at the monkeys?'

On the question of Booze, Noakes was perhaps a little more explicit. There were, he declared, three grades of liquor, Swipes, Wallop and Hard Tack. It depended on the state of a soldier's payroll as to which grade came his and his companion's way. But there was one rule that always had to be observed. No man judged another by the amount he drank, but by the way he took his liquor. The ideal indeed was that a man should take his twelve pints and a 'drop of short' added if funds ran to it, and remain on his feet. That anyone should have a list to starboard after a couple of swigs was completely deplorable, and such a one was to be despised and his company to be avoided.

As for young soldiers the same applied, but they were best confined to swipes, what did nobody any harm and flushed the kidneys; though maybe a snifter or two of hard tack at Christmas time or funerals was permissible.

All this Sos absorbed with avidity, realizing that here indeed were pearls of wisdom that came from a source which, however earthly, was born of experience. But only once did he venture to suggest that he might accompany Noakes either on one of his minor tours of square-pushing or on a round of the local public-houses.

'Come with me!' said Noakes. 'I wouldn't 'ave your company. What would a little feller like you do along of me? I'd have yer sloshed in 'arf an hour and some of them tarts gets a bit saucy.'

Sos must have looked his disappointment, for Noakes at once expounded his theme.

'I don't mean I don't like your company. But you're not in my class. It ain't your fault — you're only a kid. And what's more I don't hold with taking young fellers out and showing 'em the ropes. Let 'em find out for themselves, I say. It's not up to no older chaps to lead the little 'uns astray. Give 'em good advice as I've given you and then let 'em go.'

The long hours and early rising, the routine and restrictions were daily becoming accepted as part of a particular way of living, that was in turn becoming enjoyable.

The fatigues and drills passed so quickly and regularly that, with his complete physical fitness, Sos could turn his mind and body to athletics. He improved his boxing and his score marks on the range gradually mounted. He found life very satisfactory. He seldom thought of Highbury. Very often, he day-dreamed of the time when he, too, would carry three red stripes upon his sleeve. Then, three months almost to the day, as they broke from the afternoon's last duty, he was sent for.

'Marine Cohen. To report to the Adjutant's office, at once.'

He stepped out across the square towards the rectangular flat buildings which were Depot Headquarters. He knew which way to go in, because once he had done a fatigue there, cleaning up the surrounds. He knew, too, the proper channel of approach to the august authority that had demanded his presence, and that he must ask for the Regimental Sergeant Major. What he did not know and what filled him one moment with terrifying apprehensions, the next with fantastic surmise, was the reason for this urgent summons. In what heinous crime had he been discovered? Or had at last his as yet unrecognized merits been discovered?

He knew enough not to question the Sergeant Major as to what might be at hand. The basilisk eye flickered over him and he was curtly ordered to wait outside the Adjutant's door till he was sent for. He waited in the corridor, a prey to every hope and fear. If he couldn't recollect any of the evil he had done, he certainly couldn't remember any of the good.

When the orderly put his head out of the door and called his name he was across the corridor in a couple of strides and then he was inside the Adjutant's office and his right hand was at the salute.

The Adjutant was at his desk, running through a sheaf of papers. Sos had seen him distantly on Battalion or Church Parade. Three people sat with their backs to the light beneath the far window. Sos could just see them out of the corner of one eye, but the rest of that eye and the whole of the other were fixed on the officer.

The Adjutant snatched a file and whisked it open. He was a strikingly handsome man in the early thirties and his dark hair curled crisply from his high white forehead.

'729371 Marine Cohen, L.?'

'Yes, sir,'

'You're leaving. Hand in your kit and pack your personal belongings.'

Sos felt quite weak at the knees. The only worse thing that they could have done than this, would to have been to put him against the headquarters wall and shoot him.

'Leaving, sir?' Sos was amazed.

'You've been bought out.'

The Adjutant inclined his head towards the window. Sos let his eyes slowly wander in that direction. There they sat. Mamma in the middle, on her right Uncle Joe and on her left Blanche. Uncle Joe's top hat was on the seat beside him and his neatly gloved hands were clasped on the ivory crook of his elegant ebony stick. He looked almost as inscrutable as the sphinx. Mamma sat bolt upright, her hands folded in her lap, very white, prim and her nose a little in the air as a war-horse might flare its nostrils before the charge. Blanche, another new bonnet of pink and white over her fringe of ringlets, fluttered her eyes at the Adjutant, who smoothed back his hair and said:

'This is your man, I think. Perhaps, Madam, you would care to drop in at the Mess for a cup of tea, while your son gets himself ready?'

He spoke ostensibly to Mamma, but his attention was on Blanche. The latter contrived a delicate blush and Sos rejoiced at the memory of the times at Tankerville House, when he'd pulled her hair.

'I don't want to leave, sir,' he said. 'Please, sir —'

Uncle Joe rose to his feet. He waved Sos aside with one gesture of his hand. He addressed the Adjutant.

'Mrs Cohen and Miss Blanche Cohen will be delighted to join you in your Mess. I, if I may, will follow in a few minutes, when I have had a word with my nephew. Be good enough, Blanche, to hand me his clothes.'

Blanche passed over a brown-paper parcel. The Adjutant left his desk, put on his cap, and escorted the ladies to the door.

'There's your change of clothes,' said Uncle. 'You're coming back with us right away, but we've no wish to be seen with you in those things.'

'I want to stay here,' said Sos. 'Uncle Joe, why can't I stay here? I'm doing fine. I get on with the other fellows and you oughtn't to talk about our uniform like that. We rank with the Guards, you know.'

'Rank?' said Uncle Joe. 'That's just the point. A ranker! To think what your father would have felt, had he lived to see this day.'

'I'm not ashamed of what I've done,' said Sos.

'I don't think you know the meaning of the word. Do you ever think of anything except yourself? The anxiety you've caused. The distress to your poor Mother. The endless police enquiries.'

'I'm sorry,' said Sos. 'I didn't think anybody would miss me. And it was pretty awful in Aldersgate. I don't want to go back there. I couldn't stand it any more, Uncle.'

'They wouldn't have you after the way you've behaved,' said Uncle Joe. 'Poor Joseph was half out of his mind when you never turned up. He took it as a personal responsibility that he couldn't account for you. For a time they checked on all the accounts after making certain that the petty cash was all right. They weren't sure you hadn't made off with something. That's the humiliation you've brought to us. But this is going to be the end of it.'

Sos stood with the parcel of clothes in his arms, and he thought of that other parcel which he'd had by his bed when he first arrived and of the bowler hat on top of it. It all came back very vividly to him, with Ned mincing down the barrack-room. He didn't bear Ned any malice for that night, nor any of the others, because they'd become friends and had accepted him. But it made him rage inwardly to hear this talk of humiliation. Uncle Joe had never been swung over a bucket at the end of the ablution-benches, and he was sure that Joseph had never suspected him for a thief. This was the way it always went, had always gone. He didn't want their polite and proper ways. He wanted to do things on his own. It wasn't his fault if he wasn't like the others. Really, only Grandpapa had ever understood and Grandpapa had gone long since. He wished he could give Uncle Joe a sample of a few of the words and phrases which he had recently been taught, though he himself never used them. Uncle Joe was speaking again.

'Twenty pounds it's cost us to buy you out. Andrew Cohen's son a ranker! Imagine what people could have said! Well, we've decided what to do with you. We've had about enough of it. You're getting out of this country. As soon as we'd traced you, we arranged it all, and this time, my boy, there's going to be no funny business. You're travelling steerage on the *Pretoria Castle* for Cape Town next week to your Uncle Harry Freeman in Johannesburg who's promised to see what sort of job he can make of you!'

'Africa!'

'Exactly.'

'Absolutely marvellous!' said Sos.

'*What's* that you said?' said Uncle Joe.

Sos cleared his throat. 'I just said that's fine,' he said. 'Africa... *Africa!*'

'I'm glad you think so,' said Uncle Joe ...

1944: INTERMEZZO

Sos couldn't be quite sure at first, if the smoke driving across the perspex was growing thinner or whether the glow of the burning engine beyond was growing brighter. As far as that went it could be a fifty-fifty chance — the same toss of the coin that could decide if they were ever to reach home. He kept his eyes on the sinister glow beyond the perspex.

What was he going to do when he got home? Real home, that was to say. Not an affair of Nissen huts or requisitioned buildings, but the home he'd left in Sussex. The house known as 'Hill' in Slinfold. He was going to farm again. He'd turn more fields to arable and grow corn. He'd breed pigs. It wasn't the first time he'd dealt with stock. Years back in Lourenço Marques he'd traded in cattle, buying the half-starved beasts off the natives, fattening them up and shipping them down to the coast. And once he'd had a butcher's shop and supplied the British fleet in Delagoa Bay.

Farming. That was it. Using the earth as it should be used, feeding and caring for it, so that in turn it could care for you and yours.

It was surprising how many of the chaps had decided to farm. Not that any of them knew much about it, indeed, far less than himself. Perhaps it was because he'd so often talked about 'Hill' in the Mess, that they'd become interested. But it was easy to understand how their thoughts were led in that direction. Farming was a great life. The house was quiet and the meadows and the fields were quiet. There would be solitude and silence and there would be no sudden thundering in the night nor the clatter of machine-gun fire. There, beneath the open sky, unmenaced by raider or cannonade, there would be peace.

There was Henry again on the 'inter-com':

'Sos... How's it look?'

Sos peered through the perspex. There was less smoke. He was sure of it now.

'It's clearing a bit.'

'Is she still alight?'

'I'm afraid so.'

'I'll give her another do.'

The smoke still drifted past.

One day, perhaps, they'd all reach home. Everyone sought for an anchorage. For himself, after all his wanderings, the Sussex countryside — unless he were cheated now...

1892–1894

CHAPTER THREE: THE GOLDEN LAND OF PROMISE

All the twenty-one days to Cape Town, Sos thought of practically nothing else but his destination. He was going to the land from which Martin the African boy had come, of which he'd spoken; the land of promise, which the sailors of Tyneside knew and whose legends they had recounted over the steaming cups of tea.

He had done wrong and must admit it to himself. He'd caused no end of trouble, always had. He had pained Mamma and shocked his sisters; and his Uncle Joe thought nothing of him at all. So they'd packed him off and good riddance to bad rubbish, he supposed. Only at times a certain anger and indignation smouldered in him.

But if they'd meant to punish him they'd barked up the wrong tree and no mistake. They were sending him to Eldorado, to the golden land of promise beyond the hills, to the land where the crock of gold was waiting to be dug up at the rainbow's end.

Often he wondered what sort of fellow Uncle Harry Freeman Cohen would turn out to be, and what he'd look like and what sort of a house he had and whether it would be very grand. Since Uncle Harry was already controlling a small mining company, Sos pictured the house as a spacious bungalow surrounded by its private grounds; nothing like Tankerville House but a genial sunlit building with servants running here and there at his Uncle's bidding.

But despite the fine weather and the novelty of a sea voyage he was glad to reach Cape Town, for he felt three weeks was a long time to go before setting foot on land, ready to take the high road to fortune and fame.

He didn't take the high road, but he took the train to the last rail-head up North near Vereeniging. The train jangled and clattered across the African veldt, which stretched endlessly on either side of him. The heat seemed to increase with every mile, the sun beating on the carriage roofs so that the bare, wooden-seated compartments smelt of hot iron and oil. Only at the occasional stops could food and a glass of luke-warm water, which generally tasted of paraffin, be obtained. He was inordinately glad to arrive, his face grimed with sweat-streaked dust. He washed his face and neck and hands under a tap in the luggage yard and clambered aboard the coach for Johannesburg.

The coach was drawn by twelve mules and it jolted and swayed as it made its way along the irregular, unmetalled track. After the smell of the train and the oppressive atmosphere, it was refreshing to sit up in the boot and take stock of his surroundings.

His spirits rose, because he was near his goal, and a new, brave life was about to begin. Then as they came round a bend in the track, through the bare veldt, he had his first glimpse of the town, whose fame was so steadily rising.

He hadn't known quite what to expect, except he knew it was bound to be impressive; any great mining centre would be. A fellow passenger, who till now had sat silent and for most of the way had picked his teeth with a splinter of wood, nudged Sos's arm and jerked his thumb towards the widespread litter of tin huts and shanties on their left.

'Jo'burg,' he said.

Sos stared with dismay. There didn't seem to be a brick building anywhere. The heat shimmered over the plain and around the corrugated iron buildings. Smoke rose here and there, and now that the mules, approaching their journey's end, had dropped into a walk, he could hear a gentle confused murmuring such as is heard when a large body of men are gathered together in surrounding loneliness. Far away to the north he could see what looked like the outline of low flat-topped hills, then the coach was in the town and Sos was clambering down and searching for his luggage.

The moment he was down, the reddish dust rose about him in a cloud and there was a tumult of voices as people ran to greet the travellers or chivvied the driver with news from the south. There was for a short time quite a considerable concourse round the coach, and several 'boys' were busy outspanning the mules for the relief team.

Sos stood alone with his luggage containing all he possessed and he wasn't sure what to do, because although there were quite substantial buildings surrounding the square, there seemed little semblance of orderly planned streets.

Standing here, unwelcomed and unknown, he felt more conclusively than ever that the days of his past life were gone, and no semblance of them would return. Not only had he left his home behind him, but he had crossed an ocean and stood now, solitary and unrecognized, not merely in a strange land but on a vast continent that held every possible opportunity for triumph or disaster. But chiefly for the moment he was disconcerted and a little alarmed. Then he heard a voice behind him:

'Lionel Cohen?'

Sos turned and found himself facing what must clearly be Uncle Harry Freeman Cohen.

He saw a medium-height, slim figure in dusty dungarees and a broad-brimmed hat. The face was dark and keen and the chin carried a little goatee beard that jutted out, a trifle imperiously. Immediately behind stood an African servant.

'Uncle Harry Cohen?'

'Correct.'

They shook hands. Uncle Harry motioned to the 'boy'. He stepped forward and picked up Sos's traps.

'We'll get along to my place,' said Uncle Harry. 'How's everyone at home? Is your mother well and Uncle Joe? How are all the sisters?'

Sos answered the questions to the best of his ability. At the back of his mind another question persisted. How much of his record had preceded him? He felt sure that, given the opportunity, Uncle Joe would have laid it on pretty thick. But it was the general aspect of his new surroundings that distracted him, so that once on their way through the town, Uncle Harry had to repeat an enquiry and even at that early acquaintanceship Sos recognised a sharpness, a curtness in the repeated phrase. It was quite obvious that Uncle Harry was accustomed to have the promptest of attention paid to his authority.

They stopped at last in front of a long, low-built shed. Smoke came from a stove-pipe chimney at one end and there were windows at regular intervals down its length. A white man and a gang of workmen were busy overhauling what looked like a windlass, and there was a coil of iron cable lying alongside. Sos supposed that the shed was a workshop or a store. An attempt had been made to give it a coat of paint, but the red ochre stopped abruptly in a ragged edge half-way down the length of the building.

Uncle Harry called to the white man:

'Here's my young nephew, Wally, fresh from home.'

As the other approached he explained:

'My consulting engineer.' Then: 'Well, this is the boy. Lionel, this is Mr Walters. We've put you in the room next to him. He isn't as noisy as some of us. Take him along, Wally, and show him round.'

'This way,' said Wally.

He walked with long, lumbering steps, so that even for that short distance Sos nearly had to break into a trot. Wally's hat was pushed to the back of his head and his hair fell on his forehead. His face was streaked with grime and there were black oil smears on his bare forearms.

'It's not what you'd call luxurious,' he said. 'But I've known far worse. At least the water's laid on. The tap's at the back by the main cistern. You'll find it easy enough.'

He led the way into the shack.

'There's eleven of us put up here,' he explained, 'but we're partitioned off, you see, so you get a bit of real private.'

It was assuredly partitioned off, with a wall of canvas or hessian between each compartment. He pushed Sos into his room. His bag was already there.

'When you've unpacked, you'll find me outside, where I was before. Then we'll go for a meal. We don't eat here. But there's a good place in town. Now, make yourself at home.' He pushed the sacking aside and strode out.

Sos looked around him. Two walls were of corrugated iron, two of canvas. A wooden bed, not unlike that in his barrack-room at Deal, stood against the bleak iron wall. The single window, with a chest of drawers beneath it, was in the other. The glass of the window was totally obscured by dust, so that it might have been frosted. By the bed, with its four blankets and mattress, was a small packing case covered with a square of hessian, and there was a bucket at the foot.

Sos sat on the bed and stared with dismay at the cheerless walls and the patched and crumpled sacking of the partition. He couldn't make it out at all. At home they'd talked of Uncle Harry as a man of means, as someone who was a successful pioneer in a virgin land of promise. Uncle Harry was a mine owner. He found gold and dug it up. He could be a millionaire. But here was Uncle Harry living in a squalid settlement in the most primitive conditions and his home was something not far removed from a cow-shed.

But there was nothing to be done about it. Sos had been set upon his course and he must keep to it. Then his spirits rose again almost at once and he told himself that, after all, this was a mining town and the men all around were miners and a fortune lay beneath their very feet.

And there was no doubt, he assured himself, that Uncle Harry would put him to work where the yellow gold lay thickest. He hadn't any idea what a reef might look like or how the precious metal was mined. Sufficient for the moment that he should put a brave face on the situation, make the best of it, show himself willing and rejoice that he should have the opportunity of collecting a fortune.

Uncle Harry put him to work in the Elephant Trading Company of Johannesburg. He explained that it was impossible to employ Sos within his own activities as the mine was still only in the prospecting stage and none but skilled labour was needed. Sos thought the Elephant Trading Company was comparable only to Hell.

Like every building in Johannesburg except the very few, such as the Stock Exchange, the Elephant Trading Company's premises were of corrugated iron. It seemed to Sos in a very short time that it was a particular type of iron which had been especially invented to attract the heat. The Company traded in blankets and trinkets for the natives and household utensils for the settlers and pioneers.

But chiefly it was blankets and each one held more dust than could possibly be imagined. As a junior clerk and general assistant, it was part of his duties to keep a check on the stock. He was enveloped in clouds of the perpetual dust that came from the mining dumps and drifted incessantly through the town. He sweated and he choked.

But he learnt a great deal of the political issues which were tearing the country apart; and at Mayo's Restaurant, where for the sum of a shilling a first-rate meal could be bought, he heard that the Matabele were in revolt. To Mayo's, moreover, came the traders and merchants, the adventurers and the prospectors. In the weeks that followed he caught snatches of their conversations and overheard on most days a denunciation of the Boers, of the ill-treatment of the settlers and the lack of interest of the Imperial Government at home.

He heard the name of Kruger, the Boer President, and of his opponent, of Doctor Jameson who was the right-hand man and trusted friend of Cecil Rhodes; and always of Cecil Rhodes.

It seemed that no day passed but the name of that tremendous personality came his way. The activities of the Chartered Company, which was Rhodes's chief concern, were invariably the subject of speculation. Rhodes was intent on building an Empire and building it in his own way. The great imperialist was obsessed by his dream of an 'all red' Cape-to-Cairo railway, and everything he did was conditioned by that dream.

Sos endured the Elephant Trading Company for two months then he went to Uncle Harry and said that he had had enough of it. Uncle Harry jutted his beard out at him and asked him who the devil he thought he was. Sos made no reply to that particular query but reiterated the fact that he was not going to return to the store.

With some considerable exasperation Uncle Harry found him a position as an unauthorized clerk on the Johannesburg Stock Exchange.

It was certainly an improvement on the Trading Company, and his companions were very definitely less odorous if still less picturesque. They were indeed very much of a kin with the junior clerks whom he'd grown to recognize so readily in the streets round Charterhouse Square. Admittedly their clothes were less severe and of a slightly more dashing aspect, helped out no doubt by the ubiquitous dust, and their faces were tanned where their Aldersgate counterparts had appeared wan and pale; but nevertheless in some form or another they were tied to their desks.

Somewhere north the adventurers were gathering together. In saloons and bars and dancing booths agents were passing, moving through the throng of men thirsty for fortune. It was going on all the time.

Sos said to Uncle Harry Freeman Cohen:

'This job as a clerk is awful. What was the good of coming out here just to get my fingers inky all over again?'

'None at all,' said Uncle Harry and his beard quivered. 'None at all since that's the way you look at it, after all that everyone's done for you. You can fend for yourself.'

Smallpox broke out amongst the African miners on the Reef. It spread rapidly, a terrible scourge in a tropical climate. Two mines were closed and a quarantine compound was immediately formed for all personnel who might have been infected. The authorities well knew how fatal the consequences could be if the pestilence reached the town and circulated amongst the customers in the stores, the eating-places and the drinking shanties. Therefore the wire was of double thickness round the quarantine compound and an armed guard was posted to prevent the interned natives breaking out over the week-ends for their drink and women.

No amount of persuasion or argument could convince them that it was disaster and death, possibly to the entire community, if the scourge got the upper hand in an isolated settlement, understaffed by doctors. It served little purpose to explain laboriously that it was essential that suspected contacts should confine themselves strictly to their quarantine. Given the opportunity the whole camp would be prepared to break out. Moreover the vicious element of the 'poor white', the inevitable and loathsome flotsam of a mining town, was suspected of supplying the interned men with 'fire-water'.

The smallpox guard was strengthened. Recruits were called for. Sos homeless, penniless and out of work, applied for the job.

'Can you handle firearms?'

'I served with the Royal Marines.'

'*Goud*! But there is to be no shooting, unless by order, though you will keep a round ready, but not in the breech. Your quarters are just beyond the Reef. Report to the Police Sergeant in charge there and you will be told your duties.'

From a purely relative viewpoint, dossing down under canvas with half a dozen men or so was not so very much more unpleasant than existing in Uncle Harry's residence. Sos felt it was good, moreover, to have a weapon to handle once more, though his confidence in its ability to destroy anybody but its temporary owner rapidly declined when he inspected the barrel. The inside was blotched with rust.

But the eight men in his tent were reasonable companions. Four of them played poker half the night and all the hours they were off duty. The remainder gossiped amongst themselves, and the regular police sergeant in charge of them left them well alone, except for his inspection rounds. The trend of their conversation was invariably the same. Here in Johannesburg only the man with capital could now get a foot in. It was either that or possessing technical knowledge. For the likes of themselves, the pickings were small. If there were more profitable work to do would they waste their time keeping a poxy crowd behind the wire?

But up north it was different, up beyond Mashonaland. There, a man could fight his way to prosperity and renown. There, the prize went to the keen of eye and the swift of limb. There, no quarter was given for none was asked and the victor was the man who was there first. That was the virgin land to reach, the promised land, the realms of Eldorado.

Sos lay in his blankets and listened to the talk and the words hummed in his brain. He thought of all the way he had come and how far off still, how many hundreds of miles between, was the land of his desire. But he was no longer in Tyneside dreaming dreams, nor was he in Charterhouse Square handling the goods that came from the ends of the earth, and he, ignorant of the very air which gave them their being. Rather, he was in the presence of men who were discussing in a practical fashion the ways and means of attaining their ends. There was talk again of the British South African Police and how Rhodes was forming two punitive volunteer columns at Victoria and Salisbury. Sos rolled over in his blankets and went to sleep dreaming that he was riding at the head of the Victoria Column, with a bandolero slung round his shoulders and his rifle in its long leather holster slapping against his saddle-flaps.

It was not part of his temperament to consider the possibility of failure. He was seventeen years of age and the world was before him. Only at times when he was on duty and he saw the broken and degraded white men lounging near the compound barrier, did his heart for a moment sink, in that there, maybe, by the grace of God might any man go, in this country which he was already beginning to recognize as heartless.

No African could buy any liquor, only white men could enter the bars or stores. So in his rags, bearded and flea-bitten, the 'poor white' would wait, eager to allow the black man to drop the coins in his furtive palm, so that he might steal off and buy liquor on commission.

Now at this hour before sundown of this Saturday afternoon, at the beginning of Sos's watch, such a one was by the wire and there was considerable argumentation with the inmates beyond. Voices were raised and there was much gesticulation. It was apparent that some sort of bargain was being struck. But Sos saw no open passing of bottle or flask, which was the customary bungling of the illegal transactions by which so many of the agents were caught, though one lean black arm and grasping fingers were already outstretched through the strand of the compound wire.

Sos approached slowly, taking stock of the situation and its participants. The white man was much as any other of his kind, his beard thick and matted, his cheekbones pressing out of his hollow cheeks, and his desperate eyes staring out of his haggard face. On the other side of the wire were a score of miners, at their head one in a bright check blanket. He was an enormous man, his ears punctured and pegged with two sticks of ivory. His voice was raised to nearly a shouting pitch, his eyes rolled and the spittle ran out of the corners of his mouth. He was half-drunk, but still in control of his faculties.

Whatever might have been the difference of opinion, the matter was swiftly concluded at Sos's approach. The men snatched through the wire at the white man's hand and then before Sos could reach the group they had scattered and disappeared among the hutments of the compound.

'What's your game?' said Sos.

'I ain't up to nothing,' said the 'poor white'. 'You leave other people alone.'

He took a quick glance at the rifle slung over Sos's shoulder.

'What were you selling them?' said Sos.

'I wasn't selling nothing. They're friends of mine. I've worked down below alongside of them.'

'If you ever did any work in your life. Now get out of here.'

The other spat upon the ground, drew the back of his hand across his mouth. Even in the open air there was a sour, rank smell that emanated from him, when he moved.

'Off you go,' said Sos. 'And don't come back.'

The fellow turned about and slouched off, his arms swinging by his side, his shoulders hunched. The miners were gathering together again on the other side of the wire, enjoying the altercation. Thirty paces off the white man stopped and turned. He shook his fist in the air. He screamed out his imprecations as if he were a madman. There were no limits to his blasphemies and obscenities.

Sos unslung his rifle and slipped it to his shoulder, aligning his sights upon that shaking, insensate figure. The man flung up his arms, wheeled about and fled. From the compound rose a roar of laughter.

Sos shouldered his rifle and went on his rounds. His duty was simple enough. It was to watch the wire and see that there was no attempt at a break-out. In the normal course of events the natives were allowed out of their camps to visit the red-light quarter. This break they considered as their right, quarantine or no. There was this sundown, however, a distinct feeling of unrest in the air. Now and again, Sos could hear the faint and eerie rhythm of native drums and marimbas somewhere in the middle of the compound. Now and again a voice would rise, high-pitched and wailing. Then the drums would go on again.

He walked down the length of the wire and it seemed to him that there was undue movement between the huts as if the camp were disturbed and uneasy, and its inmates were restless and apprehensive. It would be dark soon, with the suddenness of the African twilight. He completed his tour round the compound, turned about and made his way slowly back.

The first hint of dusk was in the sky when he saw the handful of natives standing outside the wire. They were facing the camp and waving their arms excitedly. There was a crowd inside, pressing forward, then swaying back, then surging out on the flanks. The miner in the check blanket stood head and shoulders above the little group that clustered around him outside the compound. Even from the distance where he stood, Sos could see that the wire was down.

The full significance of the calamity struck him immediately. There were nearly a thousand natives in quarantine and he was certain that by now the liquor had been freely circulating. The main guard of the thirty smallpox guards was a quarter of a mile off. The man in the check blanket was exhorting his comrades to follow him and break camp. There was no doubt at all but that he was, by now, quite drunk.

Sos felt the pit of his stomach contract and he felt a little sick. He knew it was merely a matter of minutes before the mob might decide to follow their leader's invitation. The latter was shouting now and yet another of his companions picked his way through the strands of severed wire and joined the group outside. Very soon more of his companions would follow, at first a trickle and then in full spate as they poured out into the open. Sos thought to himself: What was it that Martin had said on the sands of St. Mary's Island off Whitley Bay? — a century or more ago or so, it seemed.

'None of my people would ever lay hands upon a white man, unless he showed fear.'

Sos unslung his rifle and slipped a cartridge into the breech. Then he took the whistle which they'd issued to him and he blew a long and piercing blast. He hoped with all his heart and soul that the main guard were on the alert, because one bullet wouldn't go far against a thousand antagonists, and now he saw that several of the men carried sticks. He knew what they could do with knobkerries. Then he walked across the intervening space resolutely, carrying his rifle at the ready.

'Get back,' he said. 'Get back inside.'

Nobody moved. A silence fell upon the crowd, surging round the gap in the wire. Sos couldn't see them because they were just a dark and menacing presence that he felt might overwhelm him at any minute. All he could see was the convulsed, grimacing face of the man in the check blanket, with the foam frothing at his lips and his blazing eyes.

'Tell them to go back,' said Sos to the leader. 'Order them inside at once.'

Still nobody moved. Only the man in the check blanket swayed on his feet and made as if to raise an arm. The others still gripped their sticks. Sos put his whistle to his lips again and blew long and steadily. He noticed at his feet a wire-cutter and realised what the transaction with the white derelict had been.

He gripped his rifle very tightly in case it should betray his trembling, because it was something which he couldn't control.

So he kept the butt pressed hard against his hip and his eyes steady upon his adversary. The fellow lurched forward and Sos's finger tightened on the trigger. But the man fell on his knees and started to vomit.

'Take him inside,' said Sos.

They dropped their sticks and carried the unconscious native behind the wire. Sos followed up to the outer strands and took up position by the gap, with his rifle still at the ready. The others crowded round their leader, but he lay unconscious on his back, half-suffocating himself. One of his followers prodded him in the ribs with his big toe.

'Roll him on his side,' said Sos, 'or he'll choke himself with his own spew.'

Then he heard running footsteps behind him and knew that the main guard had come up with him. The sergeant took over and they patched the wire and carried the ring-leader to the cells.

Later that night, one old-timer in Sos's tent, said to him:

'How did you get 'em to go back?'

'I told them to,' said Sos.

The other picked his nose thoughtfully. He, in his time, had once been down the mines and had also worked washing for gold-dust on the river's banks.

'Just told them to go, did you?' he said. 'And they went. Well, that's just it.'

He stared solemnly at Sos across the flickering lantern. The poker school were busy counting their chips and dealing a new hand.

'Don't you ever forget what you've learnt this afternoon,' he said. 'No, don't you ever forget it.'

The worst watch for Sos out of the twenty-four hours was the one from midnight to dawn. He would turn in at ten o'clock and snatch a couple of hours' sleep but it was a torture to wake and crawl out into the bitter cold at midnight and start his patrol, round and round the wire till daylight came. Halfway through his tour of duty, sleep would catch up with him.

At intervals along the camp were improvised sentry boxes where the guards might shelter and take rest between patrols. Below the Reef, Johannesburg slept, but always there were twinkling lights somewhere and a feeling of restlessness. It was if as the very earth softly groaned in travail in her sleep as the men on her bosom clawed at her vitals for the treasure that lay therein.

Sos thought of this all the time that he sat on the little bench in the second sentry-box this particular midnight watch of a week later, but he thought of it in no poetical fashion, being a practical young man. He thought it quite worth while for men to fight and quarrel for the sake of the gold below. There weren't any hardships he would turn his back upon, provided there was fair gain to be had in a fair and proper way. But now he was cold and hungry, because the potato soup had been rather more watery than usual and someone else had helped himself to his quarter-loaf of bread. Besides, he had no ready-made solution to this problem of making a fortune in a few minutes. Indeed, it seemed to him that practically everybody but himself was getting somewhere. That was the point. It was no good just sitting around and waiting for something to turn up. The thing to do was to go out and make things happen. This present job was no good. The hours were long, the work was hard, the pay was poor. Now, if he were a prospector, way up north, there might be something to boast about. But a smallpox guard!

He dozed off.

He woke abruptly in a flurry of thoughts and half-dreams, while his rifle, propped against the side of the sentry-box, fell clattering to the ground. A lantern was swinging in his face and he heard the sergeant's voice:

'Asleep on duty, eh?'

Sos staggered to his feet and a hand fell on his shoulder, while someone else picked up his rifle, but made no attempt to return it to him. He was blinded by the light.

'Take him along,' said the sergeant.

Before he could realize it he was in the charge-room of the Johannesburg gaol. He was still too bewildered to protest and the next thing he knew was that he was alone in a cell. It all seemed to have happened in the course of a few minutes.

He slept no more that night. He knew perfectly well that he was guilty and deserved punishment, but he had no idea what form the latter would take. The offence, if it had occurred in wartime, would have been a very serious one.

He was brought before the court in the morning and duly charged. He was asked what he had to say and he had nothing to say. By the demeanour of the bench and the court he felt he had lost his cause even before it was proved.

There was no difficulty in supporting the charge, which the sergeant preferred. He was very fair. He said that he was sorry that one of his young men, who was showing promise, should fall by the way. If it had been a mere offence against routine he would have overlooked it, as a first offender. But to sleep on duty was to betray the very essence of a special trust.

The bench, influenced no doubt by the fair-mindedness of the chief witness, concurred, adding that in view of the accused's good record they would be lenient. They fined Sos five pounds.

Five pounds! If they had fined him five shillings he would have been hard put to it to lay his hand on the sum.

He tried to explain. He had no money. He had no chance of getting any money. He'd seldom had five pounds of his own, all at one time. Five golden sovereigns! Five jimmy o' goblins! They led him back to prison.

He sat on the bench in the bare cell with his head in his hands, while the sun mounted in the brazen sky outside and beat down mercilessly on to the iron roof. Now and again he rose and sipped at the beaker that stood in a corner, but the water was warm and brackish.

He had no idea what they would do with him. He didn't much care, so disgusted was he with the whole business and with himself for his regrettable lapse. He'd made a proper muck-up of things. He'd upset Mamma and Uncle Joe and shocked his sisters. They'd slung him out of England and Uncle Harry Freeman in Africa had got fed up with him as well. He'd tried to find a job on his own, had found it, made good at it and then he'd lost it. He thought of himself in terms which were familiar to recruits in the Royal Marines. When the door of his cell was flung violently open, he was ready to go to the gallows.

'Come on. You're wanted,' said the gaoler.

He was a heavy-jowled Boer, with little eyes that were almost lustreless. He looked as if he were entirely impervious to pain and was suffering from exaggerated arrested mentality.

'What are they going to do with me?' said Sos. He wasn't particularly scared, but he wanted to know in order to prepare himself. He wasn't going to take it lying down anyway.

'Well,' he said, 'what's the answer?'

'You can clear out,' said the gaoler. 'Your fine's been paid. Be off with you. *Voetsak!*'

Sos snatched up his coat and hat from the bench and was out of the door like lightning. Then he stopped dead in his tracks, because in the corridor stood Uncle Harry Freeman Cohen.

Uncle Harry's hat was on the back of his head, his hands were in his trouser pockets and his little goatee beard was jutting out more aggressively than ever. But his eyes were very bright and now and again there was the slightest twitching at the corners of his mouth, just the same way as Grandpapa had looked sometimes when he had held the slipper ready behind his back.

'What have you got to say for yourself?' said Uncle Harry.

'Thank you for paying my fine,' said Sos. 'Thank you very much, Uncle Harry. It was very kind of you.'

'You were on your own up there, weren't you?' said Uncle Harry.

Sos tried to collect his scattered thoughts. Events had moved so rapidly in the last half-hour and he was so elated at his rescue that it was a trifle difficult to think coherently.

'Oh! that business,' he said. 'You mean when they tried to break out. I thought my last hour had come. It really was a bit frantic, Uncle Harry. Most of them were tight, you know.'

'I heard about it,' said Uncle Harry, drily.

Then he stopped and faced Sos.

'What are you going to do with yourself? They won't have you back now, you know, after this.'

'I don't want to go back,' said Sos. 'It was pretty beastly really. It wouldn't have got me anywhere.'

'Where do you want to get?'

'That's what *I* want to know,' said Sos. 'But I want to be — mixed up in things...'

'Would you like your job back with me? You can have it.'

Sos shuffled his feet.

'Uncle Harry,' he said, at last, and he felt that he looked very foolish because he was embarrassed. 'Don't get me wrong, Uncle Harry, please. It's terribly kind of you, but I couldn't stick it. I'd only turn out no good, again. I'm no good at a desk, Uncle Harry. I wasn't any good really in London, but I was happy when I was a Marine. Only Uncle Joe and Mamma wouldn't let me stay. But I hear there's an idea of recruiting people for a volunteer force up north. I want to get up there. I've heard that the Matabele are out. Everybody's been telling me. The recruiting's being done at Orange Grove.'

'All right,' said Uncle Harry Freeman and he suddenly chuckled. 'Have it your own way.' He now certainly looked very much like Grandpapa, except he wasn't quite so tall.

He drew a hand out of his pocket.

'Take that,' he said, 'to help you on your way.'

He dropped a sovereign into Sos's hand, then he was away striding down the street, towards his tin hut, again, to pick up Wally, his engineer, and set about pegging out yet another claim.

CHAPTER FOUR: A PACKING-CASE IN PRETORIA

Sos went to Orange Grove, a few miles outside Johannesburg.

'I want to join the volunteers,' he said. 'Will you please tell me how I go about it?'

'How old are you?'

'Seventeen, sir.'

'No experience in any other service, of course.'

'I was a Royal Marine, sir.'

'You can shoot?'

'I'd have got my Musketry Certificate within the year.'

'What horsemanship have you got?'

'Just a little, sir.'

'That's not enough for us. Our standard of horsemanship is very high. Besides you're under age. You understand, we have to be careful who we take.'

'I've been on the smallpox guard, sir, and I've been in the Marines. That ought to be good enough, sir.'

'We can't take you. That wouldn't apply to us. But if you could get up north to Victoria or Salisbury you might stand a chance.'

Always the north. Always the call, those hundreds of miles on.

'They could tell you more up there, if you could find your way. Good luck.'

'And the same to you, sir,' said Sos. 'And thank you.'

Well, if that was so, farewell to Johannesburg and its tin huts and dust and smallpox and on to Victoria and the North by way of Pretoria. He collected his few belongings from the tent, and with the package slung over his shoulder, set off whistling on the first lap of thirty-five miles.

He didn't whistle for long. If it were possible to shake the Jo'burg dust from his feet in one sense, it was quite impossible in another. His footsteps sent a steady cloud of floating grit around him. The sun was at its height, but he knew he must do the distance before sundown.

It was his first experience of anything approaching a forced march under tropical conditions and he found it extremely unpleasant. His feet grew sore and the sweat soaked through his clothes, but it seemed to evaporate as it met the heated air. Once he passed a wagon train of oxen with the *voorlooper* at the leading pair, but he encountered no other travellers.

At the end of three hours he took a rest, finding a patch of shade from a clump of thorn trees just off the track. He was feeling very sorry for himself. He had set out so light-heartedly, overwhelmed with his release from prison, with the sovereign in his pocket, and with the knowledge that he was set in the right direction at last. He had taken the precaution of bringing a bottle of water with him, but it was beginning to run low. When he started off again he limped for the first quarter of a mile, till his feet again grew accustomed to their discomfort. The dusty road seemed never ending, but when he first caught sight of Pretoria, some hours later, he could have cried out aloud with delight.

He was footsore and weary, grimed with dust and parched with thirst, but the town lay in the shallow valley before him, like a jewel in the palm of a bare hand. Instinctively he quickened his step and his spirits rose, because this was the first time a dream had anything like approached the truth.

The houses were white and the foliage green and there was a profusion of petunias and jacarandas in the gardens. It was an

93

hour before sundown; men and women in cool white clothes were seated on their verandahs and native 'boys' in short white jackets and narrow trousers passed between the chairs and tables. There was the clink of glasses and the murmur of conversation and now and again a woman's tinkling laughter. It was an amazing thing to think that such a place as Johannesburg could ever have existed.

He passed through the suburbs of the capital and everywhere it was the same, orderly and trim and civilized. Then he stopped outside the saloon called 'La Cigale'.

It was not a very imposing edifice, being in the first instance an affair of corrugated iron, but the interior made up for its exterior deficiencies. The furniture was elegant, for several of the chairs by the marble-topped tables possessed padded velvet backs. There were mirrors on the walls and rows and rows of bottles on the shelves behind the bar. There were spittoons with sawdust in them at every table, and it was quite clear the water in the jugs was changed every day because there was scarcely any dust on the surface. There were also three barmaids, who stood behind the counter at regular intervals. Two were dark-haired, the one in the middle, golden. Or rather near-golden. Sos made up his mind on the latter point and then, discovering there was a wash-house at the back, stripped down to the buff and washed the stains of the journey from him. Then he bathed his feet carefully and combed his hair. He felt a new man already.

He went up to the bar where the golden lady stood, and because it was advertised boldly on a card propped up against a cigar cabinet, ordered a bottle of 'ticky beer'. He had very few ideas about alcohol, except those which Noakes had passed on to him during his brief course of What a Young Soldier Should

Know. But he took it as read, that ticky beer would pass as wallop. He put down his sovereign in payment.

It was really extraordinary what a great deal of silver change came out of one little disc of gold. It was very satisfactory to drop it in a jangling handful into a pocket and to feel its reassuring weight. The ticky beer was like nectar. With the thirst of the day upon him the first glass disappeared in a twinkling. The lady behind the bar watched him with approval then poured him out another bottle. He disposed of it as rapidly and called for a third.

'What's your name?' said Sos.

'Maudie,' said Maudie.

'Then please have a drink with me,' said Sos. 'It's my birthday.'

That's ever so kind,' said Maudie. 'Many 'appy returns. First time you've been here?'

She looked him over appraisingly.

'Yes,' said Sos.

'On business?'

He looked her over, in a similar fashion.

'Prospecting,' he said, which was near enough the truth.

Thereafter everything became gradually and more delightfully confused. Each time he put his hand in his pocket the other two barmaids ranged up alongside. Now and again a customer or two who were obviously 'regulars' drifted down the counter and joined them. Everybody seemed to be very happy and glad to meet Sos and he too, was glad to be in Pretoria with its jacarandas and petunias and ticky beer.

Much later in the evening Maudie said that she had an hour's break off duty and that it was a nice night for a walk. Still later, on the return from the walk, he seemed to have lost Maudie, because he couldn't find her anywhere with the strange streets darker. Nor was he quite sure where 'La Cigale' might be. But his pockets were empty.

He was quite sure of that, because there was now no solid weight against his thigh. He searched all his pockets, including the one on the hip, but there wasn't even a sixpence. He tried to recollect how many ticky beers he'd had, but lost count, and then gave it up because it was quite impossible to remember how many drinks he'd bought the others, to say nothing of the little present for Maudie. It only went to prove the truth of Noakes's philosophy. That booze and square-pushing hit the pay-roll.

But he had to sleep. It was growing cold and the exertions of the day were beginning to tell on him. He knew that he was more or less in the centre of the city, and was surrounded with comparative comfort, if not luxury. But he was penniless.

He was not in the least remorseful. He'd achieved his first goal, and topped up the achievement with a very happy evening, in delightful and refined company. Indeed, one of the party, a bearded giant with a patch over one eye, had actually nearly succeeded in teaching him how to hit the middle of a spittoon at several yards' distance. But where to sleep? Then he saw the packing-case.

It was a large case and might have originally contained an outsize of furniture such as a sideboard or even an upright piano. It lay on its side by the President Hotel opposite the Raadsaal,[1] and even from where he stood, or rather swayed, Sos could see that it was full of shavings and straw.

He crossed the street and claimed the packing-case as his own. He put his meagre bundle of possessions into one corner,

---

[1] The site now of the Grand Hotel, one of the leading hotels of the Capital, where many years later Sos spent several nights between warmed sheets.

and then climbed in himself, pulling one or two of the planks of the lid close behind him and wedging them across the opening. Then he made a couch for himself in the shavings, arranged a bundle of straw as a pillow and pulled the rest over him. He was asleep in seconds.

He awoke from a nightmare of himself and Maudie, struggling in an icy sea of an odorous and sickly liquor which he knew must be ticky beer.

For the moment he was at a loss to remember where he was and in what astonishing kind of bed he might be. Then a distant clock chimed four and he sat up, striking his head sharply on the roof of his cabin, so that he knew at once where he was and in what plight he might be.

He was agonizingly cold. There had been little semblance of warmth in his fragile bed. His teeth were chattering and his head ached abominably. He crept out of his packing-case and started to chafe his hands and rub his limbs. He stamped his feet, and swung his arms, but it was a good five minutes before his circulation was restored. He knew that to return to his roosting place might be fatal. He must keep moving.

He walked through the streets of Pretoria till dawn. He found a tap in a stable yard, where he quenched his fiery thirst and bathed his throbbing temples. Then at last the sun came up, riding into the sky with its cursory dawn, and at last a little warmth penetrated down to him.

He must find a job. Whatever his ultimate goal might be, he must have sufficient money to eat enough to keep alive and have a roof over his head. He reminded himself that this was the capital city of an independent state and not merely a semi-exploited mining town of tin huts and dust. Here, therefore, would be a far wider market in which he could ply his many and varied talents, without being restricted to the narrow field of the engineer and the scientifically minded. Therefore, as soon as the town was fully awake and the business of the day begun, he made his rounds to seek employment.

He would, he told himself, with his experience in Aldersgate Street — to say nothing of the Elephant Trading Company and the Johannesburg Stock Exchange — find it a comparatively easy matter to get accommodated. He wondered what scale of salaries they paid in Pretoria, compared with the other places in which he'd worked.

He tried the wholesale warehouse of Loteryman's first. The man at the warehouse door listened to his application without comment and then looked over his shoulder at a companion who was handling bales in the recesses of the shed immediately behind. The latter stared in Sos's direction, shook his head, and returned to his work. The man at the door repeated the shake of the head with deliberation.

'But I'm experienced, you know,' said Sos.

'Push off,' said the man at the door.

He met with no greater success at T.W.Beckett's, General Stores. He approached the place with some confidence. He entered and asked of a spruce young man just inside the door if he could see whoever was in charge.

'I am in charge,' said the spruce young man, glanced Sos over, and then examined his own finger nails to show his disdain.

'I'm looking for work,' said Sos.

'No vacancies here.'

Sos thought it a pity that he couldn't wave a magic wand and transport them both to a barrack-room at Deal, preferably near the ablution-benches.

When he went outside, he caught sight of himself in the window of a restaurant adjoining the shop. The reflection was so striking that he must pause and examine it. Beyond the image of himself, he could see, through the plate glass, people at tables eating. The spectacle reminded him of his own hunger. He returned to the reflection.

He saw a stocky young man with a crumpled felt hat and bedraggled clothes. The jacket was creased and the trousers bagging at the knees and over at the ankles. The whole was garnished with a liberal sprinkling of shavings and sawdust. There was a distinct growth of beard upon his chin and he looked totally unwashed. He wasn't in the least surprised now at the receptions he had received.

But he didn't know what to do. He hadn't the price of a shave or a bath, let alone breakfast. The only place he knew where he could wash was 'La Cigale'. It was the last place in the present circumstances that he wished to revisit. The look of disdain from the spruce young man had been enough to go on with. He dreaded to think how Maudie would view him in the condition in which he now was — sans affluence and sans romance. The odour of coffee was wafted through to him as the restaurant door opened and closed. He forced himself to leave lest he be tempted to break in.

By midday he was very tired and growing dispirited. He wandered on, his bundle on his shoulder, till of a sudden he realized that he was back from where he had started.

The packing-case was still there, by the President Hotel. At once he saw there was a notice in the window near the main door. He crossed the road and read, 'Waiter Wanted'.

He had already, some hours ago, dusted himself down and brushed his hat against his leg, but now he went over himself again and hitched up his trousers and tightened his belt. He knew that he wasn't presentable, but a job was going and he must make the best of it, for tonight would be another night and he was tired of sleeping rough.

Nevertheless, he entered the hotel not without trepidation. He was as good as the next man, he knew all that, but it was difficult to assume any dignity with a dirty collar and a rumpled coat. He approached the reception desk with what assurance he could muster and asked the girl on duty if he could see the manager.

'What's your business, please?'

She was pert and distant. Sos felt that she ought to become acquainted with the spruce young man at Beckett's and marry him. Then if they had a baby it would probably be born in a top hat.

'You've a notice up outside, "Waiter Wanted".'

'Oh! that,' she said, as if he had referred without discretion to the drains. But she left her desk and went into an inner office.

When the manager came out, Sos was once more shaking at his jacket to rid it of the dust. It seemed a hopeless task because the cloth seemed to be impregnated with it.

'What do you know about waiting?' said the manager at once. He was a heavily built Boer.

'Nothing offhand, sir,' said Sos, 'but I can learn.'

The manager eyed him with some curiosity. He grunted.

'I'm sorry about my appearance, sir,' said Sos. 'But I walked all the way from Jo'burg yesterday and I slept out last night.'

'How old are you?'

'Just seventeen, sir.'

'Where do you come from? Where's your home?'

'England, sir. Newcastle-on-Tyne.'

'What's your father do?'

Sos hesitated. There were limits to an interrogation which could become too personal.

'My father's dead,' he said at last. 'But he was a shipowner.'

'I see,' said the manager and he gave a short laugh as if to say, 'Well, he's another one, but his remittance doesn't seem to have come along.' But his attitude was friendly and he called to the girl and told her to send for 'Nelson' and in a few seconds 'Nelson' appeared.

It was more than an appearance. He sprang into being. The lean, lithe African, in the white jacket of his office and with a napkin over his arm, pranced into the hall of the hotel, his limbs working like a marionette. Every gesture he made was a contortion.

'You callee me, sah?'

'This is your new hand. He knows nothing, so you must teach him from the beginning. Get him cleaned up and set him to work.'

'Velly good, sah,'

He turned to Sos.

'What's your name?'

'Cohen,' said Sos.

'Velly good, Kone. Me called Nelson.'

'His father had one eye,' explained the manager, pulling out a cigar from his waistcoat pocket and walking laboriously back to his office. The transaction was completed.

An hour later Sos was at work under the watchful eye of Nelson. Sos, too, now possessed a little white jacket and carried a table napkin over his arm. The barest rudiments of his craft had been explained to him, but as each day passed he grew more acquainted with its mysteries.

Nelson told him all he knew. Nelson was very proud to have a white man serve with him. There was not the slightest attempt on his part to take advantage of what could have been a very delicate situation. He danced and gambolled round his dining-room, with Sos trailing in his wake. In between short bouts of instruction he would encourage his young assistant with 'Velly good, Kone. Good boy, Kone.'

Sos grew fond of him. It was very pleasant to be looked upon with kindness and sympathy. It was gratifying to be told that improvement was showing every day and that Nelson thought him a very good boy. Sometimes, when a snatch of conversation from one of their guests was overheard and the names of Matabele and Mashonaland arose, Sos's mind would turn again to thoughts of the volunteer police, but then Nelson would be calling, 'Soup over here, Kone. More potatoes, Kone,' and he would find himself at the service hatch with his hands full.

He learnt how to lay a table. 'Big knife here, big fork there. Good boy Kone. Fish fork here, fish knife there. Plenty little glasses.' Very soon he could swing between the tables like an old-timer, flicking at the table-cloths and cruets with his napkin. He could present a menu with the necessary flourish of the wrist. He could incline his head on receipt of a tip with just that right degree of gratitude which conveyed dignity but betrayed no obsequiousness. He learnt to open a door for a guest without hurrying towards it, but by being there first, and how to strike a match so that the flame was level with the diner's cigar. He came to know, also, a little about wines and the various kinds of spirits. And all this he learnt from Nelson.

'Best dining-room in Pretoria. Plenty good food. Plenty good booze. Plenty good waiters. Three cheers for Nelson and Kone.'

Sos was not unhappy at the President Hotel. The job was serving its purpose very well until the night of the banquet.

For days Nelson had talked of nothing else. Out of all the hotels in Pretoria, theirs had been chosen. All the heads of the big business houses would be there, with the bankers and the financiers. There would be extra help for the night and the special tables would be used, so that everybody would sit together, with a head table and two wing tables, with a guest of honour at each end. The best glass was to be used and the cutlery and silver were to be given just that extra polish. Sos was instructed in every detail. On the actual night he would be second only to Nelson, with half a dozen hired African hands under him.

In the early evening of the great day, Sos himself went round placing the name-cards in each place. Then at last the guests began to arrive. The room filled up and a clerical gentleman said grace. Then they all sat down and the meal began.

Sos had no difficulty with the hors d'oeuvres, though there were several strange dishes, until he came to the young gentleman from Die Nationale Bank. Sos knew who he was and that he was called Smit, because of his name-card, and also that he was a Boer. He seemed quite a presentable young man, though Sos noticed that he wore a signet ring on the wrong finger and tucked his table-napkin into the top of his waistcoat.

Young Mr Smit devoured his portion of the preliminary course with some relish and called for olives. 'No extras,' Nelson had said. 'Boss he no serve extras at big dinners. Eat what they're given or go without, bloody-well.'

Sos made a feint towards the serving hatch and returned to the end of the wing-table where Mr Smit sat.

'No more olives, I'm afraid, sir.'

'Why the hell not?' said Mr Smit.

'They must have run out,' said Sos.

'Run out! What the hell do you mean, run out? This is a tenth-rate hotel.' He turned to the man next to him. 'I told two of the Committee men that this was the last place to come to.'

And then to Sos again: 'Get some olives or ask one of the other n*****s to fetch them.'

At first Sos could scarcely believe he had heard rightly. It seemed quite impossible that any white man could make such a remark in such circumstances, to an equal. Then, he realized that, in the eyes of young Mr Smit, he was very far from being an equal. He was some 'poor white' who was a soup-slinger with half a dozen native 'boys'.

'Good boy, Kone,' said Nelson just behind him as if voicing his thoughts. 'Soup now. Makee quick, all hot.'

Sos served his soups though his hands were shaking. Mr Smit was the last but one to be served. As Sos passed he overheard him remark, '... any job's good enough for them provided the money's there. It never occurs to them that mixing with the native lets the rest of us down.'

Sos stood back, when he had laid a full plate of mock turtle before Mr Smit's neighbour. He took no notice when Mr Smit wheeled round in his chair and asked why the hell he was being kept waiting.

'Are you the head waiter?'

'No,' said Sos. He pointed to Nelson. 'That's the head waiter. I serve under him.'

'Then it's a pity you can't learn manners even if it is off a native.'

Sos picked up a plate of soup from the dumb-waiter. It looked rich and inviting, very hot and steaming. He carried it across to Mr Smit.

'Were you asking for soup, sir?' he said.

'You damn well know I am,' said Mr Smit.

'Then this is all yours,' said Sos, and lifted the plate and poured its entire contents on to young Mr Smit's neatly brushed head.

Mr Smit gave a great shout of pain and surprise and wrath. He jumped to his feet and upset his glass so that the contents drained into his neighbour's lap. There was suddenly a babble of voices and somebody shouted 'Order!... Order!'

Nelson and two other waiters were frantically dabbing at the young Boer's evening coat. Several people at the end of the table had pushed their chairs back out of the way, others further up and at the head table had risen to their feet and were craning forward to see the fun. Somebody else was banging on the table and calling: 'Gentlemen!... *please!*' Nobody seemed to take any notice. Another voice cried out: 'What's going on there?' The place was in an uproar. In the middle of it all stood Sos, rather pale in the face but revealing his anger by his clenched fist. He wasn't in the least repentant. Even then he realized he was experiencing one of the supreme moments of his life. It compensated for many hours of disillusionment and frustration.

'Get out of my way,' said Mr Smit, thrusting Nelson and his assistants aside. 'Where's that blackguard?'

He wiped the mock turtle out of his eyes and saw Sos.

'Come on, then,' said Sos. 'Come on, then.'

There was the renewed banging of a tumbler on the table from the far end of the room.

'Come outside,' said Sos, 'and we'll talk business.'

He was out in the yard with his jacket off fully half a minute before Smit emerged. Sos could see, from where he was, right across the street to that other yard. The packing-case was still there, but he didn't allow the sight of it to worry him.

Smit stripped off his ruined coat, with its greasy, sodden lapels, and charged Sos like a young bull. Sos side-stepped him in a way he'd learnt in the gymnasium of a Royal Marine barracks, and swung a right hook that caught Smit on the cheek-bone, split the skin, and barked his own knuckles. Smit gave a bellow of pain, slithered on his feet, collected himself and came in again for more.

Sos adopted the same tactics, but his timing was inaccurate and one of Smit's knotted fists, at the end of a flailing arm, swept beneath his inadequate guard and landed squarely in his ribs. Sos, half-winded, backed away from a further onslaught and then pulled himself together and decided to box his man.

On the steps of the back door, with three of his attendants, Nelson pranced and danced in an agony of apprehension and dismay. He was wailing in a high-pitched voice of dismay, 'Kone.... Kone .... Kone!'

Sos took no notice of him, being fully occupied, and dotted a neat but not very powerful left into Smit's eye. The latter started a blow from somewhere behind his back that whistled over Sos's head, as he ducked and chanced an upper-cut that miraculously connected with Smit's mouth. The young Boer's head went up and he sat down with a very considerable thump.

'Had enough?' said Sos.

Smit spat a tooth out of his mouth and peered up at Sos with his unharmed eye. His tie was under his ear and his hair had fallen over his forehead. He had also split the back of his waistcoat and one panel of it had fallen from his shoulder. He tore the thing off, cursing, and then began to rise to his feet on all fours. Sos thought he looked more ferocious than even a wounded gorilla might appear. Moreover he was making a curious sort of hissing noise, as if he were getting up steam for the next attack.

Sos backed away from young Mr Smit somewhat fearfully because now he seemed to have changed from a gorilla into a particularly sinister and malevolent spider, such as a tarantula, which might spring into the air at any moment and launch fully fourteen stone of bone and brawn at him. But the assault never took place.

Sos's arms were firmly held before he was even aware that Nelson and his party had been reinforced by a score or more of the once assembled guests. They dragged him away from Mr Smit and they pounced on the latter and pulled him to his feet. They formed a solid wall between the two combatants and jostled Mr Smit back towards the hotel while the other half of them trundled Sos towards the open gateway of the yard, where the manager was already waiting with a bundle of clothes in his arms. His face was a dull purple, but he had turned a little yellow round the gills.

They got Sos to the end of the yard, and bundled him through the gateway. Somebody unhooked the hasp of the gates, and as they began to swing to, an assortment of garments came over the top and followed Sos out. Then the gates met with a slam and there was the rattling of a bolt being drawn and the sound of the manager's voice, bellowing from the other side:

'You're sacked!'

Sos bent down and began to pick up his belongings.

From within, wailing as a mother bereft of her child, came the last lament of Nelson:

'Kone!... Ko-one!... Ko-o-ne!'

CHAPTER FIVE: UNDER THE BLUE CEILING

But Nelson's tuition was not entirely lost. True enough, by this time acquiring a philosophy of some kind to meet all manner of exigencies, Sos was becoming accustomed to a life which seemed to lead round many unexpected corners. If he were destined to be a clerk, it appeared he must become a Royal Marine. If he wished to be a prospector he must find himself counting blankets in a store.

Now considering himself a waiter of some experience, he applied for a similar job at the restaurant next to Beckett's. No one identified him with the slight contretemps at the President Hotel, and they were very polite. They had no position for him there but suggested he might find work of a similar nature at the Albert Mines.

He went to the Albert Silver and Lead Mines and was interviewed by the consulting engineer, Mr Eisler, who didn't want a waiter at all. In fact, it was the very last thing he wanted. What he needed was a clerk. Sos said he *was* a clerk. Mr Eisler said, well, why hadn't he said so in the first place? Sos said, with some justification, that it hadn't occurred to him. Mr Eisler said he could employ him in that capacity at twenty pounds a month if that was acceptable. When Sos had recovered, he said that it was.

Twenty pounds a month! He was a millionaire.

He saw Paul Kruger, the newly elected Boer President, drive through Pretoria after his election in which he had defeated General Joubert. He became familiar with the ways of the city and felt that he was becoming a Colonial at last. He felt that he had found his niche in a somewhat turbulent life. Then the Albert Mines closed down.

They closed down without a moment's notice. With no intention of repeating the debacle of his evening at 'La Cigale', in a sober and saddened mood, with the last week's wages in his pocket, Sos found his way to a bar on the outskirts of the city.

He stood by the counter and drank a small glass of tepid beer in a disconsolate manner. Then he heard someone immediately behind him say: 'Put him alive in an ant-hill, that's what they did. There was nothing left but his head, after twenty-four hours.'

He turned to have a look at the speaker.

He was a tall lean man, with a face burnt dark by the sun, and with a short, ragged beard that reached from ear to ear and ran beneath his chin. He had a glass nearly three-quarters full of Cape Dop in his hand. His eyes glittered as he gulped at it.

'I fought against the Basuto, too —'

Sos stared at the speaker in some wonderment, because to have fought in the Basuto campaign was legendary. This fellow must be, he thought, one of the heroes of most ancient days, a veteran of the very first pioneers.[2] He was spell-bound with admiration.

'When were you there, Buck?' said one of the bearded man's companions.

'Way back, Taffy,' said Buck. 'The Mashonas aren't warriors — and they tell me the Matabele are at 'em again. They get their women and their cattle carried off every time. And that's the way it's going, I'll be bound.'

Another of the party put down his empty glass.

---

[2] He was in fact only forty-eight. Only a lad of seventeen would have regarded Buck in this way.

'Is that the last of the kitty?'

'It is,' said Buck. 'Not a penny more have we got between us. So it's fill up the billy-cans and on our way. Four hundred miles up north, so it's best foot first.'

He drained his glass. The others followed suit.

'Excuse me,' said Sos, and he was surprised at his own temerity. 'Excuse me as a stranger, but will you gentlemen have a drink?'

The gentlemen — there were five of them — regarded him with a look of astonishment mingled with suspicion.

'What's the game?' said Buck.

'I couldn't help overhearing what you said,' said Sos. 'I've got a few shillings to spare to buy a round, if you'll allow me, because there's something I'd like to ask you.'

He spoke a little breathlessly because he was rather out of his depth now that he had taken the plunge, but he knew that, in the circumstances, he couldn't have done otherwise.

'What's the catch?' said Buck.

'There isn't any catch,' said Sos. 'I promise you there isn't. But you're going up north. That's where I want to go.'

'What do you want up there?'

'I wanted to join an outfit at Orange Grove but they wouldn't have me. I was too young. But they thought that up in Victoria —'

'The Chartered Company,' said Buck. 'You know the way the rumours go, no matter the distance. They say the Doctor's[3] up there on Mr Rhodes's behalf. There'll be something doing if that's the case. There's a talk of forming a volunteer force.'

'That's what I mean,' said Sos eagerly. 'They'd probably have me. They said as much in Orange Grove.'

---

[3] Doctor Jameson, later of the Jameson Raid.

'They don't ask no questions, if that's what you mean,' said Buck. 'If you're a fit man and can fight, that's all that matters. And you don't get no pay, but gets what you can find. So you want to come with us?'

'Yes,' said Sos. 'I don't know the way and I'd get lost in the bush. Can't I come with you?'

He laid down several coins on the counter. The barman, who had been leaning across his bar in shirt-sleeves listening to the conversation, automatically picked up the glasses and began to refill them.

'Any more of that clinking stuff?' said Buck. He rubbed the beard beneath his chin thoughtfully.

'A few shillings,' said Sos.

'It all goes into the common pool,' said Buck. 'That's how we work it.'

He looked round at the half-circle of his companions. He was clearly the ringleader.

'It's all right with me, boys,' he said. 'If it's all right with you. One more or less don't make no odds. Drink up.'

An hour later the party was out of Pretoria and heading north.

The land ran flat and level on either side of them, though now and again the road dropped down into a donga or skirted the lower slopes of a kopje. If the road to Pretoria had been rough and deep in dust, this road to the north was at times little more than a wide rutted path. As they made their way along, Buck expounded his plans and arrangements to Sos.

'We sleep under the blue ceiling,' he said. He jerked his thumb up at the sky. 'It's a blasted bad road, though it's not so bad as the first time I came this way. It was as much as you could do to see it, then. We're all set more or less for Fort Victoria and maybe I might join the volunteers along with you.

Time enough for that when we get there. I reckon we'll do it in the month, if the weather holds and there aren't no accidents. We've each got a day's rations for a start and thereafter we beg, borrow or steal. It don't matter which. So that's what you're in for. Do you want to turn back?'

'No,' said Sos.

They were a strange-looking party, their packs on their backs and their billy-cans swinging at their sides. They trudged on in a straggling group, but now and again one or another of the others would range up alongside Buck or Sos, and the latter became acquainted with Robert from Scotland and Taffy from Wales.

Robert seemed in no lighthearted mood, though the adventure had just begun. He was tired of footslogging, he said, and if he'd the coin on him he'd borrow a lift from the next transport driver they passed. He looked meaningly at Sos and Buck said: 'It's all in the kitty, what there was of it.' Robert went off grumbling to drop behind with the others, but Taffy stayed behind.

'Now what would be eating him at this stage of the journey with us only just on our way? Was there anything in Africa that ever came easily and richly to the likes of us, though maybe it will one day?'

'Maybe,' said Buck.

Taffy was as lively as a cricket and his words tripped over his thoughts; but his thoughts were all of the same trend. Some time before his prospecting days were over he'd find the great diamond that was waiting for him or he'd strike the gold in an endless reef. He was quite sure of that. It had happened before, it could happen again.

'Maybe,' said Buck.

All that day they marched on and it seemed to Sos, though the heat was a great burden upon him and his mouth was bitterly dry as he had not yet learnt to control his thirst, that at last he was on the golden road of his dreams.

They broke from the track into the edge of the bush just an hour before sundown; Robert, with one of the others, prepared a fire and they all unslung their billy-cans with various messes. Taffy had a new way of fixing his can over the fire on a stick in the cleft of two forked sticks. Two of the others joined him in this new-fangled method, but the others stuck their cans in the hot ashes in the usual way.

Then a quarter of an hour later, when they were busy gathering more fuel against the night, the stick that supported the three billy-cans caught fire and snapped and the contents of the cans went into the fire. It was Buck who curbed the united outburst of wrath and dismay. Even at this early stage of proceedings Sos could see that a quarrel could flare up at a second's notice, because these men lived very near to the bare essentials which the earth might condescend to give them.

Buck soothed them down when the other two blamed Taffy for his 'fool' ideas, though he said it had never happened to him before in all his years in the bush. It was Buck, too, who led the way in sharing out his portion amongst the rest, but everyone went short and Sos knew that by the morning he would be ravenous.

When they dossed down for the night Sos kept as close to the embers of the fire as he dared, but he was cold already with a half-empty stomach and by midnight his teeth were chattering.

Later a hand groped over him in the half-light of the stars and he was momentarily startled, but it was only Buck with a stubby black bottle, proffering it in the dark. He spoke in a whisper.

'Take a sup of that. It's the last I've with me, though, so go careful.'

Sos took a gulp and the Cape Dop went down his gullet like liquid fire. He handed the bottle back.

Then Buck passed his jacket over.

'Put that round you as well. I'll do all right. I'm acclimatized.'

After that there was a faint gurgling in the darkness and a slight smacking of lips. Thereafter, Sos slept intermittently till the dawn came racing up the sky.

By noon of the following day, the discomfort of everybody's hunger was becoming quite considerable. Another forty-eight hours and it would become acute. They still marched on, hoping to intercept an oxen train or some supply transport, when they could, with their remaining pennies, attempt to make a deal. But no such luck came their way.

In the middle of the afternoon Buck made his decision. He had been silent for some time, obviously in deep thought. He called a halt and the others gathered round him. Sos noticed how everybody seemed instinctively to rely on Buck. It was Sos's first lesson in leadership in the field.

'By my reckonings,' said Buck, 'we're not all that far from Prinsloo's kraal, where there's food. We can't make a deal with him for bully, but he's got some that's on legs. Pigs and chickens and maybe a goose or two. Also I've a notion that the stockade is down in places. You, Robert and Taffy, go and look for an old ant-hill and make an oven ready. The other three of us will set off together, but we'll pick our own way and approach from all sides. The bush runs fairly near the kraal but there's a bit of open space before you actually reach it. You'll have to go careful there for Prinsloo's got two sons and they're all crack shots, and he won't hesitate to let fly. It's the accepted thing.'

'What about me?' said Sos.

'You can help to collect fuel with Taffy.'

'Not me,' said Sos. 'I want to see the fun.'

'All right,' said Buck. 'As long as you understand this isn't a game for kids.'

'I'm as hungry as the rest of you,' said Sos.

'That's fairly spoken,' said Buck. 'Now we'll take a look round.' He lead them to the edge of the bush. A hundred yards away in the centre of a clearing they could see the kraal with its low buildings and ancient stockade. Here and there, they could discern gaps in the mud wall. Smoke drifted lazily over the roofs and once they heard the gobbling of a goose.

'There's enough in there to feed an army,' whispered Buck. 'Now spread out, the lot of you, and take up your positions. I shall stay here by this dead tree. You'll see the white of its wood clear from the other side. When you see me move, in we all go. Then we rendezvous back here — with luck.'

Sos stole off, keeping within the thick scrub, till he reached a thicket a hundred or more paces away. There he lay down, his eyes now on the kraal, now on the white wood of the dead tree. It stood out like a skeleton's finger bones against the dark foliage behind. He was excited. He had no doubt whatsoever that Buck had spoken the truth and that Prinsloo would shoot on sight. It could not have been the first occasion that marauders had made an attempt on an isolated place such as this. He had no compunction to helping himself to Prinsloo's property.

Half an hour passed and no one stirred. Three pairs of eyes were fixed on the kraal and each of three men knew that Buck was watching the sky for the first hint of sundown. Once the leader had given the signal, they would have to move fast. A dog barked behind the mud walls and they heard a man whistling. The sun seemed to sink into the earth and the brief dusk was upon them.

Buck moved in front of the dead tree and Sos saw him at once, before he dropped on his hands and knees. Then he, too, was crawling slowly towards the kraal.

There was a tingling down his spine and he gritted his teeth, because this was something like the real thing at last. The dog barked again and Sos went flat, and clung close to the warm ground, motionless. In a little time, he raised his head. There seemed to be no movement before him. He went on again.

He could see a gap in the stockade, just a little to his left. Two of the stout poles, planted some four inches apart at regular intervals and lashed together with cross-pieces, had fallen out of the true as if they might have rotted at their stumps. Immediately behind stood a hut. Sos crawled forward more swiftly.

The light was fading rapidly. Already the tones of his surroundings were blending into a neutral darkness. He reached the gap and squeezed his way through. He lay for a moment between the hut wall and the stockade. Then he rose carefully to his feet, moved forward and peered round the wall.

There was an open space immediately before him and then several more huts, but between the latter and himself he saw the wire-ringed pen. It was no more than waist-high and the wire was strung almost casually around the posts. But there were shadowy and moving blurs within and now very distinct indeed was the gobble-gobble of the geese.

Sos went across the intervening space as swiftly as he'd ever sprinted in his life. He reached the pen, put an arm over and grabbed a fine goose by the neck. He swung it out of its place

116

of security and twisted its neck, while all the rest of that community flapped their frantic wings and raced round the wire in a fearful chattering.

Sos reached the corner of the hut, hugging the goose in his arms, and the dog began to bark again and he thought he heard a man's voice. He stepped swiftly round the corner of the hut, found the gap in the stockade and once again squeezed through. A whistle began to blow at the far end of the kraal. He ran through the falling darkness, towards the outline of the dead tree.

The others were already there. As he moved into the foliage Buck's hand seized his shoulder and urged him on.

'Come on! Come on!' he whispered urgently. 'Get in quickly. We'll feed tonight.'

Buck led the way, and it seemed to Sos almost by instinct, to Robert and Taffy. They had found their ant-hill and had made their oven by digging out a wide hole in the side of the narrow mound, which was as high as a man. Wood had then been piled in and set alight till now the centre of the ant-hill was a glowing mass. Buck pushed Sos forward.

'He got a goose,' he said. 'We got a piglet. We can have a two-course dinner tonight.'

He drew out his long sheath knife. The light from the oven gleamed down its blade. All around it was very silent, till a little squealing broke out. The two men came through the gloom holding a small body between them. Then they knelt on the ground before Buck. He too knelt down knife in hand. In a very little time there was no more squealing.

They cooked the sucking-pig and the goose side by side in the glowing ant-hill. The smell of the roast spread out, down wind, into the bush and Sos thought he had never smelt the like of it before. The hunger on him, tormented by the aroma, was almost more than he could bear. They carved the pig into portions and Sos took half the goose for his share. He ate it in his fingers and gnawed the bones, and the rich juice dribbled over his chin. He washed it all down with a swill of the water that Taffy had collected in the billy-cans.

But the glow of the oven was little compared to that which now filled Sos's stomach and spread into his veins. He stretched himself out, satiated and utterly content, and he felt towards his companions, and to the world which they had made theirs, a great sense of friendliness and comradeship; the hours of weary tramping through the noontide heat and the bitter hunger were forgotten. Overhead the sky was sprinkled with stars that glittered almost blindingly. He turned over on his side and went to sleep.

Dawn was breaking as he awoke, but he knew at once that it wasn't the brighter light that had aroused him, but some movement nearby.

Then he saw, dimly outlined against a thorn-bush, the dark shape of a man. He saw it was a native.

He waited for several seconds, but the man never moved. Sos wondered if at any moment a spear might come whistling towards him. Then suddenly he rolled over on his side several times in swift succession, leapt to his feet and ran towards the watcher by the thorn-bush.

The man made no attempt to evade him, but stood his ground with one arm outstretched to ward him off. Sos saw that he was unarmed.

'*Inkoss*, they have discovered the theft.'

He spoke in Bitonga.

'What do you mean?' asked Sos.

'Prinsloo and his sons, *Inkoss*. They are very angry.'

'Why do you tell me this?'

'I was a houseboy there. They beat me.'

Buck had wakened and was sitting up. He was still rubbing his eyes as he came towards them.

'What's up?' he asked.

'Prinsloo is very angry, *Inkoss*. He has reported a robbery to Pretoria. A troop of the Staats Artillery is already on the way.'

'The hell it is,' said Buck.

He was instantly fully awake. He ran from sleeping figure to figure and roused each one, and broke the news. They made up their blankets into packs, collected what accoutrement they had and struck camp with all speed.

'We've got to get to hell out of here and mighty quick,' said Buck. 'I don't want to see the inside of a Staats prison again.'

The ant-hill had burnt out and the oven was a gaping hole with white and ashy sides. All around lay tell-tale fragments of last night's feast — the mud shell, with feathers stuck into it, in which the goose had been roasted, the bones of the little pig and its tiny skull. Buck took a branch from a tree and swept the remains as well as he could into a heap and piled dry earth on it, and then he dropped the branch across it, but all the same, even to Sos's untrained eye, the signs of an encampment but recently deserted were only too obvious. Then on the instant he heard the sound of horses' hooves. Buck heard it as well. He motioned them all to silence.

The little group of men, their packs on their backs, stood uneasily round their self-appointed leader. The sound of cantering hooves came again, from the direction of Prinsloo's kraal. Any body of men wishing to join the main track would have to pass through the belt of bush in this direction.

'Wait here,' Buck whispered.

Then he was off, running doubled-up through the thorn scrub towards the direction of the sound. In a few seconds he was lost to view.

Nobody spoke. Each one was apprehensive.

When Buck returned he was breathless.

'They're here,' he said. 'I've seen 'em and they're coming this way. We've got to scatter quick. Tonight at sundown by the dead tree if we can make it.'

There was the distant sound of a voice and the blast of a whistle. Without another word Buck plunged into the thick bush, while the rest followed. Within seconds Sos was alone.

There was nobody in sight and already the branches of the bushes had ceased to sway where his companions had forced the passage of their flight. It was as if he had never been in their company and he was scared at being so suddenly alone, so that when he caught sight of a horseman approaching, he panicked and turning on his heel fled in between the close-growing thickets and high grass. But nobody shouted a challenge after him and in a little while the sound of hooves and voices died away. He still struggled on, putting as much ground between himself and his possible pursuers as he could.

The sun rose steadily in the sky and his progress became slower, till it occurred to him that a more sensible thing to do would be to retrace his footsteps, identify the dead-wood tree, which should not be difficult once he had re-established the position of the ant-hill, and then lie up till sundown, when Buck and the others would return. It was an infinitely more sensible plan than floundering on in this apparently illimitable wilderness, where he might become lost.

He turned about and made his way back.

It was quite remarkable how different the aspect of his surroundings looked in reverse. It was as if he had never come this way at all. Moreover he began to realize that in his first panic he had indeed scarcely observed which way he had been going.

The ground began to clear a little and with the greatest relief he recognized the outline of the low thorn-trees that had ringed the side of their camping-ground. He inclined his steps to the left and hurried over the rough ground as fast as he could.

He entered the clearing from what he supposed would have been the kraal side of the main track. He strode forward with confidence, but came to a halt when he saw that nowhere in the partially overgrown glade was any sign of an ant-hill.

So completely convinced was he that he had reached his appointed destination that he even searched for remnants of the feast, till he remembered they had been swept away. He looked around him, and the sun glared down, so that he fumbled for his billy-can and found to his relief that there was still a little water in it. He took a draught and looked around him again.

It was the same place and yet it wasn't. Then slowly he began to realize that in all probability, to the uninitiated, all parts of the bush looked the same, and that it was only the merest trivial details that told the experienced tracker where he might be.

He was lost. He was lost in the bush and he had no more idea of where he was than if he'd been a blind man. He was afraid, because this was a terrible thing to have happened so suddenly. He wondered whether, if he raised his voice, Buck could still hear and hasten to him, or whether by now he was far out of earshot. On the other hand to call for any kind of help might bring the troopers back again in his direction, with the possibility besides of putting his late companions in jeopardy if they were still in the vicinity. For the moment he felt he must at all costs hold his tongue. But the situation was perilous. He had no food and little water. He sat down under the shadow of a thorn-bush to try and think it out.

There was no answer to the problem. By the afternoon of the same day it was still unsolved.

Later he found himself wandering about almost aimlessly through a dreadful maze of similarity, till at last, exhausted, he sank down again in a patch of shadow; and then sundown was upon him.

It occurred to him at once that in his present circumstances the ground was no place to sleep upon. Last night he had been amongst his friends and there had been the glow of the fire from the ant-hill, so that there had been little danger of wild beasts. Now he was alone and unarmed. He climbed into a fork of the tree, beneath whose shadow he had rested.

Sometimes, during the night, he dozed, but often enough he must ease his cramped position. Once he thought he heard a sinister movement beneath of rustling foliage and something that sniffed and snuffled in the high grass below, but whatever it was passed and he heard it no more.

He climbed down from his perch at dawn and he was stiff and sore and bitterly cold. He took a sip of water and he felt his parched throat contract even as he felt his belly cave in with windy hunger. Two hours later he heard the shot.

It rang out, suddenly, startlingly, and close at hand. He turned at once in its direction, praying that it might come again. Even if it were the troopers of the Staats Artillery, better a Boer cell than this slow torture to death. He was about to shout, when the sound came again and this time it was followed by a man's voice raised in a high and rocketing pitch:

'*Wit penze*! Yoi-oi-oi-ack!'

122

And then again the sudden crack, but not, now Sos knew, of a rifle, but of a driver's whip. He ran forward, shouting, and of a sudden the bush seemed to melt away before him and he was on the main track once more.

The team of sixteen oxen trailing their transport wagon behind them was slowly approaching. On one flank the drover was whirling his splendid whip and sending the thong coiling out in a deadline over the horns of one of the team. There it would stop and break the air with the report of a pistol.

Sos waited till the wagon grew level and then he crossed the road and went to the drover. He was a young man with a broad, flat, round face and grey eyes. His hands and his feet were enormous.

'I am lost,' said Sos all in one breath. 'Which way are you going?'

'North,' said the drover. 'Lost in the bush, eh? Poor little *rooinek*!'

He opened his mouth, so wide that it looked as if Sos could have put his fist in it, and the laughter rumbled and roared out of it as if it would never stop.

'There's nothing to laugh about,' said Sos, because he was feeling very sorry for himself and the relief at his escape from a dreadful end was very nearly overwhelming.

'I always laugh,' said the drover. 'My name is Ferreira and I always laugh.'

'Can I come north with you?' said Sos. 'I want to get to Victoria.'

'You can come with me, my hop o' the thumb,' said Ferreira. 'And you can earn your passage. My *voorlooper* went sick in Pretoria and I need a man.'

'Thank you,' said Sos and then, inadvertently, he grabbed at the other's belt, for they were walking alongside the team and

Sos felt suddenly dizzy with his fasting and his aimless tramping through the bush.

Ferreira caught him by the arm to steady him, because he knew all the ways of the wild and what it could do to men. He picked up Sos as if he were a child and lifted him into the wagon. He gave him water, and a hunk of bread with a lump of biltong on it.

'Later when we outspan for the night, we talk. It will all be well.'

Sos dug his teeth into the biltong and bread, and marvelled at the godliness in men.

That evening Ferreira gave him his instructions. He would employ him as far as Victoria in the capacity of *voorlooper*, the drover's assistant who leads the leading pair of the oxen team when it crosses difficult ground, such as down a donga or across a drift. He made him the loan of an ancient single-loader Snider rifle, with half a dozen cardboard-cased cartridges.

'You can shoot?'

'Yes,' said Sos.

'It is practically only native tracks in places and there are sometimes lions. But that will be when we cross the Limpopo.'

Therefore every day at dawn Sos took up his position with the leading oxen and every day he grew more contented and happy, because the drover Ferreira was a fine and decent man, with a simple way of thought and living. He had lived all his life in Africa and his people had been amongst the early settlers. He told Sos that in his opinion this great continent, of which so little was really known, could be a Paradise on earth. There never was such a splendid country in the world, said Ferreira.

Sos agreed with him. It suited his mood of exaltation to agree, for were they not heading north, hour by hour?

He wished sometimes, though, that the days could provide a little more excitement, because it was not possible all the time to keep to such a pitch of high spirits. Often he unslung his rifle, as he plodded on at the head of the team. He examined its mechanism and raised it frequently to his shoulder and aligned the sights. The cardboard casing of the cartridges amused him, being so unlike anything that might have been seen near a Royal Marine depot, but he always kept a round in the breech in case anything unforeseen should occur. But nothing happened till they made the crossing of the Limpopo.

Sos led the leaders down the slope to the drift, while Ferreira cracked his whirling whip and shouted to the team, and the wagon lumbered on behind, grumbling and creaking.

It was as Sos stepped into the shallow water of the drift that he noticed the log. It lay half-submerged with tiny waves, raised by the breeze, lapping around it. On either side of the track the high grass and reeds rose almost shoulder-high. Sos thought it strange that a piece of a tree should be lying in such a place, where so few trees were, but he supposed it must have been washed ashore when the Limpopo was last in flood. As he was about to pass it, the log moved and opened an eye.

He knew at once what it was and how he had been deceived. He imagined he could already feel the crocodile's wicked teeth round his ankle. He brought the oxen to a sudden halt, unslung his rifle and fired point-blank.

The log sprang into momentary life, contorted in mid-air. Its jaws snapped and it plunged and wallowed at the water's edge. Then it suddenly fell quiet, and rolled over on its back with its belly upwards.

'Got him,' said Sos with pardonable pride as Ferreira came running up. He pointed to the reptile with the muzzle of his smoking rifle.

'Right across our path,' he said.

It wasn't quite the truth, but it made rather a better story of it. 'Waste of ammunition,' said Ferreira.

He half turned the creature over on its side. Then he glanced at Sos under the brim of his big broad-brimmed hat. His mouth was already stretching to a grin.

'You weren't afraid of it?' he said. 'You didn't think it was a crocodile, did you?'

'Well, isn't it?'

'No,' said Ferreira. 'Iguana.'

He gave a great bellow of laughter.

'As harmless as a little child. And hop o' my thumb had shot his first croc. Ho! Ho!'

He went back down his team, cracking his whip, and bellowing. They waded the drift of the Limpopo and the water swirled around Sos's waist; Sos kept the leaders head-on and soon they came to the far bank, where in the high grass the track began again. Indeed the grass, like the bank, seemed higher on the northern side and the oxen scrambled up the slope, straining at their traces. Sos trotted alongside, urging them on, and Ferreira was shouting all the time; then they gained the level track, which swung immediately to the left.

Sos took the leading pair round the bend in the path, and even before they had passed the corner the two oxen had thrown up their heads and were snorting. The moment they had completed the full left turn, Sos saw the lion.

It stood in a clump of grass and scrub not a dozen paces from him. There wasn't any doubt at all about it being a lion. Anyone might mistake an iguana for a crocodile, but a lion was a lion all the world over. The oxen had stopped dead and were trying to back away, so that they began to throw the rest of the team into confusion. From the rear and out of sight, Ferreira was swearing lustily. The lion's mane was risen round its shoulders and its upper lip was drawn up so that Sos could see its long, glistening teeth.

So they stood, boy and lion facing one another, and they stared at each other eye to eye. Very cautiously Sos unslung his rifle and even as he raised it, he thought the lion sank a little lower in the grass as if it were about to spring.

He managed to get the foresight of the ancient Snider somewhere near the correct alignment with the backsight, but it was not easy because the barrel seemed to be dancing in the air. Then, when he thought he was on aim as near as possible to the lion's frontal bone between the eyes, he pressed the trigger.

The Snider mechanism gave a faint click.

It was a single-barrel rifle with no magazine and Sos had forgotten to reload.

He realized on the instant what had occurred. He knew, too, that he was as near death as he was ever likely to be. The oxen by his side were snorting more loudly than ever. The lion's tail was waving ominously.

Sos kept the Snider to his shoulder and cautiously lowered his right hand to his side pocket where he kept his spare rounds. The lion's mouth opened a little wider and Sos knew that he must make no further movement, nor dare he shout for help.

Then on the instant there was a terrific explosion just behind his left ear and he felt the blast of the rifle-shot sear his cheek as it passed. The lion rose a little as if on tip-toe and then rolled slowly over into the reeds and disappeared. Sos turned round to find Ferreira at his side. He was re-loading, his eyes intent on the spot where the lion had been lost to view. He went forward slowly step by step. Then when he was within a yard of the thicket he raised his rifle and fired again. There was no further movement within the reeds. As he returned to where Sos was standing, the latter was slipping a cartridge in the breech of the Snider.

It seemed that Ferreira had taken the situation in at a glance.

'There's only one thing worse than not having a rifle,' he said, 'and that's to have an empty one.'

A bead of perspiration ran down the side of his face, from under his hat. Then, because Sos looked so woebegone, he strode forward and clapped him on the back and gave a roar of laughter, which no doubt was as much to ease his own feelings as to encourage his young *voorlooper*. The next instant his whip was cracking again and the team was on the move. Half an hour later Sos, looking back, saw a speck in the sky over the Limpopo, and then another and another, circling, until one by one the vultures dropped to where they would feast in peace and plenty.

There were no more lions on that trek, only at last a drifting of smoke over the waste of scrub and bush — the distant outline of the corrugated-iron huts that formed a settlement.

'Victoria!' said Ferreira.

CHAPTER SIX: LOBENGULA'S FIGHTING MEN

The dream was a reality. He was riding in the Victoria Column which had just joined up with the Salisbury Column at Iron Mine Hill. It was 16th October, 1893.

The Martini-Henry rifle with its long cheese-bayonet — which they had issued to him together with his horse, saddle and bridle, blanket and water-bottle, bandolero, slouch-hat and puggaree and all the remainder up to twenty pounds of kit — rested in the holster on his near side, and slapped against his saddle-flaps. It was just as he had imagined it would be, riding under the open sky with his bit a-jingle. On either side of him rode his new friends, Dawson the Colonial and Walters, the young Jew from Manchester. All three were members of No. 5 troop of the Victoria Column under Major Forbes. The combined column numbered six hundred and seventy all told: two hundred and fifty from Salisbury and four hundred from Victoria, with two seven-pounder guns, one Gatling, one Nordenfeldt and a Hotchkiss taken in a previous brush with the Portuguese at Massi Kessi, together with five Maxims, two of them with galloping carriages. There were also some five hundred native levies, engaged as carriers.

Sos knew what it was all about. Lobengula, chief of the warlike Matabele, had granted a concession in 1889 to the Chartered Company of Cecil Rhodes — so that Matabeleland might be prospected for gold and precious stones and opened up for fanning — to the tune of one hundred pounds a month, one thousand rifles and one hundred thousand rounds of ammunition. Now his warriors were disturbing the peace of a country about to prosper.

Young men of the Matabele could not marry unless they had drawn blood in battle. Therefore they had been justifying their right to connubial bliss by raiding the peaceful and timid Mashona, killing the men, seizing their women and driving off their cattle. Lobengula was warned, but notwithstanding, a Matabele impi[4] approached Victoria. The Matabele were repulsed, but even so a number of the young bloods still lurked on the border.

Rhodes felt it was time to put an end to Lobengula's activities. He decided to invade Matabeleland with three columns, one from Victoria, one from Salisbury and another consisting of the Bechuanaland Border Police from the south. The object of the campaign was to find and destroy the enemy and to occupy his capital of Bulawayo. Doctor Jameson accompanied the force as the senior Adviser. The volunteers of the Victoria Column received no pay but were promised a farm of two thousand *morgen*,[5] the right to peg out twenty gold-claims and a share of the loot.

By day Sos rode with his troop in the long column, with its transport wagons and supply carts drawn by oxen and mules, and with the meagre artillery train in the rear. They carried their cattle with them and as they progressed many of the Mashona joined them for protection.

It was a strange, fantastic spectacle, the clumsy, slow-moving procession of armed and mounted men, the covered wagons with the patient ox-teams plodding onwards under the crack of the drivers' whips, the herds of lowing cattle and always before, behind and around them wild and hostile country. At night the

---

[4] Regiment.
[5] A little over four thousand acres.

column laagered-up. A camp was formed with the wagons as a barricade and a zareba or protecting fence of 'wait-a-bit' thorn around the position. Pickets were posted with a main guard in support.

In the early days of the column, at night, rolled in his blanket with his saddle for a pillow, Sos thought it was all very splendid, because he had set out to do a thing and had succeeded. He was pleased too that the great hunter who led them, F. C. Selous, or 'Majorkala'[6] as the natives called him, had stopped one day on his way down the column and had asked Sos his name.

'Cohen, sir.'

'What's your age?'

'Seventeen, sir.'

The famous man, with his little pointed beard and keen eyes, had smiled down at Sos.

'You're very young for this sort of job, aren't you?'

'No,' said Sos, and because he could never forget it, 'once I was a Royal Marine.'

Selous had ridden off, chuckling.

Often at night Sos would think of his friends and how many of them he had made since leaving Newcastle, and how genuine in spirit they were. He thought of people like Joseph and Noakes, 'Nelson' and Buck, and now his two present comrades-in-arms, Dawson and Walters. Sometimes when rations were short, the three of them would club together, pooling their issue of Cape Dop and exchanging it with the old-timers for flour. Then they would make 'cookies' over a fire of dried cow-dung. The result was not quite as delectable as Cook's girdle cakes of Tankerville House, but the 'cookies' were sustaining.

---

[6] 'The young man.'

The first decisive action between the column and the Matabele took place at the Shangani River. The column was in laager, the latter being divided into three kraals, one for the main body and horses, another for the Mashona women who had sought protection, and a third for the cattle.

Sos with five men, including Dawson, was in charge of a picket some two hundred yards or so from the camp. In their rear was the second line of defence, the main guard covering the outer circle of the first line.

At three o'clock in the morning Sos made his rounds, going to the sentry whom he had posted forward. It was just before dawn and everything was quiet. There were no reports of any kind of enemy activity and it could be reasonably assumed that within the next two hours the camp would be struck and the column set on the move again, but when he came to Trooper Dawson Sos found his man staring towards the laager instead of looking towards his front.

It was not in the comparatively free-and-easy discipline of the column to reprimand anyone for an offence unless it were serious, but such an obvious lapse on the part of a man presumably on the watch could scarcely be overlooked.

'Face about,' said Sos in a low voice. 'That's not the direction in which you should be looking.'

Dawson motioned him to silence. The first hint of dawn was creeping into the sky. All around and before them the scrub lay dark and silent; only in the direction in which both men were now looking sounded any sign of life, the occasional stamping of a tethered horse or a low whinny. The stars were fading out of the sky.

'There's something up,' whispered Dawson. 'I've been watching it for minutes now.'

There seemed to be a movement in the scrub between the picket and the laager. It was almost imperceptible. Against the dark thickets were darker shadows, low to the ground and slowly moving. Now and again the faintest blur of white plumes showed as a dull grey, nodding against the sombre background. The scrub was infested with the Matabele.

'By God,' said Sos, 'it's them!'

He raised his rifle and was about to fire a warning shot, when small-arms fire burst out with a clattering roar from the corners of the main laager.

The situation was immediately clear to Sos. The enemy was between his picket and the laager.

The rifle fire was now incessant. Through the scrub the figures of the attackers could be clearly seen. Every warrior wore plumes and carried his black-and-white cowhide shield and stabbing assegai. Many were armed with firearms.

They ran and leapt through the scrub, sweeping forward in waves, and as they bore down upon the laager the yelling of their war cry could be heard above the din of the conflict.

The picket had by now collected round Sos and they followed him as he plunged into a thicket.

'Our only chance,' he said, 'is through the cattle kraal at the back.' It was, he knew, quite hopeless to attempt to reach the laager by the way they had come, because the main Matabele attack would be developed there, while the wings of the impis would fan out and begin an encircling movement.

It was a rough guess and one based on hearsay and not experience, but it seemed to have the merit of practicability. If they could reach the cattle kraal before the entire camp had been surrounded, they might force an entry. The six men broke from cover and with Sos leading them began to run diagonally across the defenders' front.

They had made the most of their opportunity, for there was a gap between the first wave and the second, so that they covered a hundred yards or more before they were forced to drop to the ground again, as another cloud of the Matabele surged forward.

The nearest native warrior passed the picket with less than a dozen yards to spare. It was growing rapidly lighter and Sos could see how the warriors' dark skins gleamed and glistened, and how the muscles rippled across their backs and arms. They shouted as they ran and leapt in the air, and their plumes floated above their head-rings. One Induna,[7] head and shoulders above his men, was exhorting them on as he waved his broad-bladed stabbing spear. His appearance was devilish and magnificent. He looked every inch of what he was, a Matabele aristocrat from a line of fighting men. And all the time the rifle and machine-gun fire continued.

A dozen of the enemy caught a direct burst from the Maxims, and they went down in a mass as if their legs had been cut from beneath them. One man arose from them, thrusting his way through the heap of still twitching limbs and writhing bodies. It was the Induna. And Sos saw that he carried no shield, and marvelled, for his left arm was torn away at the elbow. Yet still he ran forward with his spear on high.

Sos collected his men around him again and they made another dash and now the bullets from the laager were whistling overhead and the shells from the Hotchkiss were bursting in the paling sky. The picket ran through the scrub and a sudden outbreak of still more intense firing ahead of them told them that the flanking movement of the enemy must have commenced. Sos turned his party to a right-incline and to

---

[7] Matabele nobleman.

his infinite relief saw the cattle kraal almost immediately in front of them.

There were no natives before the zareba, so he knew that he had succeeded in reaching the kraal before the encirclement was complete. All round the small isolated party the tumult of the battle rolled, only now it seemed to Sos that it was sinking a little, as if the first attack had been partially beaten off. He ran across the open space towards the zareba and with the help of his companions began to drag the thorn branches of the barriers apart.

Immediately, rifle fire broke out from the kraal. The bullets splattered amongst the thorn and chips of wood flew all around them.

'Down!' yelled Sos. 'Picket retiring!'

Then they had all scrambled through the zareba and were pressing a way through the spaces between the wagon wheels of the laager. They made their way through the cattle kraal, while the beasts lowed and snorted in terror at the tumult around them. They ran past the horse lines of the main kraal and found their troop at the far corner, and they took their place beside them, lying beneath the wagons and firing steadily whenever a target offered itself.

Sos found Walters at his side and the little man grinned and patted him on the shoulder.

'Thought they'd got you,' he said.

He rose to his feet to get a better view, leaning across a dissel-boom and half covered by a wheel.

'They're coming on again,' he said.

Sos took up a kneeling position. It was growing quite light and now he could see the second wave advancing to the assault. It was a solid wall of black bodies with the tossing sea of ostrich feathers above. The machine guns opened up again so that the ground seemed to shake with their reverberation and the tramp of the hundreds of bare feet that thudded towards them. The Hotchkiss under Captain Lendy began to cough up its shells once more, and they exploded with a wicked crackling over the black horde before the laager. But the fire was too hot for the Matabele. Very few turned from the attack, many fell in their own tracks, though some pressed on almost up to the zareba. The advancing mass seemed literally to melt away, and the only sign of hostilities was a desultory fire from the scrub where it was thickest.

But they came on once more; and again they went down before the steady firing from the laager. All the time, intent though he was on his business of shooting, Sos marvelled at the Matabele's bravery and determination. Then he heard a cheering and the cavalry were galloping out to clear the scrub.

He turned then from the battlefield to look around him, and though the action had lasted for no great length of time, he felt exhausted and he was still shaking with excitement. Walters sat with his back against a wheel-hub, his rifle by his side and his hands clasped across his stomach. His lips looked very white and his eyes were twitching. He looked as if he were in liquor and as Sos watched him he rolled over to one side.

Beyond the zareba came the sound of galloping hooves and cries and rifle-shots, but now within the laager all was quiet. The smoke blew in wisps from the muzzles of the bigger guns, There was the acrid smell of cordite in the air.

Sos went over to Walters and tried to pull him into an upright position again, but Walters groaned, so Sos put his arm round him to support him. He felt at once that they'd never ride alongside one another any more and that No. 5 troop had lost one of their best men. All the time Walters kept his hands clasped over his stomach and now Sos noticed that the blood was bubbling out between his fingers.

'Don't go,' said Walters. 'Keep tight hold of me, because you're a good lad. I won't see Cheetham Hill no more of a Saturday night.'

And then he died.

Major Forbes, with the wit of an able soldier, ordered the column to break laager and inspan the same afternoon, in order to impress the Matabele with the apparent futility of their attack. Two hours before they moved off, the Church of England Chaplain sent for Sos.

'There is no Rabbi with us,' said the Chaplain. 'Aren't you of the same faith as your friend Trooper Walters?'

'Yes,' said Sos.

'Then you must do your best.'

Later Sos stood by the shallow grave which they'd dug for Walters, where he lay in a sacking shroud. Somebody had collected a heap of boulders to make some sort of head-stone. Sos wasn't very much good at that sort of job because it hadn't come as much his way as it should have done, despite the influence of Grandpapa and Mamma. But he had thought of Walters as his friend who had died in his arms after an action in which they had both fought side by side.

He began, a little shakily, because he felt rather a fool and moreover he was distressed. He began the opening of the Kaddish 'Hear O Israel, the Lord our God, the Lord is one...'

But he finished the job and they shovelled the sun-dried earth into the grave.

On the 30th October scouts reported the massing of large bodies of Matabele ahead and the possibility of another battle became imminent. But since the battle of the Shangani River, Sos had lost his horse. It went sick and died and he became a foot-slogger. It was the same with the entire troop. At the same time he had his first touch of fever.

Rations were cut and there was never enough water. The column had beaten off the Matabele but it was now fighting hunger and thirst and malaria. Sometimes after a night in laager a scout would be found dead, horribly mutilated. There was a grumbling in the column for men were asking themselves and each other what use gold-claims and farms and all the riches of the cattle might be, when the trail of men already doomed was rank with food for the vultures and stank of the bloated and rotting carcases of horses beneath the brassy sun.

The situation became tense. Opinions were voiced openly. Sos realized for the first time that it was, after all, mere even chances whether anyone survived the ordeal. They had ridden so blithely out of Victoria on the way to Iron Mine Hill. Now the troop colours of their puggarees were faded to one tone and their tunics were stained and torn.

Doctor Jameson ordered a parade and rode down the lines asking for complaints, so that he might give an answer. The disgruntled shuffled their feet and looked at the ground, because no one knew what the consequences might be.

There was no sound at all, when the Doctor reined up his horse and sat there facing them. He looked what he was, a fearless man.

'Good God,' he said at last, 'can't you trust me, men? Can't you trust me?'

Footsore and ragged, worn with fever and exposure and the strain of ever watching and waiting for a cunning enemy fighting on his own ground, they snatched off their hats at that and cheered him.

On the thirtieth day of the month, then, despite the privations and sickness, the morale of the column was high. By noon it was laagered up at Bembesi and the cattle and horses were led out for watering. Scouts had brought in the intelligence that Lobengula had left Bulawayo but there seemed very little likelihood of a Matabele attack while it was still daylight.

Just before one o'clock a burst of firing was heard. A picket had been surprised and a trooper killed. To the general astonishment it was realized that the enemy were definitely on the move. Volunteers were called for, to get the cattle and horses in. The latter were on every occasion the primary objective of the Matabele. Without means of transport and food, the column would soon be doomed.

As the pickets were driven in, an attack in great strength by the pick of Lobengula's fighting men, the Imbusi Impi — the Royal Regiment — was developed on the right of the laager held by the Victoria Column. The Impi was recognized at once by its black-and-white shields and ostrich plumes. When the action was completed it left five hundred of its seven hundred, dead on the field of battle.

At the height of the attack another large impi came into action and attempted an enveloping movement which was nearly successful. Some of the horses were stampeded. But the heavy fire from the machine guns and the concentrated and controlled rifle fire at last wore out the attack. The Matabele began to fall back. Major Forbes ordered the dismounted men out to clear the bush.

Sos went out with his fantastic cheese-bayonet clamped on his Martini-Henry. No. 5 troop advanced in skirmishing order. Their orders were perfectly clear and they knew how to comply with them.

The bush was still alive with the enemy, and many had climbed into the lower branches of the trees. But the dismounted men went in with the bayonet, while the Matabele bullets whistled high over their heads. They cleared the bush and fell back on the laager, and when dusk came and night fell swiftly, where had been the fearful clamour of battle was silence and the dark.

Sos remarked to Dawson later in the evening on the inaccuracy of the natives' fire. He also commented on the fact that it was strange in this particular kind of campaign against savages that anyone should be opposed by their own weapons, because everyone knew of the original arrangement between Rhodes and Lobengula and the one thousand rifles.

'That's so,' said Dawson drily. 'You can shoot straight but the Matabele can't. And for why they can't? Well, I've no doubt your sights are accurate, but before we parted with the Company's rifles, the sights were doctored. I reckon them rifles only shoot straight round corners. Besides they think that the higher they put their sights, the faster the bullet travels. I don't feel somehow that anyone of us has helped to disillusion them. As we're generally fighting at the odds of twenty to one, I don't see why we should. Have we enough flour left for a cookie?'

By the 2nd of November patrols were sent out and on their reporting that there appeared to be no sign of the enemy, the column moved away from the battlefield. The wagons travelled four abreast, with the native bearers carrying thorn, as they were now passing through open country devoid of bush.

A halt was made on the banks of the Coqui River, three miles from Ntaba Zinduna, and on the morning of the 4th of November scouts were sent on to try to reach Bulawayo, as a heavy explosion had been heard from that direction, followed by a dense cloud of smoke. Information was brought in the evening that Bulawayo had been evacuated, after its stores and the king's kraal had been destroyed and the cattle driven off.

On the following morning the column started on its last march and by two in the afternoon halted round the quarters that had been used by Colonel Colenbrander, who had been the liaison officer between the Chartered Company and Lobengula.

The information brought by the scouts was found to be correct. The greater part of the native capital was destroyed, but to everyone's delight considerable stores of native tobacco rolled in twist were found intact, together with a large number of dried pumpkins and a certain amount of Kaffir corn. Bulawayo was occupied by the Chartered Company just on three months to the day from the time the column had set out.

Sos went down with fever. He struggled against it, but to no avail. In the late nineties medical science had not as yet benefited by Dr Ross's researches into malaria and though quinine was known as an antidote, no serum had been developed for injection.

Meanwhile, though the power of the Matabele had been broken, their Impis thrashed — 'by a lot of boys', one proud Induna is reported to have said — the greater part of their cattle gone and the capital destroyed and occupied, nevertheless the king was still at large and must be captured. Major Forbes, with a strong patrol and three day's rations, started in pursuit towards Umzingwane, where it was rumoured that Lobengula might be hiding. The sortie proved to be abortive, though long years afterwards the story was revealed from a trustworthy source that one of the members of the patrol, during the heavy rain which had by then started, had lifted an old buck sail under which the king was actually sheltering, but had failed to recognize him.

Ultimately Dr Jameson sent orders to Major Forbes to proceed to Shiloh, where he would be met by Captain Napier with rations and reinforcements.

On 24th November, these combined forces continued the pursuit towards the Shangani River, but because the heavy rains had set in, Major Forbes decided to dispense with the wagon transport and go forward with the mounted men only.

The day on which this force of one hundred and forty-two officers and men reached the Shangani, a great number of armed Matabele were encountered, but their intentions appeared to be peaceful enough and they assured the party that they were tired of the war and were returning to make peace.

In point of fact the very reverse was the truth. Orders had been issued to the Matabele that they were to follow the column until it actually crossed the river, when it was to be attacked and completely destroyed.

A bivouac was decided upon by the riverside on the afternoon of 3rd December and Major Wilson, who was under Major Forbes's command, was sent on with his men to follow the king's trail. It was at that time supposed that Lobengula was just on the other side of the river, whereas, as is now known, he had retreated up north with a handful of faithful followers some days before. Wilson had been instructed to return at sundown to the main body. He failed to do so.

The failure cost him his own life and that of his party.

The opinion has been expressed that professional jealousy was responsible for this singular failure to comply with an order. The whole force was admittedly lacking in discipline and Wilson probably considered that Lobengula was as good as taken, and wished to claim full credit for the capture. Be that as it may, it seems a little significant that his party chiefly consisted of the Victoria men, of whom he was one, and who considered he should have held a higher position than he did.

Major Forbes occupied the bivouac on his own side of the river that night, with the intention of crossing to Wilson's support in the morning, it being impossible to move the column with its slaughter-cattle in the pitch darkness. Nor was it possible to form anything in the nature of a laager. The individual trooper placed his saddle facing outwards and lay down, in his single blanket or riding cape, behind it.

The following morning, as soon as it was dawn, the column assembled and set off to join Major Wilson on the far side of the Shangani. It had progressed scarcely half a mile, when violent and continued firing came from the direction in which Wilson was supposed to be. Almost at the same time a horde of the Matabele came sweeping through the bush on Major Forbes's side of the river and engaged him. It was learnt afterwards that the enemy, on the sound of the firing, had naturally supposed that the whole column had crossed the Shangani and the signal to attack had been given.

The engagement with Major Forbes's force was severe. The troopers were hopelessly outnumbered and less than a hundred rounds of ammunition had been issued to each man. Though eventually the Matabele retired, they had managed to drive off the slaughter-cattle during the action which had moreover effectively prevented the main body from joining the party on the other side of the river. When the attempt was made on the following dawn, the Shangani had risen in the night, was in full flood and was impassable. Beyond a few desultory shots nothing more was heard of Wilson's party.

It was remarked at the time that the shots were not those of rifles but of revolvers — which proved to be true. Long after, it was disclosed that the remains of Wilson's party, mostly wounded men, had shot themselves at the final approach of the Matabele, rather than fall into the savages' hands.

Thereafter, Major Forbes was entirely occupied in extricating his force from a very precarious position. The column was in a terrible condition; both the men and the horses could do little more than walk. On 9th December the column was resting for a short spell and was nearly ambushed. The fight was again severe, and while the column were laagering down for the night the Matabele, who were making shelters themselves in the bush against the heavy rain, were so close that their threats of extermination on the morrow could be plainly heard.

But despite the perilous position, Major Forbes contrived to extricate himself and his men. The laager was vacated at the dead of night. The gun carriages were left in their places and all the sick and very weak horses were left in their lines. Each man sacrificed either a riding cloak or a blanket, and these were made up as dummies. By midnight the camp was empty, and what remained of the column was threading its way in single file through the bush. Eventually open and safer country was reached, but the men were in a wretched plight, ragged and bootless.

The deception had succeeded. The Matabele were a considerable time in discovering they had been tricked and the column had a good start of them, though it was overtaken and attacked once more. But the enemy suffered heavy losses and thereafter refrained from any further actions.

At last, after the most severe privations, Major Forbes's force came up with the relief column that had set out to search for them. The relief column, of which Sos was a member, returned to Bulawayo, Cecil Rhodes riding with it.

But the fever, from which Sos had temporarily recovered, returned. He was forced to go sick again. To all intents and purposes the Matabele War was coming to its end. Wilson's last stand marked the beginning of the end. Lobengula himself succumbed to Sos's complaint, and with his passing Matabele resistance finally died.

The death of Major Wilson and his comrades was not in vain. At the time, the loss of this gallant officer and his men was a disaster; but the way in which they faced the end when it came awed the natives into great respect of the British and the story became a byword amongst legions who themselves had proved their worth on the field of battle.

The malaria took hold of Sos. When he recovered it seemed that his long-sought Eldorado had turned into a strangely shoddy reality. He sold his farming rights for fifty pounds and with the money in his pocket and the remains of the fever in his veins, made the long, slow journey back to Cape Town.

1944: INTERMEZZO

There was no longer any smoke driving past the perspex. It took a moment or two for Sos to realize the fact. The glow beneath the engine nacelle had disappeared.

He plugged in immediately on the 'inter-com'.

'Air-Gunner to Captain... the fire's out, Henry.'

'Thank God for that.'

'I've been watching it for some time now. The smoke's gone and I can't see any flame.'

'Good for you, old Evergreen.'

That was Henry's name for him and it always made him smile. Coming from anybody else to a man of his age from one so young and yet his senior, it might have sounded an impertinence. But never so with Henry. Possibly because the sobriquet was undoubtedly prompted by sincerity, without the slightest trace of impudence or malice.

He had known, of course, because of the nickname, from the very beginning what Henry had wanted to ask: how Sos managed to be serving at his age and how he'd contrived to be posted for flying duties.

The last query they had always more or less comprehended from the start. As Liaison Officer for the Royal Air Force, attached to the Admiralty, it had been reasonable to understand how it had been agreed that he should make an investigation of whatever facts might have to be examined and whatever problems. The risk was a personal affair to do with no one else but Sos. That was perfectly clear. But how had he got into uniform, first of all?

Sos let Henry ponder the problem with the rest of the crew and it amused him to observe how they each in turn so often manoeuvred the conversation round to the same subject. In the end, when the joke had been getting a little stale, he had told them.

'I formed up the Royal Air Force Volunteer Reserve. The idea cropped up in the R.A.F. Club at 128, Piccadilly, in 1937.'

'You formed the V.R.?' Henry had asked, not a little astonished.

'It grew out of the R.A.F. Ex-Officers Reserve. The subject arose one afternoon in the Club as to what would happen to the likes of us old dead-beats, if war came again. All the people there were ex-R.A.F. officers, and some of them old Royal Flying Corps and Royal Naval Air Service types. The general supposition was that we shouldn't be called up in the general shambles until it was too late and all the youngsters whose jobs we could have filled had been bumped off. We felt that people like us with Service experience could easily take certain "admin" and "ops" jobs and release the others for duties nearer the fighting. I suggested it would be a good thing to start our own Reserve. The idea was taken up and a representative meeting was called in the Club and I was elected Chairman. We decided that the Reserve would be completely voluntary and formed of all sections of the R.A.F. The meeting decided to charge ten shillings a year subscription, but I opposed that as I felt all the work should be voluntary and I myself volunteered to do it from my London office. There was to be no age limit for members. We approached the Air Ministry and were told the scheme had Air Council approval. I immediately got in touch with Lord Trenchard, who agreed to be President and was convinced that the Reserve ought to be a commitment for Air Ministry. Eventually Air Ministry took it over, files and all, and renamed the Royal Air Force Ex-Officers Reserve the Royal Air Force Volunteer Reserve. So as I was a full member of the former, I was naturally a full member of the latter. So when war came I asked for my rights, that is the commission I now hold and the rest was easy. So that's how I'm here.'

That was the story he had told Henry and it was true except for the omissions. What he had failed to tell was the fact that he had paid out of his own pocket for all the expenses of the initial organization, all correspondence, all pamphlets, and the use of a clerk. Nor did he mention that he had returned the ten-shilling subscription to each member, since it had never been used. He'd returned it as a matter of principle. It wasn't, of course, the way to get rich, but if anyone thought well of his country, it was at least a practical way of showing it.

'Captain to Air-Gunner... Sos?'

It was Henry on the 'inter-com' again.

'Yes, Henry.'

'Everything still okay?'

'Yes. No fire.'

'Well, it isn't okay this end of the line. My hydraulics have been shot up. I can't get the under-cart to move. We're not out of the wood yet, dammit.'

So the hydraulics had gone and the retractable undercarriage was useless. That meant a crash landing or baling out. The decision would be Henry's, when the time came.

When the time came...

1896–1900

CHAPTER SEVEN: THE BUTCHER AND THE BAKER

'It's a pity,' said Uncle Harry Freeman in his Johannesburg office, 'that you have to keep changing your mind, and can't settle down. How long have you been in Africa now?'

It was just on four years after the Matabele campaign.

'About five years,' said Sos.

It was 1897 and there were already remarkable signs of progress in Johannesburg. There were still tin hutments in plenty, but the partitions of Uncle Harry's quarters were no longer of hessian and old sacking. He sat now before his roll-top desk and he pointed his little goatee beard, a trifle aggressively, at Sos.

'How old are you?'

'Twenty-two,' said Sos.

'For one of so tender years you seem to have indulged in quite a fair proportion of activities. You've now been back with me on "Exchange" some time, so I suppose you feel you ought to go again. It was a newspaper, before you came back to me, after the Matabele war, wasn't it?'

'I sold the story of Sigcau to the *Graphic*. He was the paramount chief of Pondoland and was under arrest. It was the first time any native had taken legal action against the British Government under the Habeas Corpus Act.'

'Don't talk to me like a history book, even if you did write the damn thing,' said Uncle Harry. 'And before that it was a boot-shop.'

'Owned by a Quaker,' said Sos.

'What the hell's that got to do with it?' said Uncle Harry. 'And what was the game you were at before that?'

'I was a salesman in a jeweller's shop.'

'Why didn't you stay up north, when you had the chance after that Matabele business you were in?'

'Fever.'

'How's everyone at home?'

'Very well, I think,' said Sos.

He had just returned from three months' visit to England. The trip had not been an unqualified success. Piccadilly and the Empire Theatre, the Wharncliffe Rooms and the old 'Globe' had provided certain compensations, but the duty visits to his relatives had not.

Now, back in Africa, Uncle Harry sat at his desk and stared solemnly, if not a little sadly, at his nephew.

'Very well, you think,' he repeated. 'Very well, you think. I shouldn't be surprised if you never went near your people at all.'

'Of course, I did,' said Sos. 'I saw Mamma.'

'You saw Mamma! You travel back to England after all this time and you call on your mother! Well, I never!'

Uncle Harry snatched delicately at his little beard with forefinger and thumb.

'Perhaps it's just as well none of us have enquired how you *did* spend your time, though we may have our own ideas. To revert to the subject, where do you propose to go now?'

'Delagoa Bay,' said Sos.

'Why?' said Uncle Harry.

'I've heard a lot about it,' said Sos. 'There are some Portuguese that I know who I've met down town. They can give me some decent introductions.'

'I hope you're right. This raid of Doctor Jameson's when you were away hasn't helped matters. There was trouble enough before, God knows. Maybe you're right to get out before the real business starts.'

'It's not that,' said Sos. 'It isn't that at all, Uncle Harry.'

'Well, what is it, then? I've made you Managing Director of the Geldenhuis Main Reef, and you're on the Board of the Rand Collieries, South Village Deep, Bentjes Deep and the Anglian Company. It's not bad going for twenty-two, you know.'

'I owe all that to you,' said Sos.

'We can forget that,' said Uncle Harry. 'I don't put fools into responsible positions. Why do you want to leave Jo'burg?'

'I wish I could explain,' said Sos. 'It sounds so silly when you try to put it into words. It's mostly the office life, I suppose. I want to get back to the bush again. It was pretty hard going sometimes. I know all that. But there was another side to the coin. You never knew what was going to crop up next. And then, you had friends — you met people like Doctor Jameson. I'm sorry he's in trouble. He was a fine man. We thought a lot of him. I'm no good as a pen-pusher, This is the second time I've tried it. And that's not all —'

'Well, what's the rest?' said Uncle Harry quietly, because he was a judge of men and he was interested.

'Johannesburg,' said Sos. 'You know what Rhodes is supposed to have said — "Personal ambition, self-aggrandizement and money — and you can buy any man." That's what I mean.'

'You mean you don't believe in that remark?' said Uncle Harry shrewdly.

'Of course I don't believe in it.'

'And yet,' said Uncle Harry sadly, 'I've made you a Director of my Companies and you've been having instruction in mining from my consulting engineer. God knows where your idealism will lead you to, my dear boy. Well, off you go.'

Sos went down to Delagoa Bay, and since he had a little money in his pocket, put up at the Central Hotel. The town was a mixture of tin huts and stone buildings; the latter being partly the legacy from the early days of Vasco da Gama, the explorer who founded the original settlement for the Portuguese.

Sos was attracted by the place with its magnificent natural harbour and found the people sympathetic and good-natured. Therefore he was happy within himself, because he was on the track of adventure again.

He found work with a stevedore company as a tally clerk and spent his days on a lighter, ferrying between the anchored ships in the bay and the shore. The sun beat down mercilessly and the work was gruelling, so hearing of a ship-chandler's which was prospering, he paid it a visit.

The nature of his work on the lighters had made him familiar with the name of Reimann, who supplied meat as well as every other imaginable commodity to the incoming ships. His first view of the German butcher and storekeeper was in his store one sweltering afternoon, when Reimann was wielding an expert chopper on a huge side of beef. The place was filled with sea-going men and natives, women from the settlement and 'boys' buying meat for their masters. Even so Reimann towered above the crowd, his gleaming chopper in his fist, so that with his solid thick neck and square head, his knotted forearms and massive shoulders, he looked like some magnificent Germanic god who'd stepped out of the halls of Valhalla to help feed the inhabitants of Portuguese East Africa.

Sos waited his time and seized his opportunity of striking an acquaintance with the German in the bar of the Central Hotel. He found Reimann to be exactly what he'd expected him to be. His temper and generosity were on a scale with his physique. He could also swallow vast quantities of brandy without turning one stubble of a hair on his closely cropped head.

Sos asked him for a job. The next day he left the stevedore company and joined Reimann.

The arrangement was an immediate success. Sos learnt how to cut up meat and how to make corned beef, pumping in the saltpetre and leaving the huge chunks of meat in their barrels of brine. It was sold to the Union Castle line at 4½d. a pound.

He met Reimann's friends Borden, a young cattle dealer, and Protopulous, the Greek baker; but particularly he grew to like and respect Reimann himself, who knew his business well and was shrewd.

He was indeed sufficiently shrewd to take Sos in as a partner, and thus encouraged Sos grew more confident and success followed success. Even the ever-increasing rumours of the trouble between the Boers and the British seemed but distant murmurings from another far-off and less happy land.

Sos organized a supply of cattle from the natives up-country, buying at a cheap rate, fattening up the lean beasts and then trekking them down to the coast. Together with this activity he arranged for a transport service of fresh vegetables to Lourenço Marques.

When twelve ships of the British Mediterranean Fleet put into the bay to safeguard British interests, in view of Germany's sympathetic attitude to the Boers, Sos rowed out to the flagship and came back with a contract to supply the squadron as long as it was at anchorage. The following morning he raised an overdraft of £3,000 on the security of the contract alone.

But if success was easy, the work was hard and the Portuguese authorities insisted on the strictest supervision of all slaughter-cattle and killed meat. Every carcase had to bear the certificate of the Veterinary Surgeon's Department before it could be sold, and often it was killed, and out of the store within twelve hours.

Even so, despite all precautions such as these and great care in sanitation and general cleanliness of the town, blackwater fever broke out.

Protopulous, the Greek baker, brought the news to the chandler's store and explained with much gesticulation how the epidemic could spread and devastate the area. It had already, it seemed, taken hold of the native population, and the authorities were greatly concerned. No white men so far, said Protopulous, had contracted the complaint. Maybe that was because none of them were teetotallers. It was always the abstainer that went down first. Sos thought both Reimann and Protopulous stood a very good chance of survival.

There was a strange affinity between the German giant, who could lift a side of beef weighing two hundred pounds as if it were a packet of tea, and the pot-bellied little baker with his triple chin and bandy legs. They appeared to have been friends for many years and they had forgotten more about 'Portuguese East' than most people could remember. They seldom drank together in the bars around the town, but sometimes of an evening they would visit one another's houses. Often the visitor would stay the night and arrive behind his counter the following morning, hollow-eyed and grey-lipped.

The fever spread and infected some of the white population, and Sos knew that disaster could be very near to all of them.

The passing of the funeral cart, drawn by a mule, with the coffin on top and the Goanese grave-diggers in attendance became a familiar sight. It would call at a house and within minutes the corpse would be in the coffin and on the way to the cemetery.

At the height of the epidemic, Sos entertained the senior officer of the British Fleet on shore. Such a function was now well within the scope of the junior partner of Reimann's Ships' Chandlers.

It was a very pleasant party and Sos particularly enjoyed it because the senior officer of Marines was present, Brigadier Marchant, who had been Sos's company commander at Deal. The Brigadier had no recollection of his one-time marine, but it gave the one-time marine some small satisfaction to think of how different the relationship had become in the passing of a few years. Really, he thought, on the whole life could be quite easily handled.

He bade the last of his guests farewell in the best of spirits and then made his way to the store to tell Reimann of its success. The German had been away all the afternoon before and the following morning.

The store was still open, but even as he approached he realized by the small and agitated crowd that was gathered round the door, that something was wrong. As he grew nearer, the crowd suddenly scattered and ran helter-skelter down the street. A second later a customer broke out of the building, screaming. An iron bucket followed, whistling through the air and landing with a clatter a few paces behind the runner. From inside sounded the rumbling of a great shouting voice.

Sos thought that a raid had been made on the store. He had had no intimation that anything of the sort might occur and was at a loss to know what might be on hand. Reimann, a just and reasonable man, was popular and respected. Sos ran down the street and into the store.

'Get to hell out of this!' roared Reimann.

He was standing in his shirt-sleeves, the sweat pouring down his face; his arms were bare and the razor-sharp cleaver was in his hand. His jaw was working as if he were chewing. He glared at Sos and growled at him like a lion. He looked twice as big as a lion and four times as ferocious. Then with no more ado, he rocketed across the store and slashed with the chopper at his colleague.

The aim was wide and Sos ducked, for the steel chopper would have no doubt split him in twain, but it struck the sidepost of the door frame and buried itself in the hard wood.

Reimann grabbed at the handle which had slipped out of his hand with the violence of the impact and cursed at the top of his voice as he struggled to get the blade free.

'I'll get you yet!' yelled Reimann and tugged at the chopper.

'What's the matter with you?' said Sos. He picked himself up off the floor, for he'd gone down on his knees to dodge the blow. He began to dust his trousers, keeping a wary eye on his partner all the time, but Reimann turned from the fist embedded cleaver and put out a hand in front of his face as if he were collecting cobwebs.

'Wassat?' he said.

'Have you gone mad?' said Sos. 'Do you know you've just nearly succeeded in murdering me?'

'Murder!' said Reimann. 'Murder little Sos! Oh, my God!'

He tottered across towards the counter and took a seat on a half-empty barrel of dried beans. His face began to twitch and he closed his eyes. Then he opened his mouth and a prolonged and thunderous eructation issued therefrom. It seemed to ease him a little, because his shoulders sank and his figure relaxed into itself, like one of the inflated rubber whistling pigs that Sos had once played with in the nursery of Tankerville House.

'Come here,' said Reimann and opened his eyes. 'You know I'd never murder you,' he said. 'Never touch a hair of your head, *mein Kind*. Too many people dead already. My poor friend. Oh! my poor friend, Protopulous. He is dead of the blackwater. Where's the brandy?'

The brandy was in its usual place at the back of the counter. Sos fetched the bottle and Reimann put it to his lips and drank as if the liquor were water. Then he belched again.

'That is better,' he said. '*Mein Gott*, where am I?'

'You're in the store, you fool,' said Sos.

A head appeared round the doorway and an urgent Kaffir voice whispered: 'Is it safe now? I left my meat.'

She stood in the doorway, all twenty stone of her, and her white teeth gleamed in her ebony face. She wore a yellow rag round her head and her feet were bare. Sos recognized her as a regular customer. Reimann appeared to have gone asleep, for he was snoring.

'What happened?' said Sos.

'He drove us out. All his customers. He said we were devils. Not for a long time has he done this.'

'Not for a long time?'

'Not since you have been here. Now the madness out of a bottle has come back to him.'

'You mean he's got d.t.s!'

'He has been drinking again. His friend the Greek baker has died of the fever. He was telling us, how only last night they were together and how he heard this morning that his friend was dead and how he sent a wreath to the cemetery for him. He was weeping when he told us. Then he suddenly started to drive us out.'

'You must help me get him into the back room,' said Sos. 'Then we'll find your meat, and you can go.'

Together they managed to get Reimann on to a couch in the office at the back. Sos covered him over with some sacking and went off for the doctor. He was full of misgivings. Only an hour ago all prospects for the future had seemed golden; he had that very morning completed a contract to supply the local police and the military with meat. The party with the naval officers had seemed so characteristic of this period of success. Now Protopulous had succumbed to the dreaded fever and Reimann was in the throes of delirium tremens.

He found the doctor, who knew his patient of old. He accompanied Sos back, bringing a stomach-pump with him.

On the following morning a strange case came before the Court of Justice in Lourenço Marques. The story was told by the chief witness, the headman of a party of Goanese grave-diggers, and by two of the police who had arrested the accused.

The accused had been found lying on the ground on the outskirts of the town by the party of grave-diggers on their way back to the cemetery. It appeared to be quite apparent that the accused had been making his way into Lourenço Marques, possibly for medical assistance, when the fever had overcome him and he had succumbed. There appeared to be no life in him and it was felt that as the burial party was for once returning empty-handed to the cemetery the opportunity should be taken to provide the accused with a free ride to his last resting-place.

His identity had been established by the discovery of a letter in his jacket. The time of day had been just about dawn.

An ingenious expedient was now explained to the Court by the chief witness. By reason of the epidemic, labour was becoming very scarce in direct proportion to the number of dying. Not only was there a shortage of grave-diggers, but also of carpenters to supply coffins.

To save time and trouble a special coffin was carried on a mule-drawn truck, which called from door to door. It had a lid, as it were, both top and bottom. That on the top opened in the usual manner, so that the corpse could be viewed in all its placid indifference, but that on the bottom was in the nature of a sliding panel. On arrival at the cemetery, it was merely a matter of moments to strip the corpse of its outer garments and wrap it in a shroud, replacing it in its coffin. The mule was then led to the newly dug grave, the improvised hearse was drawn astride of it, the sliding panel of the coffin was pulled out, and the body dropped neatly into the place prepared for it below. The hearse then moved on. Two bucketfuls of lime were pitched into the grave, and then the entire party wheeled in an about-turn towards the entrance to the cemetery and made its way back to the town, where there would assuredly be more customers awaiting attention.

In this way, as the chief witness explained, much unnecessary work was avoided and there was moreover a very great saving in wood, which was highly commendable. This special coffin, the chief witness assured the Court, had already served on some eighty occasions and everybody had been well pleased.

This, then, he continued, was what had occurred on the morning in question. The dead man had been picked up, lifted into the coffin, driven up the hill, and just outside the cemetery gates had been properly and decently shrouded, after his jacket and trousers had been removed.

The body was then replaced in the coffin, wheeled to the appointed grave, dropped in, dusted with lime and the bearers had moved on.

The rest, indeed, should have been silence.

It was not.

A frantic cry from one of the bearer party had startled the others, who had turned to see the fearful spectacle of an apparition in white arising from the grave they had just left. This terrible and ghastly spectre had rushed towards them with a staggering gait, so that it tripped several times over its long winding cloth, being somewhat short in the leg and rotund of body.

The grave-diggers and bearers had taken immediate fright and run for their lives and had not been seen since, which was very unfortunate owing to the labour shortage. The mule had bolted and fallen into another open grave, wrecked the hearse and had itself to be destroyed. Altogether a most unprofitable dawn.

On the evidence of the police, it was stated that the accused was found later in a dazed condition, with his head covered in lime, walking about Lourenço Marques with no jacket or trousers and clad in nothing but what appeared to be an outsize shirt.

When questioned, he appeared to be a trifle incoherent, only insisting that he had spent the evening and the night before with an old friend on a mild carousal. The accused was then incarcerated. The Court fined him three thousand *reis* for indecent exposure.

The surname of the accused was Protopulous, a Greek baker of Lourenço Marques.

Thereafter the situation deteriorated, with the relations between the partners in the chandlery business becoming more and more strained.

Protopulous made no effort to return Reimann's wreath or repay him what he had spent on it. This upset the German considerably, because, as explained to Sos in the brief intervals between brandy bottles, it was like obtaining a funeral by false pretences.

The Greek, on the other hand, insisted that during the later part of that fatal evening Reimann had substituted 'Dop' brandy for the better-class brand with which they had started the debauch. That alone was an insult which could certainly never be condoned when it was followed by the injury of being buried alive.

The quarrel upset Reimann, at least sufficiently to provide an excuse for the further drowning of his sorrows. The frequency of his drunken bouts increased, and what was more regrettable, he began to carry his habits into the bars and saloons of the town.

No doubt, already doubly primed before he set out, it was only inevitable that he should collapse before he reached home. The police began to take an interest in the German's activities. They cultivated the habit of picking him up and running him in.

Reimann in a cell was of no more use to Sos than Reimann stretched out paralytic on his back. Somebody had to cut up the meat and it needed a skilled man.

There followed a regular and tedious round of bargaining and arguing with the police, every time Reimann was taken inside. Sos would go round to the station and demand the release of his partner. If Reimann was then still detained, Sos would refuse to deliver the contract meat to the police. As there was no other source of supply, he generally won the day. It was a case of no Reimann, no meat. But it was all very exasperating.

It became more exasperating when Reimann took in yet another partner. Sos decided to leave. As always he had kept his wits about him and when he visited the bars of the town he had listened to the conversation around him, and though most of it had been concerned with the growing unrest in the Transvaal and the Orange Free State, there was also talk of many kinds of trading, not least that of native labour recruitment for the gold mines.

Sos said goodbye to Reimann with regret. The German had been fair and just and generous. If he had been able to keep off the liquor no doubt the partnership might have continued. But the business had become more or less of a routine and the market had reached its saturation point, so that while there was a good living to be made, the element of enterprise and adventure was slowly receding.

Reimann was genuinely upset, thumping his fists on his great knees, as he sat by his counter.

'Leaving me! Leaving your old friend! *Ach, Gott im Himmel,* what shall I do?'

'Gott knows,' said Sos; but he left.

He entered into a contract with the Consolidated Gold Fields of South Africa to supply the combine with native labour. The terms were £5 per head per native and 5s. a month for every man that stayed over six months. Sos was to cover the district of Gaza, including the district of Inhambane. All the natives came under the military authority of the Portuguese, and they were allowed to repudiate the bargain at any time after six months.

The duties of an organizer were strenuous but straightforward, though at times hazardous. Before any native could marry he must find the *lobola*[8] to pay his father-in-law for his wife. Ten selected cattle could provide a basis for domestic

---

[8] Price of a wife.

bliss. The oxen, however, had first to be acquired and one way of going about this matter was for the prospective bridegroom to serve a few years down the mines and earn sufficient money to return to his own people. It was with this argument at his fingertips that Sos would approach a local chieftain.

He had, however, previous to the actual campaign of recruitment, already had a compound constructed — a very large kraal, with his own quarters stationed nearby. Here the volunteers could be assembled and at specified times, and when their numbers were sufficient, they were marched to Inkomati for their ultimate destination. But beyond the distant prize of a wife a more immediate bait was offered. A party would be arranged.

The parties that Sos arranged were most unconventional in one sense, in that party manners were not always over-delicate, but in another sense they conformed to the universal idea of fun, being a nicely adjusted combination of alcohol and dancing. But whereas the drawing-rooms of the Mayfair of that day regaled their guests with claret-cup and a rendering of Tennyson's 'Maud' and lasted till midnight, Sos's parties consisted of a liberal issue of fire-water, an ox roasted whole, and a band of native drummers, and the parties lasted day and night for as long as a week.

They danced and drank and ate. They fell exhausted to the ground and other dancers trampled on them. The moon came up and still the drums went on, a steady, rhythmic, eerie tap-tapping and shuffling of fingertips that could rise to a gale-like diapason or drop to a secretive and sinister murmuring in the gloom. Then after a little time, when the ardours of the body had been dissipated, opportunity came for a little business talk. But there could be difficult occasions.

Sos sat outside his hut at Chungwani, where he had established a very successful recruiting centre in conjunction with a Canadian, Jack Pierce. The compound was more than adequate, the liquor plentiful and the meat fresh and good. His own quarters were reasonably comfortable, though the centre was more isolated than usual, being just over ten miles from the nearest village, Chai-Chai. At the rear of the hut Sos had built a run for three dozen chickens which he had had specially sent up from Durban. It was a source of considerable satisfaction to him to have a constant supply of fresh eggs. It was also of equal satisfaction to the native dogs who howled and bayed the moon down inside and in the vicinity of the compound, when they'd finished scratching their fleas.

The curs belonged to the natives, mostly of the Machopi tribe, in whose village the compound was. And the dogs stole eggs. Night and day they prowled round Sos's hut and sniffed at the wire and wooden stockade of the chicken run. Then they broke in and raided the nest-boxes.

It was as impossible to keep the dogs out as it was to keep constant watch. Even now one gaunt grey beast with a mangy back was loping along the stockade, its ears pricked and its tail waving. Sos jumped to his feet, picked up a stone and flung it with accuracy. It hit the mongrel in the ribs and sent it yelping towards the entrance to the compound. Even before it reached there, several natives were ready to greet it.

'They like their dogs,' said Pierce who had come to the door. 'They're mighty proud of those dogs.'

'I'd be proud of a dog that stole eggs for me if it were mine,' said Sos. Pierce stroked his chin ruminatively. He was a big, florid man, some five years senior to his partner.

'They're a curse,' he said.

'I'm going to put a stop to it,' said Sos.

'You'll be a clever man. Nobody ever owns up to ownership of a dog what's been raiding. None of our friends over there are going to confess that it's their dog what's to blame.'

'We'll see,' said Sos.

He picked up his hat, which lay on the ground beside him, put it on his head and crossed over the compound. There were several natives just inside the barrier and two were fondling the grey cur that he had hit. Their display of affection increased as he approached.

'In future,' said Sos, 'you'll keep your dogs under control.'

There were expostulations at once. This dog was not theirs. Indeed, they had no dog at all. Even so it was not right to throw stones.

'Fetch your chieftain, Chiachalo,' said Sos. In a little time Chiachalo came out, wrapped in a gaudy blanket. Sos came to the point, at once.

'You're chief, here. So when I speak to you, I speak to everyone in this kraal. What I now say to you is to be made known to every man here. Whoever owns a dog is responsible for it and is to keep it under proper control. If I see a dog near my hut again, I shoot it.'

It was early in the following morning that he carried out his threat. He had gone out to feed the chickens, and there, sure enough, nosing in the nest-boxes, was a mottled brown beast for all the world like a jackal. It fled as Sos dropped the bucket of chicken-food, searching frantically for a stick, and leapt the side of the pen with ease. Then it trotted to the centre of the open ground between the hut and the compound, turned about and sat down, with a maddening air of self-assurance. It was quite clear that it was only waiting for Sos to complete his business and go back into his hut, when it would make its way back and continue its investigations.

Sos went inside, took his rifle from the rack and went to the door. He took steady aim and fired. The cur rolled over, dead. Sos ran the pull-through through his rifle barrel and replaced the rifle on its rack. Then he went in once more to help Pierce get ready the morning meal.

It was a busy morning, as the stores had to be checked, and it was not until midday that Pierce made any mention of having heard a shot in the morning.

'One of those damn dogs,' said Sos. 'I shot it. I told them I would.'

He looked out across the compound.

'It's still there,' he said, with some surprise.

The dog lay where it had fallen. Over the ground heat-waves danced and shimmered and no breeze stirred the dusty leaves of the single tree that provided the only spot of shade. The atmosphere was heavy and oppressive. From the back of the hut, Neptune, the old bay gelding that the partners used for transport, neighed as Mesulitalan the police-boy went to him with a bucket of water. There was no one in sight or at the barrier of the compound. Very high overhead a single vulture was circling.

About three of the afternoon, while they were sorting out a packing case of groceries, both men simultaneously became aware of the low rumbling undercurrent that had been going on for some time and which was now unmistakably the sound of drums. It was a steady, ominous beat, and when they looked out from their hut they could see above the walls of the compound a small light cloud of dust such as might have been raised by the stamping of many feet.

There was no one in sight, and the body of the dog had gone.

Both white men returned inside once more and Sos looked across at his companion, who was still listening intently.

'Well?' said Sos at last. 'What do you make of it?'

For answer, Pierce moved to the rack, took his own rifle down and slipped a round into the breech, then propped it up in the corner.

'Just in case something proves to be what I think it may be,' he said enigmatically. 'Come on, let's get on with this job. Seven pounds of flour, three of sugar...'

Less than an hour later, there was no mistaking the nature of the activity within the kraal; a war-dance was taking place. In such a manner had Lobengula primed his impis to battle, inducing into his warriors a blood-lust frenzy. Now, within the recruitment compound, would-be peaceful labourers, bound for some centre of civilization to earn their *lobola*, were reverting to type.

Pierce picked up his rifle and Sos joined him outside, with a loaded revolver strapped to his belt.

'Somebody's enjoying a celebration,' said Pierce, 'but I don't think it's in honour of us.'

The next moment the entrance to the compound was swarming with its inmates. The sound of the drums continued. Sos thought he could hear a low and steady chanting from the recesses of the kraal. Then the Africans were streaming out into the open.

They fanned out to the left and right as they emerged, squatting along the stockade or leaning against it. They formed an audience with a stage entrance, as it were, in their centre. The affair had something of the air of a ritual, drunk though many of them might be.

Almost before the crowd had assembled, three men carried out a large calabash. It was obviously filled with liquor, because as soon as they rested it on the ground others rushed forward with small gourds cut in half to form cups, and began to dip out the contents, swilling it into their mouths. No sooner had they dispersed than a native in war paint, carrying an assegai, bore out what was unmistakably the corpse of the shot dog. He laid it beside the calabash. Then as the drums beat louder, Chiachalo, chief of the Machopi, appeared.

No longer were his shoulders covered with a ragged-edged blanket. Now rose from his head the dancing plumes of a chieftain's headdress, round his neck was a necklace of lion's teeth, a leopard's skin girdled his middle and the tail swung down between his buttocks. He carried his shield and stabbing spear in his left hand, and his knobkerry club was strapped to his wrist. He came out of the compound, leaping high.

Then he stood his ground and spoke.

He raised his shield and stabbing spear aloft, and his voice rang out, so that he wasn't any more one of the Machopi in a fine blanket sitting on his haunches outside his hut, but a warrior with a purpose on hand, a mission to complete. He was very drunk, but wholly magnificent.

He told everyone, all the world at large, who he was. He told everyone of the tribes he ruled and the lesser tribes that his own tribes had enslaved and 'eaten'. He described his lineage from ancient times to the present day. He went on to enlarge upon his own personal prowess and of the battles he had fought and the victories he had won. He declared that a chieftain's property was sacrosanct. That to defy that law meant death to whoever committed the foul deed, because he himself was Chiachalo, chief of the Machopi, whose sacred property, a most valued and trusted dog, a hound which was beyond the price of the white man's gold, was dead, dead, dead!

And by whose hand?

'This,' said Pierce, 'is where we make our own entrance into the concert party, before it's too late and the curtain comes down on us.'

And he pressed up the safety catch of his rifle and raised it to his shoulder.

'For God's sake, no,' said Sos. 'Put your rifle down, man.'

For answer Pierce squinted along the sights.

'I've got a bead on his navel,' he said. 'I wish he'd keep still.'

'Put your rifle down, man. Are you crazy?'

'I'll drill a hole in a few of those sons of hell before they open up my bowels,' said Pierce.

'Don't shoot,' said Sos. 'Chiachalo's our only trump card. What's the good of knocking off a score of them? They'd only get us in the end. It's three hundred to one in numbers against us. Leave this to me. Keep me covered, while I go out to them and you get a bit of rope ready.'

Then Sos stepped out into the open ground, took his revolver out of its holster and went forward at a steady pace. The drums from inside the kraal had ceased to beat now at sight of the short stocky figure of the white man advancing; Chiachalo's diatribe died away, but he took a bold stance. His followers craned forward and there was a great silence. The dog still lay by the half-empty calabash. In another land, in a former age, it might have been a boy with a sling and a pebble against a giant of the Philistines, with a little brook running in between.

'People of the Machopi and people of the Chungwani area,' said Sos in their native tongue, and he kept his revolver levelled at Chiachalo's chest. 'Listen to me. I made an edict that no dog should come near my kraal to thieve again. This was told to you by your chieftain, Chiachalo. Then a dog comes again and there the dog lies dead. It was not in my knowledge that it was a chieftain's dog, but that means but little to me. It would have died just the same.'

There was an ominous growl from the crowd and Sos thought he saw from the corner of his eye the glint of a spear blade, upraised. He spoke on.

'While you are in this compound — and you all came here of your own free will and accord and have been treated justly — you will obey my orders. Go back to your huts. If anyone makes one movement now against me or my companion, I shoot your chieftain till he lies as dead as his dead dog lies there. Now let that be understood.'

Sos looked around the crowd and no one moved and it seemed that no one breathed; only the sun beat down till the heat waves shimmered over the ground and the flies buzzed and settled round the dead cur's eyes and nostrils.

'As for you,' said Sos to Chiachalo. 'You will come with me. You will drop your shield and spear and go to that tree.'

They stood and faced one another and Chiachalo glared at Sos and bared his teeth. Sos raised the barrel of his revolver by half an inch.

'I shan't hesitate to shoot,' he said.

He knew that every word was understood.

'Put down your shield,' said Sos.

Chiachalo was panting as if he were engaged in a fierce struggle.

'Quickly now,' said Sos.

The chieftain flung his shield on the ground.

'Now your spear.'

The biceps muscles of Chiachalo's arm bulged as his arm stiffened and those of his forearm began to swell as his grip tightened on the haft of his assegai. Sos knew that the man could spring like a leopard, as swiftly and as suddenly, and that even before his feet reached the ground again the steel spearhead could rip into his vitals.

He knew, too, that hundreds of eyes were intent upon him and that a surging sea of dark figures would overwhelm him if ever a blow fell or if ever a shot were fired. Either way lay death. So he fought Chiachalo with the power of his will, as he had learnt to do in the very beginning, when he'd fought in a smallpox camp, many miles from where he was now, and seemingly many years ago.

But now Chiachalo was almost imperceptibly lifting his arm up, as if the very muscles had control of the limb, and beyond the volition of his brain would take charge and strike the fatal blow. So in the same way Sos's fingers tightened on the trigger and the hammer slowly began to rise, very slowly, but very steadily, till it would reach the apex of the cocking-piece and snap down to send a leaden bullet to tear Chiachalo's chest apart.

Then suddenly, with a great sigh, Chiachalo dropped his assegai from nerveless fingers, and it fell rattling on to the ground. Sos indicated the direction of the tree and Chiachalo stumbled off towards it and his forearm was across his forehead, as if he must shade his eyes from his shame.

He reached the tree and Sos ordered him to turn about and then Pierce was by their side. He carried a length of rope, and while Sos covered Chiachalo with his revolver, Pierce lashed the chieftain to the tree.

'Mesulitalan is going for the Esquadrilha de Gaza,' said Pierce.

At the back of the white man's hut, the native boy was swinging himself across the bare back of the bay gelding. He was as naked as the day he was born. He shook the rein, the bay tossed its head and as Mesulitalan drove his heels home, set off in a hard gallop. They swung round the track as it turned into the scrub, and disappeared.

Pierce brought out a couple of old packing cases, and he sat on one with his rifle across his knees watching the entrance to the compound, while Sos, on the other, kept guard over the chieftain.

The heat of the sun was intense and Sos grew thirsty, so that it became an anguish, but he dared not leave his post. So they waited there and the afternoon advanced towards evening. After the sudden dusk, there would be the night and in the darkness there would surely be an attempt on the part of the natives to rescue their chief. The hours crept slowly on and the sun began to sink and Sos's hopes sank with it, because he knew that once night fell it would probably be the last night he would know on earth. And all the time there was a silent throng of Chiachalo's followers at the entrance to the compound, waiting, intent and watching. He spoke no word to Pierce, because it would need shouting and he felt he must not break the silence of what seemed a monstrous dream, with the silent camp teeming with life and the black contorted figure lashed against the tree.

He heard the sound of hooves, through the still air, when they were certainly a mile away, because it was several minutes before the troop of the Esquadrilha de Gaza broke out of the bush, their officer galloping at their head.

They came into view with the dust rising in a cloud about them, some troopers of the police in their grey uniforms and wide hats and with their swords in scabbards at the side of their high-pommelled saddles. At their rear, his own legs and thighs smothered white with the bay gelding's sweat, rode Mesulitalan the compound police boy.

The *Alferes* in charge of the troop cantered up to where Sos now stood, his revolver at last hanging from its lanyard.

'We are in time, senhor?'

'You are,' said Sos. 'Just.'

He pointed to the tree.

'And that's your man.'

CHAPTER EIGHT: GREEN MAMBA

There was no further trouble at Chungwani. The example which had been made of Chiachalo had an immediate effect not only on the inmates of the recruiting centre but on the entire district.

Sos became prosperous. The first intakes of labour now established in their various mines were showing returns, there was a steady influx of recruits and there seemed no possibility of unforeseen misfortune. He put the police-boy Mesulitalan to work outside on the patch of ground which he hoped one day would resemble a garden, and engaged his sister of fifteen, Majasse, in the house. Jack Pierce departed to set up his own centre and Sos was left in sole charge.

He thought that it was very agreeable being king of his own castle although most of it was made of reeds and had floors of beaten cow-dung. But his word was law. He was, moreover, successfully trading in cattle. His bank balance went steadily upwards and every month he had the supreme satisfaction of knowing that whatever success had come to him was of his own contriving.

But it was not only through the agencies of prancing chieftains, swearing revenge when in their liquor, that danger could arise. The fever he had contracted during the Matabele campaign had been kept under control, but the country swarmed with venomous reptiles and insects; the tarantula, the poisonous spider that sprang for the eyes, the scorpion with its terrible sting and the dreaded green mamba, the snake from whose bite, it was believed, no white man had ever survived.

In the early afternoon of this particular day, within a month of Jack Pierce's departure, Sos turned in for an hour's siesta on the bunk in his hut. In the shade of the tree where Chiachalo had learnt his lesson, Majasse was washing clothes in a tub, the way Sos had taught her. He could hear her singing contentedly to herself.

He was also well content with a week's hard work behind him and the possibility of a day or two off down-country. He had just completed a successful deal over twenty oxen and had had good reports of his cattle in Lourenço Marques. He stretched himself out on his bunk and fell asleep.

He awoke with a start, crying out involuntarily at the sudden pain in his hand. It was in his right hand, which had fallen over the side of the bunk as he slept, and reached the floor.

He jerked his arm away from the ground, and as he did so the snake fell from the first joint of his middle finger.[9] He saw it momentarily as it dropped off and as it writhed away towards the door. He knew it at once for a green mamba.

The pain in his hand increased to an agony as the hand began to swell. He staggered to the door and called for help. Majasse heard him and dropped her dripping washing over the edge of the tub, while Mesulitalan came running round from the back with a spade still in his hand.

'Green mamba,' said Sos, and clutched at the doorpost because the pain was appalling, and the knowledge that he was poisoned in a most deadly fashion took all the strength out of him.

Majasse caught her brother by the arm and she pointed to the compound and she had only to say one word, because these two young natives knew what peril beset their master and what they must do.

---

[9] Sos carried this scar to his final day.

Mesulitalan ran across the compound and his sister led Sos back to his camp bed. He sat there in mortal anguish while the girl clasped his knees. It was almost as if she were praying. Then she rose and pulled him to his feet and kept him walking till Mesulitalan was back with a demijohn full of alcohol.

Majasse took a glass and a knife and she blew at the fire and put a steel skewer into it. Mesulitalan took the glass from her and filled it with the raw liquor.

'Drink, Inkoss. And then drink again. And you mustn't sit still.'

The stuff tasted like cheap brandy, and it burnt the lining of Sos's stomach like a draught of boiling oil. He drank the glass and then another and the native boy kept him on his feet.

Majasse took Sos's hand, and in the flesh where the green mamba had bitten she cut a slit, and it was as deep as the bone. The blood spurted out and Majasse put the finger to her mouth and sucked at the wound. She spat the blood out on the floor and put her lips back to the wounded hand again. Mesulitalan filled yet another glass with the fire-water, and supported Sos while the girl continued to suck the poison out. And Sos knew that she might very well fail and that it would be at the very peril of her own life; but because he was 'Inkoss', master to her and to her kith and kin, it was a mere matter of duty.

By the time she had drawn off all the blood she could he was practically drunk with the fiery brew. Which was as well and no doubt intended, for she cauterized the wound with the white-hot skewer and the flesh sizzled as it burnt. Then when her brother went across to the compound to organize a party to take Sos down to the Limpopo River bar, where a Portuguese gunboat lay with a doctor on board, she kept Sos still on his feet despite his protests.

They carried him down to the mouth of the Limpopo in a *mechila* — a hammock slung on a pole supported by two native boys at each end, with a relief of fourteen others marching in the rear.

It was fifteen miles to where the gunboat lay, through bush tracks, and the going was rough at any time. Now, Sos lay in agony in the swinging, dipping *mechila*. The carriers had been told by Majasse that speed was the essence of the journey. When they reached the Limpopo he was practically unconscious.

They carried him aboard the gunboat and the medical officer took charge of him immediately. The head-boy of the carrier party waited to hear the doctor's verdict, before he led his party back to Chungwani, because he knew that Majasse would be waiting for the news, as would so many others of their people.

The doctor sent a message, at last.

'He'll live. But we only got him just in time.'

The head-boy of the carriers went back on shore, where his team was anxiously waiting for him, and told them that Sos would not die; they broke into a chattering like pleased children, and started off on the way home.

The Portuguese treated Sos with great consideration, and while he was convalescing he would look forward to a talk with any of the officers who dropped in from time to time to see how their patient was getting on. Always it seemed the talk was of coming trouble.

Sos had been entirely absorbed in his recruiting job, and the rumours of war which he sometimes heard when he visited Lourenço Marques became relegated to the back of his mind, with more urgent matters on hand. But it seemed that matters were coming to a head. The Jameson Raid had widened the breach between Boer and British, and not only were the *uitlanders* suffering still increased taxation at the hands of Kruger, with no further promise of enfranchisement, but incidents of an ugly nature were continually arising. War seemed, to the Portuguese at any rate, inevitable.

For their own part, they were engaged in subduing a revolt at Magigoun in their own territory, in which Sos held a licence for the recruitment of native labour. Nevertheless he could not allow his spirits to be damped because he was rapidly recovering and he knew that he had escaped death by inches. He thanked the doctor when he left.

'Don't thank me,' said the medical officer. 'Thank the girl, who by her promptitude saved your life. But for her you would have been dead.'

Three weeks later Sos was riding, with two horses on the lead, along a bridle-path on the frontier of Gazaland, as fit as he had ever been. He was very pleased with himself, for his recovery was complete and he had not been sick long enough for his business to be seriously affected. He was, indeed, now returning from a mission at Inkomati in Gazaland on behalf of the Consolidated Gold Fields combine, and the trip had been successful. He had, moreover, during the last year or so gained considerable confidence in himself It was lonely at times out in the bush, but if the life was hard it had its compensations. One day he would tell Uncle Harry Freeman how everything had prospered, since he'd left for Delagoa Bay. Or maybe he'd write him a letter. Yes, he'd write him a letter.

They were upon him before he had the slightest indication that there was anyone within a couple of miles of him. The reins were snatched from his hand and the two spare horses halted by their bridles. The muzzles of two loaded carbines were in each side of his ribs and the officer in charge of the troop had drawn his sword and was barring his path.

Sos recognized his assailants at once as members of the Portuguese Lancers.

'What the devil —' said Sos.

The *Alferes* snapped out an order and two troopers lashed Sos's arms behind his back, before he could imagine what they might be about. Then they turned the horses round and set off along the track in the direction from which they had come.

'What's all this about?' said Sos and he was white with anger.

'You'll hear about this.'

The Portuguese lieutenant swung round in his saddle, and he looked very scornful and contemptuous.

'You know well enough,' he said.

'I'm certain I don't,' said Sos.

'That remains to be seen.'

'Where are you taking me?'

'Chibuto.'

Chibuto was the capital, and two days' trek away.

'What are you charging me with?'

The officer turned in his saddle again. They rode on in silence and in single file.

The track narrowed and the thorn bush and cactus clawed at Sos's arms and shoulders. Bound as he was he could not avoid the onslaught. His sleeves soon became torn to tatters and the thorns ripped at his bare flesh.

He demanded again an explanation of this outrageous treatment and received no answer. He declared that he was being treated as the lowest cattle thief or border blackguard. No reply was made, but one trooper looked him over, across his shoulder, as if he could spit in his face.

They kept guard on him all that night after they had made their bivouac, with an armed trooper at his side, watch by watch. He received a bowl of beans and a can of water, and one arm was released so that he might eat and drink, but a carbine was levelled at his chest all the time. If he had been a triple murderer he could not have received more stringent treatment.

By the late afternoon of the following day they reached Chibuto. The reception which he received was characteristic of the ordeal to date. As the prisoner and escort entered the camp, passers-by stopped and stared, and in a very short time a crowd was gathering.

Sos sat on his horse, with his hands bound behind his back and his arms and shoulders caked with blood. A soldier in the crowd shook his fist at him and shouted:

'*Fillio de pouta!*'[10]

Then someone threw a stone, so that it struck the flank of Sos's horse and it reared, nearly unseating him. Everybody seemed to know who he was and why he had been arrested and what manner of foul crime he had committed. Everybody, that is, except Sos. He sat with bowed head as the stones flew round him or hit him. The pain of his torn, lacerated shoulders and the bruises from the stones was terrible.

The roadway led through the camp and uphill to where the fort stood. The crowd followed them all the way and twice the *Alferes* in charge of the escort was forced to wheel his horse and threaten the crowd with the flat of his sword. As his frightened horse plunged and shied between the troopers who held it on either side, Sos knew that should he fall and the escort pass over him the mob would be upon him and tear him limb from limb.

---

[10] 'Son of a bitch!'

They helped him down off his horse and frog-marched him off to a building on the far side of the square. Because he was stiff and sore, he stumbled a little as he walked, which was no doubt the reason they were so rough with him. Two troopers held him outside while the lieutenant went in. In a few seconds he emerged and waved them aside.

Sos found himself in a big bare room, with rough planking walls covered with maps and printed sheets. It reminded him of an orderly room. There was a table with a lantern on it and its harsh yellow glare — since it was now sundown — lit up the features of those gathered there.

Seated behind the table was a man of some forty years, whom Sos judged to be the Governor, as all those present addressed him as 'Excellency'. By his side stood a gigantic African, with the distinguishing ring-kop on his head. Four Portuguese officers formed the remainder of the company. Through a door at the far end of the room Sos could see the shadowy outlines of several tribesmen gathered together just beyond the threshold.

The Governor turned to the native at his side.

'Juan Masublana, this is your man.' Then he turned to Sos.

'Sam Heine, what have you to say?'

'Why am I here?' said Sos desperately. 'What have I done? I'm not Sam Heine. Lionel Cohen is my name. I'm an Englishman, I can prove it.'

'Do you think we are likely to believe that, after all the trouble you've given us?'

'But I have my credentials from Delagoa Bay, my Bilhete de Residencia. It's the proof of who I am. I'm a British subject and I'm employed with the Consolidated Gold Mines of South Africa as a recruiting agent.'

'How do we know it isn't forged?'

'You can have it identified.'

'What time have we to do that? Don't you realize that the rebellion of Magigoun is on our hands? Well you do! Since you fought against us at Uanetzi on the native rebels' side.'

'Fought against you?' said Sos aghast. 'How could I have fought against you? I've been sick with a snake-bite.'

'And you are also charged,' continued the Governor remorselessly, 'with inciting the natives to revolt and supplying them with arms.'

'I swear on my honour, sir, that you are making a mistake,' said Sos.

'*Your* honour!' The Governor turned to the officer who had led the escort.

'You caught him on the border with three horses did you not, Alferes Praça? And he admitted coming from Komati Poort?'

'Precisely, Excellency.'

'He tallies exactly with the description of the man, Heine, whom you were sent out to apprehend and who was reported in that area with three horses?'

'Precisely, Excellency.'

'Very well. Bring in your witnesses, Juan Masublana. We will prove the case.'

The huge African beckoned toward the doorway and called a name. He was clearly a man of considerable authority and was acting moreover as interpreter. An old tribesman shuffled into the room.

'You recognize this man as the German-American, Sam Heine?'

'*Yebo, Inkoss.*'

Sos was stunned.

'But you can't examine him like that,' he cried. 'You put the words you want into his mouth. I've never seen the man before.'

'You gave this man Heine shelter for the night in your hut?'

'*Yebo.*'

'He's lying,' said Sos. 'He's never seen me in his life. I'm a British subject and I demand my rights. This witness is suborned.'

'Silence!'

The Governor motioned to the chieftain called Juan Masublana.

'Bring in the rest of them.'

They were brought in one by one. In every case the approach and the result were the same.

'You are a rebel prisoner taken at Uanetzi?'

'Yes.'

'This is the man Heine, who fought alongside you against the Portuguese?'

'Yes.'

'He's trying to get himself off,' cried Sos. 'Can't you see that's what it is?'

'Silence!'

And then another.

'This man supplied you with a rifle and one hundred rounds of ball ammunition?'

'*Yebo.*'

So the pitiful farce was played out to its finish. It was abundantly clear that Juan Masublana was convinced that in Sos he had the man he sought, but it was just as apparent to Sos that the last point to be considered by any of the witnesses was the veracity of their statement, while the first was to answer their chieftain in the manner he so obviously desired.

That an innocent man might suffer was of little importance as long as Juan Masublana was satisfied.[11]

The evidence, presented in such a fashion from witnesses over-willing to please regardless of the truth and cross-examined by a scries of leading questions and implications, was utterly damning.

Sos stood between his escort of two troopers, the sweat running down his dust-grimed face as he listened, and he knew what the meaning of the phrase could be when a man's 'bowels turned to water'. There was no attempt at forming an authorized council or any attendance to legal routine. There was no deliberate intention of dealing corruptly with the accused, but no court could have been more unjust. Sam Heine must have been a very painful thorn in the side of the Portuguese.

The last witness shuffled out, and Juan Masublana sat down and folded his arms. The Governor leant forward a little across the table with his fingers lightly clasped together. The light of the lantern glowed starkly on the little group, the bloodstained young man between his guards, the ebony-black face and the not ignoble features of the chieftain with the Induna's ring-kop, the Portuguese officers erect in their trim uniforms. The Governor started to deliver sentence.

'Sir!' said Sos in utter desperation. 'Sir, I beg of you... This is a case of mistaken identity. Look at my papers, sir, send them to the coast ... I can prove who I am, if you'll only let me —'

'You are found guilty,' said the Governor coldly, 'of all the charges. Tomorrow, you will be shot. Take him away.'

---

[11] It should be pointed out, in all fairness to Masublana, that he was convinced of Sos being Heine. Years later prosecutor and accused met and discussed the case. They became firm friends — a friendship based on mutual respect.

They took him away and hustled him along to a bare room. He was alone with his thoughts.

His first reaction to his plight was still one of stupefaction. It seemed incredible that such a travesty of justice could be sponsored by people of repute. In a little time the mood passed and gave way to one of great anguish of mind, in that he knew that he was to die. He was not going to be killed in battle with his friends around him nor was he even to depart in any attitude that could be remotely designated as heroic. He was going to die the death of a traitor, a blackguard and a cur. He was going to die for something he'd never done, and of which he had never heard.

He prayed because he was in extremity and for all his adventures was still very young and inexperienced, when death came to gibber and grimace at him in the loneliness and stillness of the night. He wished that he knew how to pray better and that he'd attended the outward forms of his religion instead of stealing off and playing with glass-alleys at the back of Tankerville House.

He thought of Mamma bending over to kiss him goodnight and the scent and rustle of her progress; of Grandpapa warming his toes under his night-shirt and searching for peppermint bull's-eyes in a little silver box; of Papa in a magnificent new hat and cut-away coat; of Joseph and his great moustaches, and Noakes and Nelson, and Buck, who'd led the way. He heard Ferreira's mighty laugh again and heard the pistol-crack of his whip, and he saw Uncle Harry Freeman wagging his goatee beard at him, and Jack Pierce dropping the safety catch on his rifle as Chiachalo shouted his imprecations and his plumes danced over his ring-kop. He could see Reimann in the bar of the Central Hotel in Delagoa Bay drinking down brandy after brandy while Protopulous, the

Greek baker, gazed at him goggle-eyed with his hands clasped across his little pot-belly. He heard the girl Majasse singing at her wash-tub under the tree by the compound, and the boy Mesulitalan digging the hard-baked soil of the garden plot.

He saw them all and heard them all and he knew that in all their diversity of kind and colour and race they were his friends and he loved them as he had loved Walters who had died in his arms, and whom he'd buried while the Matabele still ranged the scrub. Now they were only ghosts, as soon he would be a ghost.

In the morning a priest came in to see him. He was a tall cadaverous man, in the cowl and cassock of his order. He urged Sos to take Extreme Unction. Sos refused.

'You are a very obstinate young man, my son, with your end so near.'

'You are not of my faith,' said Sos.

'It is my duty to put you on the path to God. You are fortunate to have the opportunity. They could have shot you on sight when they first captured you. I don't know why they didn't. We are *Estado citio*. We have proclaimed martial law.'

'I'm not going to change my faith,' said Sos, just because I've got to die for something which I haven't done.'

'*Interrado com um cão*! Then you will be buried like a dog.'

'There were better men than I,' said Sos, 'who lay unshrived and unburied in the Matabele bush across the Shangani River.'

That was unanswerable and the priest flushed a little beneath his sallow skin.

'Then if I can do nothing for your soul,' he said, 'is there one last request I can try to arrange for you on earth?'

'Yes,' said Sos. 'I'd like to see the outside world just once again before they finish me off.'

'I will see what I can do,' said the priest, and left him.

187

An hour later Sos heard the steady tramp of approaching footsteps outside his cell and the rattle of carbine butts on the stone floor of the corridor. The key turned in the lock and he thought his hour was come, for the troopers stood there waiting for him.

He tried to square his shoulders and put on a brave air, and hoped he didn't look what he felt to be, a stricken creature who couldn't help being scared at the prospect of death. Nevertheless, he walked steadily up to the two waiting men and placed himself between them. He wondered if at the end they would tie him to a stake against a wall and bandage his eyes. He hoped he would have the courage to refuse the bandage and that it wasn't too far to the place of execution.

The sunlight blazing across the quadrangle of the fort blinded him as he stepped out of the shadow of the building.

'Which way?' he asked.

'Whichever way you like,' was the reply. 'This was your request, wasn't it?'

He wished then that he had made no request such as this, for he had steeled himself to the final act and now must needs repeat the effort again when the time came. But the priest had been as good as his word, so Sos looked around him to take every advantage of the courtesy that had been afforded him.

He saw the sun and the brazen sky, the brown-grey buildings of the Fort and the white dust swirling in little whorls across the quadrangle. He thought for how short a time he could look upon these things and then how very short a time a few minutes could be, or what — in reverse — an eternity it could be, when death as a guest stood waiting as the first arrival of the feast to come. Then he saw the Picador.

The Picador was the Riding-Master to the Viceroy, and had occupied the same position under Mousinho d'Albuquerque, the great Portuguese empire-builder and former Viceroy. He was responsible for all cavalry training and the care and schooling of all horseflesh of the command. He was a striking figure, with bristling moustaches. Not so very long ago at Chungwani he had 'chopped' a horse with Sos, to the satisfaction of both, but not to the knowledge of the authorities. Officially he was the Picador to His Excellency. Unofficially he coped some of His Excellency's horses. Sos and he had done many deals together, off the record. He saw Sos as the latter recognized him. The recognition was mutual and immediate.

'Whatever are you doing here, senhor? What a state you are in! What is this escort for?'

'I'm to be shot,' said Sos.

'Impossible! Who is going mad? Tell me what's happened.'

Sos told him and the escort lolled on their carbines and grinned across at one another because it was all a great joke, and as long as the Picador was there the responsibility for the prisoner was his, since he was the senior officer.

'But *I* know who you are,' cried the Picador. 'Come with me.'

They crossed the quadrangle to the headquarters office and past the door of the room where Sos had stood the mockery of his trial the previous night. The Picador went into the Commandant's office and saw his Adjutant. The Adjutant turned the Picador on to the Governor's aide-de-camp and the Governor's aide-de-camp directed the Picador to the *Alferes* who stood as duty officer of the day. Then they reviewed the whole proceedings, with the Picador demanding an interview with the Governor, only to be assured that he mustn't be disturbed as he was sleeping. He had had a trying experience the previous evening, condemning a man to death, and it had upset his nerves.

In the end the Picador, who was a soldier and knew his business, traced the officer who had picked up Sos on the Gaza border and from him traced the source of the signal that had set the troop in motion. The signal had been sent by heliograph and the original message read that the wanted man had set out from Komati Poort with two horses for the border. The Picador pointed out, besides himself entirely establishing Sos's identity, that while Sos had admittedly led two horses, he had started out from Inkomati and not Komati Poort — a difference of half a dozen signalled letters, becoming confused by a method by no means infallible.

Everybody was very apologetic. The Governor when he woke up, his nerves restored to tranquillity, sent for Sos and explained everything. The officer of the escort apologized for the rough treatment he had meted out. Then they let him go.

Sos went down to Lourenço Marques before he returned to his Centre, and asked to see the British Consul-General. It took him a whole day to get an audition with the Consul-General, whose name was Roger Casement.[12]

He presented his case with some vigour. Casement agreed that it was an affair justifying a protest. He would take the matter up with the Portuguese authorities. A British subject had been outrageously treated and had very nearly lost his life through a gross miscarriage of justice.

Sos had hope of good news, but none came. The negotiations dragged on and on. In the Consulate all the talk was of trouble up the Zambesi with the Portuguese, concerning gunboats. It became quite clear to Sos that the interests of the Consul lay with the major issue.

---

[12] Shot by the British Authorities as a spy and traitor sixteen years later in the First World War.

Disgusted and disillusioned with the official attitude towards his case, he packed his maps and returned to Gaza. He had work to do. He had been away from his business too long.

The news of the actual outbreak of war between Great Britain and the Boer Republic reached Sos on the day of the 'smelling-out'.

He had been back at Chungwani just over a month. The Boer ultimatum to the British, directing them to remove the troops massed on the Transvaal border within forty-eight hours, had been delivered but its time limit had as yet not expired. The camp had been running fairly smoothly during his absence, but it was quite apparent that his presence was needed.

Chiachalo's successor as chieftain of the Machopi tribe was a far older man and his powers of discipline were not to be compared with his predecessor's. Nevertheless Sos liked the old man, who was wise in his generation and well disposed towards the white man in general. It was, therefore, unfortunate, if understandable, that amongst the younger element a certain disrespect and mild contempt for the older order had arisen. For a time the results of any disagreement between the younger generation and the old regime were solely domestic matters, contained within the circle which they immediately affected. In a short while, however, the occasional flouting of internal authority had its reactions beyond the confines of the main kraal. The repercussion fell upon Sos.

At all times it was necessary to carry about with him a large sum of money in gold. Opportunities in trading for cattle could arise at any time and demanded cash payment. There were running repairs that constantly needed attention and which must be paid for, and the wages of certain 'boys' employed in various capacities. He had, therefore, no other option but to keep money by him and he kept his sovereigns and silver in a leather bag, which reposed by his pillow at night.

He found himself twenty pounds short. He was quite certain that he had not lost that amount, because he kept the closest possible guard and a regular tally over his portable bank. He was just as certain that the sum of money had been stolen. But how or when it had been stolen was completely beyond him.

He retraced to the best of his ability his movements of the preceding days, but could remember no occasion when he had given a thief any reasonable opportunity to do his work. He felt positive that neither of his house-servants were guilty so that the culprit must be one amongst three hundred recruits in the compound.

Without a vestige of any clue, nor the least suspicion of who the thief might be, he realized that he was faced with a problem which was practically insoluble.

But twenty pounds were twenty pounds, and represented some very hard work. He took his trouble to Melampa Quehania, the witch doctor, whose hut-tax he had paid, and who was therefore under an obligation to him.

The old man listened intently to what Sos had to say, squatting outside his hut with his blanket around him and looking very patriarchal with his grey hair and deeply wrinkled face.

'What can the police do, if I call them in from Chai-Chai?'

'Nothing, Inkoss. No white man has a magic for this; but I have. You shall have your money back, Inkoss. There are young men amongst my people who are of a new generation and think too much of themselves and get out of hand and may have dared to rob. They mock the mysteries of their father's fathers and so they need a lesson taught to them. I, Melampa Quehania, will find the thief.'

'You know him?'

'No more than you do, Inkoss. But I will smell him out.'

The old man took snuff from a former Martini-Henry cartridge fitted with an ivory stopper.

'You doubt my power, Inkoss. I can see it written in your face. I have never known a white man to be permitted to attend a smelling-out before, but you shall come as my guest and you shall see for yourself. We shall smell out the thief at noon tomorrow.'

Sos passed through the compound gates precisely two minutes before noon the following day. There was no need to ask where the ceremony of the 'smelling-out' was to be held, because the drums were already throbbing, and led him to the open ground in the centre of the kraal.

He had been in two minds to keep the appointment, feeling quite ridiculous at attending such an affair in any air of good faith and embarrassed at the thought of himself so doing. Moreover, the news coming through from the coast was more and more disquieting. It was the general opinion that the Boers would fight, and in some quarters it was said that Kruger had declared that he could easily 'drive the British into the sea'. The Boer opinion of the British fighting qualities was very low.

War would not necessarily involve Sos. He was not on British territory, nor under any obligation to offer his services. But war would mean a dislocation of industry with the consequence that the business of native recruitment would close down. Moreover, on his last visit to Lourenço Marques he had heard many views expressed as to the outcome of any possible war; only one issue seemed clear. The British attitude towards the Transvaal found no favour in eyes other than those of the Portuguese.

The entire population of the kraal were gathered in the central clearing, seated in a circle on the ground. The sun was beating down relentlessly and the heat seemed to surge forwards in waves as if in harmony with the rhythmic pulsation of the drums.

The strange, eerie beat was by no means unknown to him, from the smallpox camp at Johannesburg to Chiachalo's war dance, but now under this midday sky the sound seemed vastly more sinister. He was astonished at finding such a reaction within himself, because he was not given to flights of the imagination. It was, he supposed, because he was so very definitely one of the audience, amongst an assembly of people who were in a state of the highest nervous tension.

He knew that this was so, because of the uncanny and utter silence and the impassivity of every face. It was as if no one dared to breathe, and despite himself he felt that he might be upon the verge of something that was known only to the people of the bush and that, despite the sunlight, the powers of darkness hovered on the fringe of the circle. It was the oddest feeling, but it persisted.

There was a huge clay pot in the centre of the assembly and a fire burnt beneath it. From where he sat, Sos could see the occasional wisp of steam blowing over the rim. A native stood beside the cauldron, a great carved wooden spoon in his hand.

The drums sank to a mere whispering and then of a sudden rose to a violent and almost painful throbbing. The sound seemed to fill the ear, so that the sound-waves beat against the ear-drums, producing an extraordinary sensation of elation. It was as if, at the height of a Black Mass, the Devil was about to appear.

He appeared. He leapt fully a foot over the heads of a section of the crowd opposite the chieftain and into the ring. His face was smeared with ochre and the plumes danced from his head-ring. He was naked except for a brief kirtle about his loins. Round his waist a girdle carried the horrid emblems of his trade, the mummified remains of a monkey, a handful of bones knotted together, a long hank of giraffe and elephant hair. It was Melampa Quehania, the witch doctor.

He was grotesque. He was fantastic. He was something that only the primitive mind could have conceived. He should have been completely ridiculous with his magical trappings, but he wasn't. He leapt round the circle of his audience in tremendous bounds that carried him four feet in the air at a time. The drums rose to a frenzy as he made his way round the second time, and Sos saw that, as the witch-doctor passed, that section of the crowd nearest to him inclined away as if in silent terror. It was like the breath of a wind of evil passing across a circular field of corn.

Sos knew that it was all on a par with All Hallows' E'en in Newcastle-on-Tyne seemingly all those years ago; and he knew that Melampa Quehania was probably the biggest rascal and charlatan on earth. But though, to preserve his own sense of proportion, he told himself that Melampa Quehania was making a damn silly ass of himself, Sos knew that he was doing nothing of the sort, and that he was in his element and was magnificent and was holding his audience spell-bound. And though he was reluctant to admit it, Sos was spell-bound too.

Three times the witch doctor made his magic circuit and then he halted before the steaming cauldron. There was a bundle on the ground, covered with coarse native cloth. The drums dropped to a rustling whisper as the wizard began his incantation.

195

As he chanted he uncovered the bundle at his feet. The contents were even more deplorable than the ornaments about his midriff. There was a dried frog and a snake; a small crocodile, the fresh entrails of a monkey and a cockerel's head; an assortment of bones and a bundle of dried herbs. There were many other things which Sos could only suppose to be indescribable. One by one they were named in the invocation that accompanied their passage to the cauldron.

They all went in, from the snake to the entrails, and the water bubbled and seethed and a fearful stench arose with the steam. The wizard stirred his unholy broth and his voice rose and fell to the tremolo of the drums.

All the time the sun blazed down so that the glare from the dusty ground made Sos's eyes ache and his temples began to throb a little. The smell of the infernal brew came in his direction from time to time and mingled with the acrid odour of the black perspiring bodies pressed close around him.

He wished that he hadn't come to the ritual, because it was beastly and sinister and there was something beneath all its mumbo-jumbo that was significant and real. Then he saw that Melampa Quehania had left his cauldron and with his great wooden spoon, filled with his devilish concoction, was again making a round of the circle. Only now he no longer leapt, but glided forward in long strides which reminded Sos in the most forcible manner of a leopard stalking its prey.

Now and again he would pause in his stride, his eyes rolling and glaring and his nostrils distended, while he drew in great draughts of air, as if already he smelt his victim. Then he would side-step swiftly, delicately as a dancer might and the next moment the spoon was at one of his audience's lips.

Sos knew that to whomever the spoon was presented, so they must drink. The innocent would survive, the guilty man would drop immediately dead. He wondered what on earth would happen if the witch doctor challenged him, himself. There was nothing to stop him. He was no respecter of persons and Sos's story could have been a conspiratorial lie.

Then he realized that every single person present, being who they were, was feeling precisely the same thing as himself.

There was no sound anywhere, save for the shuffling footsteps of the wizard in the sandy circle. He presented his spoon a dozen times or more. Still nobody moved and still the sun burned down and still the spoon went its rounds.

No one fell dead and no one left the circle and still all were wrapt in the poisoned, magic air, and though with repetition the ceremony was beginning to pall a little to a Western mind, nevertheless, the spell was still there. And then suddenly it happened.

There arose a strange and terrifying cry as of a man tortured beyond endurance. It rose, strangulated, wailing, intolerable to the ear. The whole assembly quivered and grew ever more still, and Sos felt little chilly tremors running down his spine, because the whole business was getting quite beyond a joke.

Melampa Quehania stopped dead in his tracks, crouched like a wild beast, and Sos could see the stringy, bunched muscles of his naked thigh and calf. He held out his spoon and very slowly began to tip-toe across the arena.

'Come forth,' he said.

The cry arose again, teetering into high hysteria, and a young man, whom Sos recognized as an assistant storekeeper, crept out from the assembled, squatting ranks.

The witch doctor moved on and the young African stood utterly still. It was like a stoat with a rabbit. Very slowly Melampa Quehania made his approach, and now he was holding out his spoon again and raising it a little as he went forward.

The young storekeeper could move neither hand nor foot. Sos could see the way his eyes rolled, first in one direction then in another as if to find a way out of an invisible maze in which he was lost, while his tormentor and destroyer descended upon him. Then when the outstretched spoon was not a foot from his lips, he fell flat upon the ground, his hands clasped behind his head.

Sos could hear his babbling voice as he confessed to the theft. Melampa Quehania stood astride him, a fearful and victorious figure, and there was nothing ridiculous about him at all now, because he had vindicated his profession, and no one could say him nay.

They led the young storekeeper away and Sos never knew what happened to him, but he got his twenty pounds back and he gave a golden sovereign to Melampa Quehania with which to buy more spells, though he was inclined to imagine that Melampa Quehania would probably dissipate the entire fortune in Kaffir beer.

Later on he thought to himself what a very clever man the witch doctor had proved to be. And since in those earlier days the psychiatrists had not found a word for it, Sos could only sum it up that Melampa Quehania was a first-rate showman and, had he been of another colour but of the same talent, well worth his hundred a week on Broadway or Piccadilly, since he could hold an audience and play on a guilty man's fear.

Sos returned to his hut and found that the weekly supply of newspapers had come up from the coast. The Boer ultimatum to the British authorities had terminated at 5 p.m. on the 11th October, 1899. On the following day a British armoured train had been attacked at Kraaipan, south of Mafeking.

The first shots of the Boer War had been fired.

CHAPTER NINE: THE WATCH ON THE FRONTIER

Sos went down to Delagoa Bay because there was a war in progress and one, moreover, being waged against his own countrymen. It was therefore quite unthinkable that he should be left out of it.

He went to the Consul-General's office, and he had forgotten in his excitement all about the trouble of Chibuto, as he had almost forgotten about his job as a recruiting agent.

They told him at the Consulate that there were several possible courses he might pursue. It was difficult to foresee at this early stage of the conflict what kind of volunteer forces might be formed. On the other hand, it was well known that the British Regular forces were being relied upon and were massed in Cape Colony and Natal. It seemed doubtful if a trip to Cape Town would bring any immediate satisfaction. Within days, news of the Boer invasion and the investment of Mafeking, Kimberley and Ladysmith came through.

Sos stayed in Lourenço Marques, a little crestfallen after his first attempt; then he called at the Consulate again. This time he was interviewed by an official who was well acquainted with Sos's activities.

'I think,' he said, 'I have come across something that might suit you. There's not much honour and glory in it, and it may prove very dangerous work. Nor do I know what guarantee the Portuguese or even ourselves could give you. You may be liable to be shot on sight, if you get involved. But it's an unusual job.'

'Go on,' said Sos.

'The Portuguese are our oldest allies, and though they're neutral in this present business, they're on our side in every way they can be except actual fighting in the field. On the other hand, the rest of the world — notably Germany — is very opposed to our attitude to the Boers and they think of us as a lot of freebooters. There is only one port here that's any good and this is it — Delagoa Bay. There isn't the least doubt that sympathetic foreign powers will attempt gun-running and heavens knows what, landing arms and agents here, moving up to the Portuguese border and slipping them over into the Transvaal.'

'The Portuguese have got their frontier posts,' said Sos.

'They're sufficient for peace, but not for the exigencies of war. They want an espionage network set up along the border, getting information in order to forestall enemy activities. In fact, you would be working behind the Boer lines and in the bush.'

'A secret agent!' said Sos. 'I'd be as scared as a frightened canary, but it sounds pretty good to me.'

'Then the people to see are the Field Intelligence. You will of course come under the Portuguese and be paid by them. But the work you'll be doing would be of infinitely more value than it would be as a mere trooper in the field. Besides, you have experience of the country and a knowledge of the people.'

Sos went off to the Portuguese Field Intelligence Headquarters and learnt more of the nature of the proposed scheme. The frontier was covered by a series of armed camps, rather than forts, with Portuguese troops, mainly cavalry, based on them. Patrols were constantly maintained between the camps.

He was told that if he accepted the task of organizing and implementing the scheme, he would receive full support from the Portuguese authorities. A horse and equipment would be found for him, together with the necessary firearms. He would have under his control some hundred or more *informadores* — native irregulars. His territory of some three hundred miles would be from Inkomati to the Limpopo River.

He was, in the essence of the job, to be the eyes of the regular Portuguese in their screen of encampments. He was to patrol continually from post to post, where all facilities would be granted to him, and to organize in small camps his *informadores*, who would be armed together with such other tribal levies as might be called in.

His duty would be to stop the passage of unauthorized or suspected persons attempting to cross the border, to intercept any dispatches or messages coming through from the Continent — especially from Holland where Doctor Leyds, a former colleague of Kruger, was the Boer plenipotentiary to the Dutch Court — and to give instant warning to the nearest Portuguese post of any attempt at gun-running. There would be, moreover, a no less important obligation — the reporting of any significant Boer movements, which might be passed on through the Field Intelligence to the British authorities.

It all sounded on paper extremely entertaining. It was work after Sos's own heart. He would be his own master on a roving commission, with *carte blanche* to organize, administer and direct his own command in any way he should think fit. From time to time he would be called upon to report to Portuguese Headquarters in Lourenço Marques, otherwise he would be on constant duty, drawing no rations but living on the country.

Sos accepted the post with alacrity. A week later he was on the frontier.

He decided first of all to make a comprehensive tour of his territory, both sides of the border, making the acquaintance of his *informadores* and organizing them. Within a short time his organization was in working order.

It was on his return from his northern region that he encountered the ant-hill and its tenant. He came upon it suddenly, riding out of the bush into the scrub in a wild and desolate district that many years later was to become the Sabi game preserve. The nearest post was some fifteen miles away.

He thought the ant-hill looked somewhat unusual, as it had on its summit an irregular excrescence. When he rode up to it the mound reached up to his waist. The leaf-and-twig mould of the ant-hill, chewed into a solid by a million or more worker-ants, was smooth and baked hard under the sun, but the crown was broken as if it had been torn away. And at the very peak, to his amazement, Sos saw the head of a man.

His horse, downwind of the corpse, threw up its head and snorted, so that Sos turned his mount to windward. Here the smooth shell had been broken open, as from a violent thrust from the interior. It was quite apparent where such a thrust had originated. A bare human arm, with a length of fibre rope hanging from the wrist, was hanging down the side of the ant-hill. It was utterly bare of flesh. Even so, the white and glistening bones were spotted with the huge voracious ants.

Sos stared in horror, watching how even now the ants were swarming over the head of the corpse. What was buried in this insect citadel could now be only a skeleton, devoid of flesh and muscle and tissue, and each morsel had been torn away from the living whole by thousand upon thousand of tigerish tiny jaws. He swung his horse into the bridle path and broke into a canter.

He asked the meaning of it all from his head *informador* when he reached the post.

'I have not heard of that for many years, Inkoss,' said the man. 'But now there is war, and there is unrest on the border and there is pillaging and looting between the wandering bandits. One party has caught a member of another party. So they have buried him with the ant-hill torture. Shall I report it to the Portuguese camp?'

'No,' said Sos. 'We've other things to think about.'

But it was a long time before those other things drove to the back of his mind the memory of that fearful face, crawling with ants, and the empty, eaten eye-holes.

A month later, Sos met with his first success. The days in the open, covering forty miles or more in the saddle, were a mode of life which suited him. He lived on the country. He drank Kaffir beer and ate mealies and killed his own game, making his own biltong.[13] At night he would sleep in a native hut, which he had swept out, with his blanket wrapped around him and his horse hobbled outside.

If he were lonely, as indeed he was, with no other white man as companion, nevertheless he was well content. All the wild world around him was his.

Some five days' trek from the spot where he had encountered the atrocious ant-hill, he picked up several of his men returning from a patrol. They informed him at once that two strange white men were in the district and that they had had them under observation for the last ten days. They were camped at the edge of the bush.

Sos went forward to his encampment, collected ten of his small garrison, and set out fully armed in search of the visitors.

He found them precisely as had been described, encamped at the border of the scrub, under the tall trees. Both men were in

---

[13] Strips of venison, dried in the sun. Easily carried and very sustaining.

civilian clothes and occupied in cooking their midday meal near a small tent. They were still on the Portuguese side of the border. Sos dispersed his men in a circle around the encampment and then himself went forward, revolver in hand.

He was cordially greeted. Both of the newcomers spoke English, but with a slight foreign inflection. They were, they declared, looking for territory in which to settle and had worked their way up all the way from Lourenço Marques.

'In wartime?' said Sos. 'A little dangerous, isn't it?'

'We are neutrals. Who should interfere with us?'

'You have your permits?'

'But yes, indeed. Our *bilhetes de residentia.*'

They produced the two permits. They were perfectly in order, in the names of Johann Malzer and Ernst Leimann. Sos looked them through, completely unconvinced.

'Where do you come from?'

'Switzerland. If there is any trouble made for us, our Government will intervene.'

'Nobody's making any trouble,' said Sos, and his mind was working fast.

'No,' he repeated, 'nobody's making any trouble. But I, of course, have my duty to do as a member of the Field Intelligence. Part of that duty, I take it, is to see that no innocent party becomes involved in this affair.'

'That is well spoken,' said the taller of the two and he smiled down at Sos. He had a square, bony face and it looked as if his teeth were filed. He smiled most genially and Sos thought he had the look of a quite uncompanionable hyena. Sos knew that he must move most warily.

'Then I must wish you good fortune,' said Sos.

The two settlers exchanged a swift glance.

'Good day and good hunting, then,' said Sos, and on the moment's inspiration slightly inclined his head, in the politest of almost imperceptible bows.

The visitors reacted at once. Sos had hoped for such a piece of luck, but not on so generous a scale. The day was theirs and they knew it. Their *bilhetes de residencia* had paved the way for their effortless effrontery. They bowed and clicked their heels in acknowledgment of Sos's courtesy, as one gentleman to another. They bowed from the waist and their heels came together simultaneously and though they were a score and a score of leagues from their native land, the ingrained habit of years had unconsciously persisted.

'Your hands above your heads,' said Sos, 'and please not to move.'

He raised his revolver and took his whistle by the lanyard from his breast pocket, and he blew a shrill blast. His twelve men came running out of the bush and the two 'Swiss' were surrounded.

They made a great noise in their protestations, and all the pleasant semblance of civilized gentility of a few moments before disappeared. The mighty wrath of the Swiss nation should fall upon Sos for this outrage.

'Forgive me,' said Sos, 'but I too was once falsely arrested so I know what it feels like if that should be the case. Nevertheless I must ask you to accompany me to the nearest Portuguese post.'

'*Verdammt noch mal!*' said the taller of the two.

'I know a great many of the Swiss speak German,' said Sos. 'But as a non-military nation, I've yet to see them bow like a Prussian officer. Now, if you please...'

A month later, Sos received confirmation that the two suspects he had arrested went by the names of Baron von

Maltzheim and Major Rennenbart, regular officers of the Imperial German Army, in sympathy with the Boers and intent on crossing the Portuguese border as saboteurs.

Thereafter for a little time the border was free of incidents, but there was no opportunity to relax. Always and at any time, particularly in the dense bush, traversing the single native tracks, it was possible to stumble upon the unsuspected. It was ideal country for the ambush, and often it reminded Sos of the forced marches of the Victoria Column. But now he was alone and no vanguard or flankers were screening his path.

On the evening that he reached the native village, on his second tour north, he was in good spirits. He was hospitably entertained by the headman and a clean hut was prepared for him. After the evening meal he was about to leave for his quarters, when the chief detained him.

'When I heard you were coming, Inkoss, I sent for one of your *informadores*. I felt the news would come better from him than from me.'

'What news?' said Sos.

'Everyone is speaking of it. Everyone knows. I think you should go back to the coast, Inkoss, and stay there. We have known you and like you well.'

He could say no more, no matter how Sos pressed him; and at length the *informador* arrived. He came to the point at once.

'While you were down south, Inkoss, a small Boer Commando crossed the border, under a field cornet. His name is Tomas Kelly, and he and his men were hunting for game. That is how the story spread.'

'What story?'

'General Beyers of the Boers has said that this war is between white men and white men only. If anyone employs our people to fight on his side, he will be punished. And you employ us, Inkoss, and we are armed.'

'I see,' said Sos. 'So General Beyers is angry, because I caught two of his men.'

'He says, Inkoss — so the story goes — that he will capture you. He will send a special party to capture you. Then when you are taken, you will be stripped and bound and buried in an ant-hill.'

'Very thoughtful of General Beyers,' said Sos.

But the night he spent was restless and time and again he woke up as if at the sound of voices or horses' hooves outside the kraal. And sometimes in his troubled sleep he saw again an eyeless head, and the ants, swarming.

In the middle of the game country Sos encountered Tomas Kelly's Commando. Hearing several shots in quick succession, Sos cantered through the scrub in their direction, till a herd of frightened wildebeest stampeding across his path told him he was near a raiding party. He went forward cautiously, taking cover whenever possible, till he saw the Boers disappearing round the corner of a kopje, a quarter of a mile away.

He returned immediately to his nearest encampment and set half a dozen of his men on the Boers' trail, with instructions to keep in touch with the force until reinforcements could be brought up. He then made contact with the nearest Portuguese post and contrived to get a message through to the British South African Police. Tom Kelly and all the members of his hunting party were captured. It was all extremely satisfactory, until recollection of General Beyers's threats returned.

But the strain was beginning to tell. The long weeks, that had drifted into months, in the wilderness; the lack of companionship and the fear of treachery; the necessity of keeping constant watch night and day, with no relief; and the lengthy hours in the saddle, often without food or drink, began to show their mark.

His nerves became on edge so that in the interminable bush silences the slightest small noise would make him start; and often he wondered if, at nights, he slept with one eye open.

It was, he told himself, no more than many other men did, in what they considered to be their duty, but it was the responsibility and the absence of any other white man in whom to confide or with whom to scheme and plan, that rendered his position unique. Nevertheless his tally of suspects, detained and interned, kept a steady level.

When the Lourenço Marques lighters began to freight pianos ashore in their hundreds, Sos and his men were kept twice as busy on the border. There had never been a better container for contraband fire-arms and ammunition than a piano packing-case, but it was not until well on in the second year of the war that General Beyers made any serious attempt to carry out his threat.

Sos slept that particular night amongst his own men in one of his small encampments.

He lay beneath a rough shelter, his saddle for a pillow and his revolver cocked and ready at his side. He drowsed off in a little time, having ridden over forty miles that day and feeling confidently secure. Tomorrow he would be on his way again in an attempt to intercept a suspect, an officer named Martinsen of the 3rd U.S. Cavalry. Martinsen was carrying dispatches across the frontier to Colonel Blake,[14] an Irishman who ran his own Commando on behalf of the Boers.

In the early hours of the morning Sos was awakened by one of his carriers, who told him an *informador* wished urgently to

[14] Just over twelve years later he was fighting for Great Britain in the 1914-18 war and later was a Member of Parliament.

see him. The man, it appeared, had been running all through the night from the next encampment. He brought a message that was brief and explicit. One of General Beyers's field cornets was over the border with fifty men, with the sole object of capturing Sos.

He made his way, therefore, through what remained of the night towards the east, putting as many miles between himself and the frontier as he could. When morning came, he was in comparatively open country, and mounting a small kopje he took a survey of the route he had taken.

The ground fell away directly before him and the scrub was sparse. Far away to the north was a long range of hills and at their base the dense bush, through which he'd passed. He had little doubt but his pursuers were on his heels, for they would have their Kaffir trackers with them and his own spoor would be easily traced. He was at a loss to know what to do, because while his natural inclinations were to make good his escape, nevertheless his sense of duty warned him that the American whom he in turn was after might already be approaching the frontier. Then he saw his pursuers advancing beneath him.

They were coming on in a slow lope and from where he was, he could see the two trackers, their hands to the stirrup leathers, running smoothly alongside the leader and one of his men. Behind them the remainder of the troop came in a ragged four abreast. They all wore the typical slouch hat of the Boer, with bandoleros across their shoulders and their rifles slung across their backs. They looked very business-like and formidable. Even as he watched, the field cornet swung his arm above his head and the column fanned out into two encircling arms.

Sos galloped down the slope on the reverse side, and the shale and loose stones rattled beneath his horse's hooves and set it stumbling. He gathered his mount up and they reached the base of the kopje, smothered in dust and the horse's near wither bleeding from the cut of a cactus thorn. He galloped on, and the stunted thickets flashed past and any moment he expected to hear a shout and a volley of shots.

He rode on as straight as he could till he reckoned he must have passed through the gap of the encircling flanks, then he turned towards the north. There was no means of telling whether he was within the circle of armed men or whether he had slipped through. He had only been able to make a rough estimate of the distance in that one hurried glimpse which he had taken, but after a quarter of an hour's riding he found a bridle-path turning in a westerly direction and he chose that way since it would lead him back to the border. Two hours later, he turned about on higher ground, but he could see no sign of his enemies and was confident that he had outwitted them.

This indeed, later proved to be the truth, but the determination of Beyers's men to fulfill their mission was exemplified by the fact that they themselves were over twenty miles into Portuguese territory. Two days later Sos encountered the American envoy.

There was no mistaking the man, and he was taken to a local *informador*'s camp for interrogation. It was impossible to get any final proof of the nature of the dispatches which Sos had extracted from him, without making contact with headquarters, and as this meant delay and there were no proper facilities for confining a prisoner, Sos accepted the American officer's parole. Within an hour he had broken it.

Sos had left him outside his hut while he wrote out his own memorandum to cover the query over the dispatches. When he looked out of the door again, the man had gone.

211

The alarm was immediately raised. Sos led the pursuit himself, for if his prisoner managed to elude him and cross the border, his own life again would be in immediate jeopardy, as his position had been disclosed.

They found their man and Sos threatened to shoot him, but they carried the American across country to the nearest Portuguese strong-post and there left him, in safe custody.

The incident was trivial enough and it would in the ordinary course of circumstances never have passed a second time through Sos's mind, but coming as it did, when Beyers had made so determined an attempt to capture him and with the fearful threat of his vengeance, it became something of an obsession. It made him think still more often of the daily hazards he must run and the burden of the weary and anxious hours of his duty became very heavy. He was reaching breaking-point. For a long time he had been carrying his life in his hands.

But the tide of the war had turned. The Boer leader Cronje had been surrounded and captured with 4,000 of his men at Paardeburg. Ladysmith had been relieved on the same date. Kimberley and Mafeking were relieved. The core of Boer resistance was rapidly crumbling, though the bitter guerilla warfare was to continue for another two years. The influx of contraband and saboteurs over the Portuguese border had become a mere trickle. Sos was recalled to the coast and returned to Chai-Chai. It was considered expedient to send him by sea.

He contrived to find a vessel ready to make a passage north along the coast to the Limpopo, where he would land and continue his way by road.

The vessel was a converted trawler, used as a coaster, under the command of Captain Ferrandez, that remarkable seaman.

He agreed, quite readily, at a price, to take a passenger and indeed regaled him for a time in his cabin with brandy and coffee, while the cockroaches crept rustling in the bulkheads and behind the dilapidated panelling of the cabin.

Captain Ferrandez was a big man with a moist and sympathetic eye and a moustache which he would blow from his upper lip from time to time in a somewhat flaunting manner. He wore on his peaked cap a linen sun-cover. It had once been white, and was quite strikingly smart for the type of vessel of which he was master. He had as a mate, a Portuguese by the name of Manoel, who very soon hinted that he was not unconnected with the gentry, which made Sos wonder if the Portuguese nobility were above noticing that the buttons were off their shirt-fronts and if it were considered beneath their dignity to wash the backs of their necks. The engineer, Ian MacPherson, was a gaunt Scotsman of some fifty winters. He was not inclined to be communicative and spent all his time, of necessity, in the noisome sump which was his engine-room.

There were other members of the crew, but Sos tried to keep a distance from them. It was very hot weather.

The Captain looked his passenger over critically.

'You are in the army?'

'More or less,' said Sos.

'You should have gone to sea,' said Captain Ferrandez. 'That's the place for a young feller like you. Romance. Adventure. It would put some meat on your bones, too.'

Sos was well aware how he must appear, thin almost to emaciation and burnt mahogany-brown with a skin of parchment stretched over his cheek-bones. It had been a long, arduous and perilous sojourn in the bush.

They had turned out a cabin forward of the engine-room for him and he spent the first night stripped because of the heat, but later he dressed again. He had many companions in his cabin, and though they were small, they were most attentive. At dawn he joined the Captain and Manoel on the bridge.

The weather was calm, though seawards a bank of mist lay heavily along the horizon. The little ship chugged her way steadily forward at some five knots. Captain Ferrandez leant upon his bridge-rail and picked up the thread of his theme where he had left it the evening before. He enquired politely if Sos had spent a good restful night and Sos said 'Yes, thank you' and scratched his ribs.

'The mighty main,' said Captain Ferrandez. 'I should not care to think how many years I have spent upon it. Since a boy. And I have had remarkable occasions, I can say. In the ports, women! Ah! Out in the ocean the romance of the unexpected. It takes the nerve, senhor, to stand the strain.'

'You're not at war,' said Sos.

'There are warships all around us.'

'When I was gun-running in the Philippines —' said Manoel.

'Tush,' said Captain Ferrandez. 'Well do I remember a brush with the enemy. He had ten guns and we but one. I was not a Captain then, I tell you, but I was a gun-layer. In with the roundshot and tamp the charge. Then I would take my taper — and pouf! Out with the mop then and swill the barrel out. Ah! the smoke, the blood, the carnage!'

'Where might that have been?' said Sos. 'Trafalgar?'

'I can't remember, I have seen so much of it.'

'When I was in the Philippines, gun-running —' said Manoel.

'Tush,' said Captain Ferrandez.

'I think there's somebody wanting you over there,' said Sos and he pointed towards the horizon.

She was coming out of the mist, a grey lean shape, -with the ripple of white high about her cutwater. Sos could see the

214

white ensign at her peak and she was signalling, dash-dot in flashes from her bridge. He was no authority on naval craft but he knew her for a British gunboat.

'What's she saying?' said Sos.

'Ah! take no notice.'

There was a string of flags now fluttering along her signal halyard.

'That's one of my country's ships,' said Sos. 'She's a man o' war. Hadn't you better answer her?'

'I think she tells us to stop,' said Manoel. He had his eye screwed to a battered telescope.

'Tush,' said Captain Ferrandez. 'For why should we stop?'

'She may want to examine your credentials,' said Sos. 'I think I would take a little notice of her. She may feel herself entitled to blow us out of the water. She's quite capable of it, you know.'

The signal lamp from the gunboat's bridge was flashing rapidly. She swung in her track, heeling over, till she took a parallel course to the trawler. Sos supposed it enabled her to bring her main armament to bear. He was not at all happy.

'Heave to!' he said. 'Don't be an ass.'

'I am the Captain,' said Captain Ferrandez. 'I give the orders. Nor how can I stop my engines? How do I know the bloody things will start again?'

'When I was gun-running in the Philippines' said Manoel.

The first shot went whistling overhead and landed in the sea a hundred yards to leeward of the coaster. A column of water spouted up and smoke drifted away from the muzzle of the forward gun. The trawler continued cheerfully on her way.

'What did I tell you?' cried Sos, and turned in indignation to Captain Ferrandez.

There was no sign of Captain Ferrandez nor of Manoel. There wasn't anybody on the bridge at all, except himself. He thought they must have dived clean through the deck-planking to have reached the doubtful security of their quarters below. The gunboat was signalling violently, almost viciously.

'Stop this blasted ship!' roared Sos.

There was no answer, because there was nobody to answer. There was another puff of smoke and a second shell screamed overhead and carried away the coaster's semi-dilapidated forestay. Sos heard the sound of a hatch being slammed down forward. There wasn't a sign of anybody on deck at all.

The gunboat had eased in nearer, so that he could see the rippling of her ensign in the wind, and, what was infinitely more disconcerting, the swinging muzzle of the bow gun. He clutched at the bridge telegraph and grabbed the lever.

He swung the lever to 'Stop' and it slid back to 'Full speed astern'. He clawed it forward and it overran and slipped into 'Slow ahead.' He went round all the range of speeds and there was a muffled clanging of bells from the awesome recesses of the hulk beneath him. Then a wrathful face, smeared with oil and with matted hair plastered to its head, appeared round the corner of the deck-house immediately astern of the bridge.

'What in the name of the Lo-r-r-d do you imagine you're up to, you son of a bitch?' enquired Ian MacPherson, the engineer.

'Stop this damn ship,' said Sos.

'And for why should I stop this vessel at all?' said Ian MacPherson, coming round the deck-house. He carried an immense spanner in his right hand and a huge lump of tow in the other.

'For Heaven's sake, Jock —' said Sos.

'My name's Ian,' said MacPherson. 'And that's the richt name of me and no other. I was christened by it and I stand by it. For why should I stop my engines? There's a rat got oot o' the bilge an' I think it's in the condenser.'

There was a whistling sound overhead, very shrill and very menacing. It passed, taking the roof of the deck-house with it.

'Now you know,' said Sos.

Ian MacPherson went down his hatchway like a rabbit. Sos leapt from the bridge and ran to the gunwale of the trawler, waving his arm in any kind of a signal. The bow gun raised its smoking nose as if it were sniffing the air. Two minutes later a fearful rumbling from below indicated that Ian MacPherson, engineer, was making some adjustments to the machinery he was paid to control. A trail of blue smoke from burning oil drifted up out of the hatch. An ominous silence enveloped the coaster. She hove-to.

They lowered a ship's boat from Her Majesty's gunboat *Dwarf* and a sub-lieutenant clambered aboard.

Sos stood at the wheel while the trawler wallowed in the swell, then he took charge of the sub-lieutenant and went to find Captain Ferrandez.

He was in his cabin, but he was not apparent in the first instance, being under his bunk, and it was some little time before an exchange of confidences could take place because the free-board of the bunk was quite inadequate for Captain Ferrandez's girth; but in the end they extricated him and poured some of his own rum down him and the Royal Navy expressed its satisfaction that the ship's papers were in order and bade farewell.

Later Sos enquired of Captain Ferrandez how he felt.

'That is not good for my nerves.'

'You deserted your post in action,' said Sos, with severity.

'Tush,' said Captain Ferrandez. 'There are limits to all things. That gun was too noisy. I didn't like it.'

And later again, they crossed the bar of the Limpopo, with Manoel in the bows swinging the lead.

'*Uma braço e meio!... Uma braço scarço!*'

The water over the bar, in cross waves and in a riot of white horses seethed about them in an inferno and it seemed to Sos that a speedy end at the hands of Her Majesty's gunboat *Dwarf* might have been preferable to the prolonged anguish of observing Captain Ferrandez's navigation. But at last they slipped across the bar and were steaming slowly and steadily in deep and smooth water.

Captain Ferrandez landed Sos up-river. There were tears in his eyes. He held on to Sos's hand with his own large fleshy paws and for one agonizing moment Sos thought he might be kissed on either cheek. The effluvia of garlic about Captain Ferrandez was quite oppressive.

'I shall never forget our trip,' said the gallant Captain. 'I shall tell my grandchildren of how we faced the British Navy, the Inglese Colonel-General and myself. "Comrades-in-arms," I shall say. Outnumbered but shoulder to shoulder. *Tel logo, senhor.*'

'Goodbye,' said Sos. 'There is only one thing I shall ever regret.'

'And what is that, *senhor*?'

'That I shall never know what happened to Manoel in the Philippines.'

'It is of no interest, *senhor*. There is no need to know. It would all be lies. He is a terrible liar. *Adeus.*'

Thereafter Sos came very little in contact with the active side of the war. He joined the Rand Rifles, but saw no further action. He soon recovered from the stresses of his activities, but the war had drifted into that most difficult phase of dealing with the guerilla Boer commandos. He was glad when at last the end came. The chapter seemed completed. He turned his face to the south...

1944: INTERMEZZO

There had been no further message from Henry on the 'intercom'. That meant they must be coping on the three engines but how long that state of affairs would last was beyond Sos. At the very best if they reached base they would have to crash-land.

This state of being readily confident in any emergency was something to which one never seemed to get accustomed. Familiarity should have bred contempt of disaster, but it never did. The only people who thought it should were the people who sat in armchairs and talked about war.

It was just the same attitude of mind that imagined a uniform changed what was inside it. There never had been a man who'd never been afraid. And now it was happening all over again, this appalling suspense and the horrible feeling of frustration, in that there was nothing to be done about anything.

This wasn't the first time it had happened. After all he'd flown operationally from Iceland to the Azores, he'd been over Brest in a Blenheim where the 'Scharnhorst', the 'Gneisenau' and the 'Prinz Eugen' were berthed, he'd been based in Cornwall and the North and he'd faced every kind of weather.

There was always some humorous slant on the most perilous occasions. It was, he supposed, the sort of grim humour which necessity called forth.

They had been flying from an English base, and had caught fire. He couldn't remember now what had actually happened, but they were nearly home when it occurred. One thing was certain, as they made their circuit at the regulation 'aerodrome two thousand', they were alight. They asked permission to land.

'K for Katie calling... K for Katie … can I come in?'

And flying control answering — a woman's voice, a W.A.A.F.

'Speedwell calling K for Katie... Continue to circuit... Over.'

Then, '... K for Katie... I'm on fire... Over.'

And in return, 'Speedwell calling Katie... Continue to circuit... Over.'

A fat lot she'd cared. But they'd got in before the aircraft tried to blow up.

Then there'd been that ticklish business when he'd been with the Australian Squadron at Mount Batten. They were on reconnaissance in a Sunderland over the Bay of Biscay when they caught their enemy submarine surfacing.

They went in at low level and the U-boat gave back as good as she got. The stick of bombs was a near miss and the submarine's guns scored a direct hit on the flying boat.

Everyone felt the impact, but the pilot went round for the second time and, holed as he was, beat up the submarine again, before it crash-dived. It had been a cool and daring operation. When they reached base they all scrambled out on to the wings as soon as they landed. Nobody had known whether the aircraft would sink or not as soon as she touched water.

Well, they hadn't had to swim for it that time. And maybe this time they'd get away with it. It all depended on Henry.

There, again, was the repetition of a theme. Time and again the situation would depend on one man. And nobody ever seemed to fail anyone else. There were occasions, naturally, when something snapped and one amongst a myriad fell by the wayside, but it was astonishingly rare.

They were extraordinary young men, because despite the amazing things they did they were very ordinary young men. Very much given, too, at times to the sort of pranks which higher authority and more dignified years looked upon with a rather grave concern.

It didn't seem right to pile all the furniture, tables and chairs, into a monstrous pyramid and then climb to the top, all for the sole purpose of writing one's name on the ceiling. There was always the chance of breaking a leg, or even a neck.

Playing Rugger in a fully furnished anteroom with the waste-paper basket as the ball was another unconventional way of amusement, as also was the custom of holding a newly decorated companion upside down, while everyone else lay on the floor on their backs, in order to see if he'd got the stripes of his Distinguished Flying Cross the right way up. While for a change there was nothing like climbing the glass partition doors of the mess, with a very fair risk of falling through and severing an artery. Of course, nobody but lunatics would do these things.

But then again, only lunatics perhaps would walk into the furnace of a burning aeroplane and try to pull someone out, whom they'd never met before, just because he was someone burning to death; and only crazy people perhaps would have the cool, calm courage to fly through the bursting flak and drop their bombs with calculated determination.

All these things were being done every day, and not by mature men, but youngsters. There were Wing-Commanders, ranking with a Lieutenant-Colonel, that had scarcely reached their majority. He knew one who was only twenty-two and already carried the D.S.O. and the D.F.C.

It made Sos think of that proud Induna of the Matabele Royal Regiment, who had complained so bitterly that his impi had been defeated by a 'handful of boys'.

A handful of boys! That's what it was. 'Age shall not weary them, nor the years condemn.' The young men of Great Britain and the British Empire, who thought so little of death yet loved their lives so well!

So maybe, in the end, come what might, in all the travels and wanderings of his own life, in times of joy and pleasure, in times of sorrow and distress, at adventure's height or when the slow hours of suspense dragged, here maybe was the Eldorado he had always sought and which had so often eluded him; here, in a battered aeroplane with a broken engine, amongst his crew and comrades; here, come death come life, amongst these young men who had taken him to their hearts, 'among the very brave, the very true'...

1903–1939

CHAPTER TEN: THE WHEEL SPINS

The scrap of blotting paper lay on the desk of the Editor's office of the *Rand Daily Mail*, beside a copy of the paper and before a calendar which gave the date of a summer month of 1903.

Scrawled on the piece of paper in the Editor's writing were the words:

'E.W. — Finis!'

Sos picked up the scrap, handed it to Jack Andrew, his brother, and said, 'Rubbish, he's only just beginning.'

'If that's how he feels,' said Jack Andrew, 'it saves us the trouble of sacking him — I should say, asking him to resign.'

Edgar Wallace had been the editor of the paper, originally the *Standard and Digger's News*, for the last two years; ever since Sos and his brother, newly arrived in Africa, had taken over the joint directorship from Uncle Harry Freeman just after the Boer War.

There were many distinguished journalists in South Africa at the time: Gwynne of the *Morning Post*, Dawson, later to become editor of the London *Times*, Frank Blake and half a dozen others, among whom had been Wallace.

He had come under something of a cloud at the time Sos first met him, because as war correspondent of the *London Mail* he had telegraphed his paper the victory terms of the British with the Boers, without the authority of the official Censor.

Lord Kitchener, Commander-in-Chief of the armed forces, had sent for the irrepressible Wallace and there had been a stormy interview. It had not seemed to upset the correspondent of the *Mail* unduly. He had achieved a remarkable scoop for his paper and to his way of thinking the end had justified the means.

Both Jack Andrew and Sos had been with Uncle Harry Freeman on the Jo'burg Exchange when the paper had been acquired and Wallace installed, and were still members. True to form, Uncle Harry had settled both nephews in comfort and security and then, dying, rounded a life of generosity and human kindliness by underwriting the Boer Rehabilitation Fund, founded for Boers in distress through the war, for a quarter of a million pounds.

With the discovery of the Premier Mine, famous now for the Cullinan Diamond,[15] a bitter controversy had arisen as to the sharing of the profits. Sos and the majority of the Board had agreed on continuing the policy of Uncle Harry Freeman within their newspaper of sixty per cent to the Government and forty per cent to the owners. The policy had been passed at a Board meeting specially convened to discuss the subject, and Wallace had been given his instructions. To everybody's amazement, when the leading article appeared the *Rand Daily Mail* was found to be in favour of the owners, the precisely reverse policy to that decided upon.

'He'll have to go,' said Sos. 'It's a matter of principle. He's flouting our authority.'

'No one,' said Jack Andrew, 'can afford to play fast and loose with principle.'

'That's right,' said Sos.

Of course, Jack Andrew was right, because in Sos's opinion he always was. He was the chap with the brains. Sos was always telling people that. Moreover, he was perfectly prepared to leave it all to his brother. Things were going very well and

---

[15] The greatest diamond in the world. Its component parts are now in the Crown Jewels.

when they'd got rid of Wallace, they'd go better still. They already had a new man in mind. There was also the organization of the printing works to be overhauled.

Edgar Wallace, as typical, departed with good grace. There seemed little doubt but he had already foreseen the coming storm. His own 'obituary' seemed to confirm the point.

In the early days when Sos had slept in a packing-case and served as a waiter, it had always seemed to him that fortune spun as a wheel. He rejoiced now that a bright patch was his. He enjoyed his position on the paper, edited the financial column and wrote dramatic criticisms.

The paper could have done better, but it had some considerable consequence in the political world. Nevertheless, because of Wallace's delinquencies, neither Sos nor Jack Andrew was averse to selling should a favourable offer occur.

The offer that came was very fair. It came through E. P. Solomon, who was now on the Board and was an intimate friend of H. C. Hull, one of the leading members of the Responsible Government Party, who were pressing for full Boer representation in the newly formed constitution.

The offer was made to the two brothers by Solomon in person. There was no question whatsoever of any manipulation of policy or goodwill. The affair was purely a matter of business. It was very good business.

In short, if the brothers sold the property to H. C. Hull and his friends, the representatives of the Responsible Government Party, who would use the paper as a medium for propaganda in support of their cause, Sos and Jack Andrew would receive, beyond the purchasing price, the guarantee of a retainer on the Board for each of them, running into four figures. The arrangement, to all intents and purposes, to be in force in perpetuity. It would mean that whatever happened, in the years ahead, a settled and secure income of not less than £1,000 a year would be theirs.

Jack Andrew said that it was a most excellent business deal. Sos agreed.

Two days later Lord Milner, the High Commissioner, sent for Sos and his brother at Pretoria. Lord Milner told Sos that he had heard that the brothers were possibly selling the *Rand Daily Mail* to the Responsible Government Party.

'Yes,' said Sos, a little surprised that the news was out. 'We have had a remarkable offer.'

The High Commissioner asked Sos if he fully appreciated the potentialities of such a sale.

'My brother and I, sir,' said Sos, 'are simply business people who want to do the best for themselves in fair dealing. We have certainly had an offer and it's one that it's quite impossible to refuse.'

'It must be very good,' said Lord Milner. 'But that's not what I am asking. You understand that the *Mail* is a very valuable weapon in the hands of whichever party acquires it. That, of course, is why you have had this remarkable offer.'

'I'm not interested in politics, sir,' said Sos, 'I'm a business man.'

'But you're interested in your country,' said Lord Milner.

Sos made no answer to that, because somehow the trend of this interview was becoming obscure to him and at the same time he was becoming a little worried at the possible outcome. There was an undercurrent present which he had not suspected.

'The British Government', said Lord Milner, 'do not agree at all with the views of the Responsible Government Party. Indeed His Majesty's Government are completely opposed to them. They consider it is far too soon after the late war for full representation. Wounds are still open, feelings are apt to run high. The days are too early for the enemies of only yesterday to sit side by side in council. The future of South Africa is at stake.'

'I see,' said Sos, a little uneasily.

'Therefore anything that is done to help the Responsible Government Party is in direct opposition to the wishes of the British Government.'

'Politics aren't my concern,' repeated Sos. 'We want to sell the paper, sir. We're both members of "Exchange" and it occupies a great deal of our time.'

'Abe Bailey would buy your paper,' said the High Commissioner.

'I'm sure he'd never offer such terms as Mr Hull has put up.'

'That may be,' said Lord Milner. 'I can't dispute that part. But if you sell to Mr Hull you are doing the Empire a disservice. If you sell to Abe Bailey, who is one of our greatest Imperialists, you are doing the Empire a very good turn. It's just as simple as that.'

'I don't think it's fair,' said Sos, 'to put both my brother and me in such a position as this. This is the offer of a lifetime —'

'Nobody', said Lord Milner, 'is putting anybody in any position. The position happens to be there. That's all. You choose between yourself and your country. The decision is entirely for you. Nobody can force you.'

Sos sat silent for a moment, because he knew what the High Commissioner said was the truth. He knew, too, that he had a choice to make and that it was a very hard one.

'I know,' said Milner, 'what would have been the answer from another patriot and the late proprietor of the *Mail*, by the name of Harry Freeman Cohen, had he been alive today.'

Sos and his brother got up then, because they realized the interview was at an end whatever more might be said. They talked it over at lunch, at considerable length. Then Sos went off to Abe Bailey.

Lord Milner's information proved correct. Abe Bailey wished to buy the *Rand Daily Mail* and he made a fair offer.

'My brother and I,' said Sos, 'are salaried directors at present. How shall we stand?'

'I'll see you boys are all right,' said Abe Bailey. 'You're doing the proper thing by the country. I'll watch your interests.'

It was only a verbal agreement. Six months later Abe Bailey sold forty-nine per cent of the holdings in the *Rand Daily Mail* to the Central News Agency. No provision of any kind had been made for Jack Andrew Cohen nor his brother Lionel Cohen. They were no longer members of the Board. The contract with the Central News Agency had been completed. There were no further emoluments from the *Rand Daily Mail*, nor any redress. Sos wondered if Uncle Harry Freeman had managed to turn in his grave.

But the Stock Exchange still showed a very fair profit. It showed enough, at any rate, to allow the occasional extravagance; a 'pony' on the favourite, a holiday up-country, but particularly a jaunt with Spelterini.

Sos had always been interested in the air, and Spelterini the famous balloonist was making a tour of South Africa at the time. For the sum of sixty pounds a head he was prepared to take passengers for a trip. Sos had already flown in one of the biplanes of General Livingstone's 'circus' over a five-furlong straight course, and reached the dizzy height of some twenty-five feet in two hops, but the idea of riding in a balloon thousands of feet above the earth was entrancing. He paid Spelterini his fee, and in company with Kingswell of the *Owl*, as a recording journalist, and with another companion, left the Jeppestown Stadium in Johannesburg for a journey wherever the wind and fate and Spelterini's skill might take them. Their ballast was augmented by a case of champagne.

It was all a very spectacular business. The town turned out to see the fun and there was a band playing and people brought their newest motor-cars to follow the flight by road. Sos, most pleasantly exhilarated with the prospect of seeing Africa literally at his feet, drank champagne and assured Kingswell that they were going to have no end of an expedition. It was to prove quite true.

The mooring ropes were cast off and they soared aloft. It was the most exhilarating and exciting sensation. There was no sound at all of a rushing wind or a roaring propeller. There was no bouncing or bumping such as there had been in the General's aeroplane over its five furlongs. It was just a question of soaring away like a bird on the tilt of the wind. Beneath, the ground receded as if the earth were being drawn away from them, while they themselves remained motionless. Johannesburg took on a shape like a town on a map. On the road below, the following train of motors looked like ladybirds in a row.

'Higher,' said Sos.

It wasn't any good, he argued, going up in a balloon if it didn't go very high. That, after all, was what balloons were for, so have some champagne.

Kingswell said that he didn't mind if he did and anyway he was quite determined to have his money's worth and was there any reason why anyone shouldn't pass the bottle? Spelterini looked a little glum because, after all, he was responsible for the party; but no doubt he realized that his passengers had already paid their fares. They went up still higher.

At sixteen thousand feet it was bitterly cold, but the wine was still in circulation. It was, however, not possible to ascend any higher because everybody seemed to have been flinging bags of sand out of the basket, followed at intervals by an empty champagne bottle. Kingswell had ceased making notes because, as he explained, he was surrounded by so much of nothing that there wasn't very much he could say about it and had anybody got the wire-cutters because this damn cork had stuck?

'Higher,' said Sos.

An hour before dusk, they sighted the Drakensberg Mountains. The balloon was still moving at the same level, but was not answering accurately to its trail rope.

'We must land,' said Spelterini. He consulted his watch. 'It will be getting dark soon.'

He leant out over the edge of the basket, surveying the ground far beneath.

'We may be in difficulties,' he said.

'What's the matter?' asked Sos.

'Your insistence on going so high. You have thrown all our ballast overboard. I have none left to land with. It may be a rough landing. However, I will pull the release-cord and let the gas out. We mustn't drift over the mountains in the dark.'

'Go ahead,' said Sos. 'You know best. Who's pinched all the glasses?'

But Spelterini was staring aloft where the great gas-filled envelope swung in the air.

'The cord,' he said. 'It is adrift.'

'What's that?' said Sos.

'The release-cord. It should be fastened to this cleat. Someone has been tampering.'

'Well, what's the odds?' said Sos.

'None,' said Spelterini. 'None at all, except I cannot reach the cord and so I cannot release the gas, so we cannot go down and all the time we are driving into the Drakensberg and night is coming.'

'That isn't funny,' said Kingswell.

'I am not trying to be funny,' said Spelterini. 'But this joke has gone far enough and is no longer a joke. I am not very eager to die.'

Sos stared up as Spelterini had done and he saw the release-cord floating away from its contact point with the valve in the mouth of the balloon. The loose end was a dozen or more feet away from the edge of the basket. It was quite impossible to reach it. There was only one way to retrieve it and that was to pick it up where it joined the envelope. The point where it joined the envelope was twenty feet above Sos's head. He glanced away from the swinging, swaying bag with its netting and straining guy-ropes, towards the east. The Drakensberg Mountains looked very dark and menacing in the evening light.

In the immediate foreground the floating, jigging rope of the release-cord lay far beyond Sos's grasp. He took a firm hold of one of the guy-ropes and swung himself on to the edge of the basket.

At once, trimmed out of balance, the basket swung away from under him, so that while he still held firmly to the rope, his legs slipped over the wicker-work rim as far as his knees. He glanced down instinctively and saw swimming between his thighs the dizzy panorama of the earth, over fifteen thousand feet below.

The spectacle, presented in such an original manner, combined with the gyrations of the balloon, sent him suddenly weak with the nausea of vertigo and his hands seemed to slip on the rope. Kingswell grabbed at Sos's legs and hung on there, and the grip was reassuring.

Sos was quite certain that he wasn't going to look down any more. The guy-rope was close to his face. He could see the separate coarse fibres of its strands. He told himself that he would concentrate on the rope, creeping closely up it, and never glancing again at the awful abyss below. Then he began to go up.

The moment his feet left the edge of the basket, he knew that he was in the utmost peril of his life. The inspiration to climb aloft and solve their problem had been the work of an instant. Now he was set upon his course and could not possibly afford to fail. All their lives were at stake.

He had learnt to climb a rope as a boy, swarming up hand over hand, with the rope between his knees, one bight twisted round his left calf, and the rope gripped by the heel of his right foot against the instep of the left. There was nothing in it. But the ropes that fell from the sides of ships in Delagoa Bay, or had hung from the roof of a Royal Marines gymnasium in England, had been ropes intended for men to climb, fast at the head and free at the foot, and of a thickness to fit the clasp of a hand.

But the rope that Sos now climbed was thin, so that it cut his hands. It was not free at its foot but firmly fastened to the weighty basket, so that it was extremely difficult to encourage a few inches of slack to maintain a foot-hold. It was like climbing a wire that, with the movements of the basket, was taut one minute and loose the next, so that the climber must be prepared for the bow-like whip of the line which, as it tightened, could throw him into space like a stone from a catapult.

The first time it happened, Sos was not prepared, and his right arm was wrenched free and he swung outwards as the entire balloon spun sickeningly on its axis. He lay horizontal in the empty air and he slipped down the rope a little. The rope bit at his knees and he knew the skin was gone from the palm of his left hand, because it felt as if he was holding a red-hot bar of iron. But he recovered his hold and though he heard what he thought was Kingswell below, shouting to come down, he clawed his way up.

He went foot by foot, and every time he brought his legs up he spun in an arc. He wondered whether, if he lost his grip and fell, he would be unconscious before he hit the ground. He imagined he'd burst like a paper bag from that height. Then he was beneath the valve of the envelope.

He passed his arm through a link of the netting that connected the guy-ropes to the balloon. He snatched at the length of release cord and caught it. Then, because he knew he would need both his hands and all his strength to return in anything like safety, he pulled the cord up foot by foot to tuck the loose end into his belt.

He reached the end of the softer slender cord and was about to push the end past his belt buckle, when the balloon lurched in an air-pocket and the cord flew out of his grasp as he clutched at the guy-rope.

He tried again, but the cord eluded him as the balloon careered on drunkenly; so he rested a little because he knew it was impossible for him to last very much longer. His hand was an agony and every muscle in his body seemed to be strained to breaking point. Then as the cord drifted past him once more he caught it and made the end fast to the buckle. It was no easy matter, for he had only one hand with which to work, with his other arm crooked in the netting loop as support, but at last the job was done and he began to descend.

It was far worse than the ascent. The guy-ropes continually slipped in his hands and once his feet were nearly shot from their precarious hold as the rope strained to another sudden lurch of the balloon; and with the basket all the time hopelessly out of trim, he was again hanging almost parallel to the surface of the earth beneath.

But he reached the basket and tried to get his ankles over. They slipped and for one moment he thought he had gone, for the wicker-work reeled away from under him and all his weight was suddenly on his hands. He thought he heard a muscle crack in a joint at the sudden strain and then Kingswell had one of his legs in his grasp and his companion had another and Spelterini himself had struggled between, and with his arms around Sos's waist was tugging him into the basket. It tilted and tipped beneath their weight, now all concentrated on the one side, so that for the moment it looked as if it would pour them, four writhing figures, over its rim, but they fell in a heap on the floor and lay there for a moment panting.

Sos sat up, undid the release-cord and handed it to Spelterini.

'Now pull the plug and let's go home,' he said.

He struggled to his feet.

'Has anybody got a drink?' he said.

'There's one glass left in the magnum we brought as a spare,' said Kingswell.

He poured out a drink. It annoyed Sos very much that the glass rattled against his teeth when he drank. He was shaking quite uncontrollably.

Half an hour later they had landed and Sos was in one of the attendant cars, being driven back to Johannesburg. His hand had already been roughly bandaged. Kingswell slept peacefully beside him. Every now and then he snored and muttered. It had been rather an exhausting day.

'Sammy' Marks, of Lewis and Marks, the richest member of the exclusive Rand Club in Johannesburg, delighted in a simple little riddle of his own invention. 'When is a millionaire not a millionaire?'

The answer was, 'Nine times out of ten.'

It was probably very near the truth in the spring of 1913. There was considerable unrest in the mining community, with trouble between the owners and the miners on the question of an increase of pay. Moreover, in sharp contrast to the preceding years, there was general trade depression and the Stock Exchange was immediately affected. Business fell off and Sos was heard to comment that most of his friends 'hadn't got two sixpences to jingle on a tombstone'.

He had fully reckoned by now to have turned his back upon poverty and had married and had one daughter.

The lady had played the lead in *The Quaker Girl*, which had been touring South Africa, at the time. Sos had paid a visit to the theatre, had been instantly overcome and had married her forthwith.

The Management, together with the Stage Director, had joined the company at the wedding breakfast. Everyone had enjoyed the occasion very much. Especially the Management, who had returned later with the police and arrested the newly married bride on a charge of breaking her contract in the middle of the tour. But somehow things had been smoothed over. Since then, Sos had been very well content. The tempo of his life was serene. Sometimes he thought a little regretfully of the lost connection with the *Mail*, but on the whole he prospered, though times were growing difficult.

The first indication of really serious trouble was the outbreak of a strike at the Kleinfontein Mine on the East Rand, on 27th May 1913. The strike, encouraged by agitators, rapidly spread. It was decided, in the event of emergency, to support the police with the military and at the same time to enlist volunteers. Sos went with his friends to the police headquarters in Von Brandeis Square to draw arms and then returned to the Rand Club — the 'Millionaires' Club'. It was generally realized that should rioting break out the club would be threatened. Sos was appointed by General Byron to take charge of the ground floor. He set about barricading the windows of his 'command' and putting the place in a state of defence.

On 4th July an unauthorized meeting was held by the strikers in the market square in Johannesburg. The authorities had previously decided to prohibit the meeting. On the day in question the square was packed with the strikers and their supporters, who also had occupied the roofs of surrounding houses.

The Chief Magistrate, the Commissioner and Deputy Commissioner of Police went to the square and attempted to placate the assembly. They were attacked with stones and bottles and the police were ordered to clear the area.

Not only were missiles of every kind used, but unfortunately firearms were employed and there were very considerable casualties. The offices of Johannesburg's evening paper, the *Star*, were set on fire and many of the employees were only rescued with the greatest difficulty, as the fire brigade was attacked when it arrived. The building was completely gutted.

The Park Railway Station was also fired, and a police officer was dragged from his horse and beaten senseless. An attempt was made to fling the unconscious man into the burning buildings.

Meanwhile Sos was at his post in the Rand Club, and snipers were firing from the roofs of the houses opposite. The mob had by now reached Loveday Street, where the club was situated. The situation grew extremely ugly and Sos found it a far from agreeable position being responsible for shooting his fellow citizens, with whom he had no personal quarrel.

A company of the 10th Royal Dragoons had now formed into skirmishing order in the adjoining street, and the crowd were told that if they did not disperse they would be fired upon. They immediately grew more aggressive and one of the ringleaders, by the name of Labuschagne, stepped out into the street before the line of troops. Sos could see him quite clearly through his window.

The man strode into the open, bared his chest and shouted:

'Shoot, you bastards! Shoot!'

No notice was taken of him, while the strikers' bullets continued to rip along the walls of the Club. As Labuschagne repeated his challenge, baring his chest and ripping his shirt apart, an officer of the Dragoons, Lieutenant Turner, was struck by a sniper's bullet, and the troops were ordered to open fire. The agitator fell dead. The Dragoons then advanced and cleared the street.

But though General Botha and General Smuts contrived within the next forty-eight hours to effect a settlement, it only proved a temporary remedy. In January of the following year, 1914, the Reef was again torn in conflict in a general strike. Sos enlisted as a special constable and patrolled the streets. He attempted, moreover, to intercede with the strike leaders but was unsuccessful.

The strike continued to spread but now the Government, acting out of past experience, decided to declare martial law. On the day of the proclamation the ringleaders in Pretoria were arrested. Several burgher Commandos were called up and the Boers rode in from the veldt in the varied garb which Sos remembered so well from the Boer War.

The strike leaders in Johannesburg, hearing of the fate of their comrades in the Capital, barricaded themselves in the Trades Hall. The building was surrounded immediately by the police and armed burghers and the area sealed off, and the inhabitants of the immediate neighbourhood evacuated. It was not until a field gun of the Transvaal Artillery had been trained upon the building and the strikers told that they would be blown sky-high, that they decided to surrender. The strike leaders were eventually deported.

But if the year 1914 was to prove fateful and tragic to the world at large, to Sos it was to prove how fickle any one man's fortune might be.

On the London Stock Exchange they 'hammer' a man who fails to meet his liabilities. An official calls the attention of members, by the striking of a gavel on a rostrum. There are no such formalities on the Johannesburg Exchange. Instead, a defaulting broker writes to the Secretary of the Exchange and states that he cannot meet his engagements. The letter is acknowledged and the defaulter ceases to become a member. He is expelled.

On either Exchange the disgrace is identical.

It was not Sos's fault. The avalanche started in a small way. A client unexpectedly went bankrupt, a matter for personal regret for an old and valued friend. Then another followed immediately on the heels of the first, which caused concern for the goodwill of broker as well as client. Then, swiftly, three or four more, which meant that all reserve funds must be called upon; and then no abatement of the terror, but indeed an acceleration, a gigantic downpour, an avalanche, smothering everything, everyone before it, carrying away the structure of years, destroying, implacable.

He was at first quite stunned and bewildered by the outrageous blow, because it all happened so suddenly that it was difficult to realize that his life was secure, as a reasonably wealthy man, one minute, and in the next he was without the means to pay the rent. It became more intolerable with a young wife and a small daughter at hand.

He had many friends. He had been in Africa over twenty years. Through his various activities he was well known throughout the Rand. He could have gone to his friends, for help. No one would have turned him away. Instead, he went to Jack Andrew.

He went to his brother for no other reason but that Jack Andrew was a director of the Luipardsvlei Mine. Jack Andrew asked him what he wanted, and Sos said he wanted to be a miner.

That made Jack Andrew laugh, and he asked Sos what the devil he thought he knew about mining.

'I was once under instruction from Uncle Harry's general manager in the days of the Geldenhuis, and anyway everybody's got to start.'

'At five bob a day? Learner's pay?'

'At five bob a day,' said Sos. 'Good money for a man who's broke.'

'Five years to go,' said Jack Andrew, 'before you qualify as a manager. It'll break your heart.'

'It won't.'

'Let me help you. We'll tide you over somehow.'

'This is the way you can help me,' said Sos. 'There isn't any other. This is my picnic and I've got to solve my own problems.'

Jack Andrew gave him an introduction to the Luipardsvlei general manager, R. B. Saner, who agreed to take him on. Sos returned to his wife and told her that he'd found work. She was no more impressed with the solution to their troubles than he was, but she never raised one word of protest when they all three moved into one combined room.

Sos worked very hard. The years of hard living and harder experience had taught him adaptability. Whatever regrets he may have had for the past, and happier days, he never voiced them. It seemed to him that in the end, perhaps, this was the way of all life: that there could never be any retreat, but always a man must advance, however bludgeoned by his fate. He thought, too, that maybe the cardinal sin, in the eyes of the ultimate Providence, was cowardice. If the battle did not necessarily go to the strong, it could certainly never go to the faint of heart.

But it wasn't always easy to keep his courage up. His very determination to fight his way through raised a barrier in his path. His keenness and energy put him ahead of his fellows long before his time. At the club, at meetings of the Mine Managers' Association, in bars and saloons, it became a standing joke to jeer good-naturedly at Mr Saner and tell him that he'd be losing his job to Sos Cohen if he didn't look out. But it was not the mine manager's fault that Sos was put in charge of a 'raise' that had not been 'lashed out'.

When a reef of gold runs diagonally upwards a shaft, known as a 'raise', is driven in a steep upward incline to another level. As the face is blasted away the rubble of rock and ore piles up in the raise, and since the latter is at a steep angle the debris very swiftly obstructs the passage and must be 'lashed out', or cleared out by manually removing the mass of broken rock. If the 'lashing-out' has been neglected anyone working that particular reach of the reef must climb and clamber over the obstruction, and at times force a passage through a gap scarcely high enough to allow a man to pass. The task allotted to Sos, in circumstances such as these, was not enviable.

It was eleven o'clock of that particular morning some weeks after he had been taken off the raise, that as shift-boss (to which position he had been promoted) he was making his rounds. It was his duty to inspect every part of his section of the mine. He took with him, as customary, a boss-boy, who carried the acetylene lamp. There was no reason to suppose that the morning would bring forth any incident in the least out of the ordinary. The general working of the mine was satisfactory in every way.

A gang of 'hammer-boys' were drilling in a stope on one of the levels which had been blasted out from the raise, as Sos entered from the 'box' — a passage with a rough wooden ladder on which to climb up the stope, which was at an angle of about twenty-five degrees.

The half-stripped black figures were still drilling in the face and the white miners, whose job it was to charge these holes with dynamite when they were finished, had not yet arrived.

The usual procedure for the shift-boss was to test the 'hanging wall' — the ceiling of the stope — on entering any place where natives were working, to tell by the sound if it were solid. Evidently there was a fault here, for a few moments after Sos had tested it, the 'hanging wall' collapsed.

The massive rock fell in great slabs that broke into portions as they fell. The main galleys of the mine reverberated with the roar and thunder of the collapse and the stope was a fog of thick dust.

Sos went down in a shower of rock that piled upon him, while the dust blinded and choked him. The terrifying roaring was still in his ears as he lay pinned on the floor with a weight of shattered rock upon his leg. On all sides of him in the suffocating darkness he could hear moans, and somewhere near by a man was screaming.

For a few seconds Sos lay very still, because he scarcely knew whether he was dead or alive, then he attempted to move and found that he couldn't.

He had no idea whether he was seriously injured or not. He felt at the moment no pain, but knew that shock might have numbed him. Very cautiously he attempted to tense each muscle in turn, of an arm, a leg, of the back and the abdomen. They seemed to be all right, but he still found it impossible to move and was fearful of increasing his efforts lest he disturb the balance of the rock resting on him and cause more to roll upon him. Moreover, it was not improbable that a further fall might occur. Someone, within reach of him if he could have stretched out an arm, was crying in a strange, shrill, child-like way that was utterly horrifying. Somewhere in the distance an alarm bell began to clang, then another and another. Voices sounded from the drive. He heard the clatter of picks and shovels. A light seemed to flicker through the interstices of the rubble, and he thought he heard a voice calling in English. Then for a little time it seemed that he heard no more and his senses went dull, till there was a clamour about him and the unmistakable gleam of a lamp and hands were helping him to his feet.

Eighteen men were killed that morning, among them the bossboy who had been carrying the lamp at Sos's side. Sos himself, having been buried alive for over two hours, suffered no more than a severe bruising and an injured ankle which was treated in the Krugersdrop Hospital.

244

In the following week Great Britain declared war on Germany.

CHAPTER ELEVEN: CO-FORCE AND COLONEL TAFEL

The German Commander in East Africa, Von Lettow-Vorbeck, was one of the outstanding characters engaged in hostilities on either side, in any theatre of war, from 1914 to 1918. Though forced to retreat from German soil, his armed forces never actually surrendered of their own accord. Von Lettow-Vorbeck was still fighting brilliant rearguard actions when the Armistice was declared in November 1918, and he was instructed from Berlin to give up the fight.

The struggle fell into three phases: on the outbreak of war, the Germans invaded British East Africa, with the British on the defensive and only attacking as part of their strategic defence; in the second phase, from 1916 to 1917, the British under the brilliant leadership of General Smuts, assumed the offensive and, under General Hoskins and the Boer General Van Deventer, drove the Germans into their own territory and finally swept them out of it; in the final phase, Von Lettow-Vorbeck was pursued into Portuguese East Africa.

The invasion of German East Africa took place under General Smuts in three main thrusts with General Van Deventer in the centre, driving down from the north. Van Deventer was in command of the Mounted Brigade, and he was directly under the Commander-in-Chief. The Brigade included the 1st South African Horse. It was the 1st South African Horse which Sos joined in Pretoria in 1915.

Before joining the regiment, he had enlisted as a trooper and had been sent recruiting through the Free State. He was therefore extremely glad to be with a combatant corps and was not a little amused at the comment made by Major Wilkins, the second-in-command, when his commission came through.

'Commissioned *him*? What, that fellow? We don't want no *rooineks* here,' the Boer had said. 'Turn him round three times in the bush and he'd be lost.'

The Brigade were moved from Pretoria to Mombasa, by way of Durban, and were sent up to Nairobi and trained in the Game Reserves of the Mbegathi Plain. They were eventually based on Mbuyuni when the advance began.

Sos, with two pips up, was in command of a troop. It was the beginning of his third war.

He first saw action at Kahe, when the Germans were fighting a stubborn rearguard action as they fell back over the Pangani River, and then on 3rd April he set out from Arusha, lying fifty miles west of Moshi, to attack the enemy's position on Lol Kisale Hill.

With the horses left under cover, Sos led his men forward dismounted through the scrub in the early hours of the morning. They passed through tall elephant grass, which reached up to their armpits. Immediately they emerged from the scrub they were met with a withering fire from the enemy, who were in position in the distant foothills. Sos had no option but to order his men to drop down out of sight.

From their position in the small kopjes, the enemy had a commanding field of fire over all the few hundred yards of open ground that lay between Lol Kisale and the scrub. When, a quarter of an hour later, Sos raised his head to take stock of the situation, a burst of machine-gun fire at once greeted him. He ducked down immediately.

It was apparent that the enemy were in a very superior position. Not only had they a clear field of fire but they were concealed and protected by the natural cover. Far to the left and right flanks there was a desultory rifle-fire with the intermittent chattering of machine guns. It was clear to Sos that the attack was developing, but for his part he was too occupied with his troop to speculate what was happening elsewhere. He had an uncomfortable feeling that the enemy would have any advance he made covered foot by foot and had already ranged the terrain directly before him. He decided to find out.

In order not to disclose his position he made his way a hundred yards or so to his right, crouching low beneath the elephant grass. His little batman, a fellow 'Geordie' from Krugersdorp, accompanied him. He was indeed always at Sos's heels, a little bantam of a man with an inimitable sense of humour and of great courage.

'Give me your rifle and helmet,' said Sos.

He raised the helmet on the rifle, above the high grass. At once a burst of machine-gun fire swept over them, the bullets rustling through the grass, mowing a swathe-like path immediately behind them.

'That's altogether too hot,' said Sos.

It took him half an hour to regain his former position, crawling most of the way on hands and knees. Every now and again there would come another burst and he wondered if the enemy could follow his movements through the grass. But there was no doubt whatsoever that the area was under the closest observation from the higher ground. There was nothing to do until orders came through but to remain where he was.

They were still pinned down in the middle of the afternoon. The heat was relentless and their water was practically gone, together with their rations. No instructions had come through from the Captain in command of the squadron, and Sos was growing restless, as were his men.

Beyond the discomfort of heat and thirst, which could soon become a torment, there was the added anxiety of not knowing what the enemy might be contemplating, though it seemed doubtful whether the Germans and their Askaris would turn to the assault on what was still admittedly a rearguard action. Nevertheless it was completely exasperating and a little humiliating to lie, helpless and hopelessly immobilized, within sight of the objective.

Half an hour later he sent his runner back with a message asking for instructions. There were none forthcoming. It was getting on for some thirty hours since the force had set out from its original base. If no solution to his problem came from his commander, it appeared that he would have to find one for himself.

He cudgelled his brains to find a way out of the impasse. It was no good staying where he was, but equally it was impossible to remain. Whatever source of water there might be would assuredly be within the enemy lines. There was every likelihood that he and his men would not be able to assuage their thirst till they had taken their objective, which seemed as distant now as it had ever been. Then on a moment's inspiration he saw a possible answer to the riddle.

Between the scrub and the enemy's lines was only one area completely uncovered by the latter's fire. The belt of elephant grass and the barren, broken ground beyond afforded very little cover, but at the very foot of the low kopjes where the enemy lay would be a blind area, beneath the angle not only of his fire, but of his observation.

The plan, then, should be to rush the intervening space till the shelter of the broken, rocky ground at the foot of the hill was reached.

It was a daring enough proposition, and the movement would have to be carried out with great resolution. Nevertheless, Sos felt confident that he knew his men well enough to rely upon their dash and determination, while the audacity of the movement might catch the enemy off his guard.

He detailed the proposal on a sheet from his Field Service notebook and dispatched it to the rear. Ten minutes later he received the reply. He could put his plan into operation.

Keeping low under cover Sos brought his troop to the edge of the grass belt. On hands and knees, peering out, he could now distinctly see the foothills ahead. In the late afternoon they lay brown and bare, with never a sign of human life anywhere in their vicinity. He marshalled his men into skirmishing order and then broke cover.

He had rushed the first hundred yards before the enemy opened fire. He signalled his men down and they went flat to the ground. Ahead, a wisp of smoke showed here and there between the rocks. The whine of a bullet passed overhead and the dust spurted up thirty yards behind them.

A more concentrated fire was brought upon the troop, but did no damage. Sos carried his men steadily and swiftly forward and in a short time they were once more under cover, but now behind the boulders at the foot of the hill. What he had surmised turned out to be correct. They had reached the dead ground and were in comparative safety.

Moreover, the initiative had passed to him. In the high grass he had been pinned down so completely that the enemy had, no doubt, been able to dismiss his troop as an effective force and had contented himself with merely keeping a watch on the area. That he had been taken by surprise accounted very possibly for the absence of any opposition from machine-guns.[16]

But now the disadvantage had passed to the defenders of the hill. Their enemy was at the very threshold of their defences, and while able to choose the time and opportunity to strike, was himself immune from anything other than a desperate frontal attack, which would rapidly resolve itself into hand-to-hand conflict.

This, then, was the position as dusk fell. The exchange of rifle-fire died down as the night rapidly followed, and only now and again a single shot would betray the agitation of an enemy sentry.

During the night the main body moved further forward in an enveloping movement, but as far as Sos was concerned his attention was concentrated entirely on his troop, resting his hungry and tired men as far as he could against what the morning might bring.

It brought a white flag. It was the first thing that Sos saw as dawn came into the sky. The piece of white rag fluttered from a stick of thorn, fixed in a cleft of rock on the crest of the hill. Sos called his runner to him and wrote a hurried message. The little Geordie ran back across the open ground towards the high grass. Sos watched him go, his short legs twinkling as he ran. Then he turned to look at the top of the hill. There was no sign of life. It was strange, in this eerie silence, to think that the enemy must be teeming there.

Within minutes an instruction was in Sos's hands. The runner stood panting by his side.

'Investigate. But suspect trap.'

It was not the most inspiring of messages.

'Come on', said Sos.

---

[16] It was found later that the enemy had only two machine-guns on Lol Kisale.

251

They went up the hill together, the stocky subaltern and his fellow townsman. It was a stiff climb and the rubble was loose under their feet. Nor was there anything enjoyable about that brief passage, which two rifle shots could bring to an end. Then he saw, by the flag, the German officer.

He stood with his arms folded and as Sos scrambled up towards him, he threw a brief order over his shoulder. Sos kept his hand on his revolver and his batman carried his rifle at the ready. Then two Feldwebels joined their officer. Sos came level with them, and indicated the flag.

'Surrender?' said Sos.

'*Ja.*'

The German officer, Leutnant Hergott, broke into a torrent of German.

'Why don't 'e talk sense?' said Sos's batman.

The German gestured with his hand sweeping the horizon.

'Surrounded,' he said. '*Kaput.*'

He pointed at the fluttering white flag. Almost, Sos thought, with disgust and contempt. Then he gestured again, behind him.

There were over four hundred of them there, collected together in two ragged ranks, the German Askaris and their carriers.

'You're getting some exercise this morning,' said Sos and gave his runner another message. Then he sat down with his back against a rock. His thirst was becoming a torment, but he couldn't borrow of his enemy, yet.

It was nearly half an hour before he received a reply.

'Remove bolts from all rifles. March prisoners down to foothills.'

So it came that on that April morning Sos went down the hill of Lol Kisale at the head of three Germans and four hundred and thirty native troops, with the added prize of two machine guns; and the water he drained from a prisoner's water-bottle was like a draught of wine.

On the 12th of April Van Deventer's mounted Brigade reached Ufiome, with the objective in view of the important strategical point of Kondoa Irangi. Late that night, while on his tour of the camp as duty officer, Sos stumbled upon a Boer picket, asleep in their blankets.

He roused them and asked their corporal what he thought he was doing, and if he realized the seriousness of the offence and what the penalty could be.

The reply was that no one was sleeping, but the mosquitoes were so bad that he and his men were sheltering from them beneath their blankets.

'And every time they bite, they make you snore,' said Sos.

He told his orderly to take the men's names and see that they were reported. It was a step he was reluctant to take, because the death penalty would automatically be enforced. Some days later he enquired of their Boer Colonel whether the men had been before him.

'Yes. But I have taken no action.'

'No action!'

'No. You did your duty, but I have let them off this time. They fought so well at Lol Kisale!'

On the 13th of April Van Deventer's force reached Galai and, still advancing, were in touch with the enemy four miles north of Kondoa Irangi. The weather was appalling with the heavy rains and mist, but by noon of the following day the town was in Van Deventer's hands. During the next three weeks Van Deventer was joined by his Infantry Brigade and the 4th South African Horse and Sos and his troop were sent out scouting.

The task was eminently to his liking. He was his own master and he could use his own initiative. He crossed the Kilombero River and moved south, in which direction Von Lettow was supposedly still retreating after the fall of Kondoa Irangi.

No contact was made with the enemy so he pressed on, confident that sooner or later he would locate the position where the enemy might be deciding to make a stand. As the fortunes of war go, it was the enemy who located Sos.

He met them well south of the Kilombero, but they were heading north, so that they met face to face. He was taken by surprise and very nearly surrounded. But he managed to re-cross the river and at once sent the message back that Von Lettow was now advancing, returning to the attack. As it afterwards transpired, realizing only too clearly the strategic importance of Kondoa Irangi, Von Lettow had transferred troops from the Usambara railway to the Central Railway and had some 4,000 troops under his command, together with two naval 4.7 guns which had been taken with their crews from the German cruiser *Königsberg* after she had been beached.

Sos held on north of the river, awaiting instructions. They arrived in the person of Van Deventer himself. The Dutch General had decided, on receiving Sos's information, on a reconnaissance in force, bringing a battery of South African Artillery with him under Colonel 'Toby' Taylor, D.S.O.[17]

Sos was very pleased that his information should have proved so valuable. It compensated for the risks he had taken, driving so far south in the first instance. Van Deventer sent his Boer troops across the Kilombero with instructions to make contact with Von Lettow and then to hold on as long as they could and get their information back at the earliest possible moment. It made Sos quite comfortably warm within, to think

---

[17] Now Brigadier Taylor, Q.C., C.M.G., D.S.O., and Sos's firm friend.

what a splendid smack on the nose the German would get when he came on to find Van Deventer with his cavalry waiting for him and Colonel Taylor with his guns.

Von Lettow didn't come on, but the Dutchmen came back. They had seen no sign of the enemy. Van Deventer stormed round his headquarters.

'*Waar is die vyand?*' he stormed and sent for Sos. '*Waar is die vyand?* Where is the enemy?'

'South of the river, sir,' said Sos. 'And advancing.'

'He is not there. There is nothings of him at all there.'

'Then your troop didn't go deep enough and press home their reconnaissance. Because I know Von Lettow's there and if you let me take my troop, I'll prove it.'

'These *rooineks,*' said Van Deventer. 'The things they'll say.'

'The best place for you,' said Colonel Taylor, who was equally furious, 'is to get out of here and get back to your bucket-shop. Bringing us here on a fool's errand!'

But they left Sos behind when they fell back to Kondoa Irangi. That is to say they requested him to stay out as a scout screen and he complied with their request because he wasn't overfond of their company for the moment. He disliked having his word doubted when he'd risked his skin to get the facts.

Von Lettow came on in due course, as Sos knew he would, and his advance guard drove Sos and his troop slowly further back. All the time Sos preserved his lines of communication intact and kept Van Deventer's headquarters duly informed of all that was happening. Indeed, to be strictly truthful, he was glad to be able to pass on the news.

Colonel Nussey of the Dutch forces instructed Sos, in a brief message from the comparative safety of his headquarters:

'Lead them on.'

As he had nearly been outflanked that very day, Sos was of the opinion that they didn't need much leading on. It was the first week in May.

On the following day one of Von Lettow's 4.7-inch shells went soaring hundreds of feet over Sos's head as he lay with his men on a small kopje outside Kondoa Irangi, and landed with a *crump* in Van Deventer's headquarters in the town.

As the only person who knew that a gun of that calibre was within two hundred miles of the vicinity was Von Lettow himself, a most stimulating surprise was enjoyed by all. Particularly by Sos.

Von Lettow, after four fierce attacks upon Kondoa Irangi, was driven off and before the end of the month Van Deventer was strongly reinforced.

When the signal came through that the force was to be provided with air support, Sos was immediately involved. Despite his previous encounter with the General over the enemy advance, Sos was well liked by Van Deventer, not least because he could speak Afrikaans. Sos in turn held the Boer General in considerable respect, knowing his prowess as a fighter. It gave him great satisfaction to hear the commander detail an operation expertly and point out on the map the references to which he referred. References, indeed, seldom recognized at first sight, as the Boer's immense hands nearly covered the entire map.

There were aeroplanes arriving, said Van Deventer, and a place must be made ready for them. He would know what to do with horses, but what sort of stabling did 'die Lugskip'[18] require? Someone suggested that they had got to land. They couldn't be tethered like a nag, nor hove-to like a ship at anchor. Van Deventer supposed they could not, though he had

---

[18] 'The air ship.'

little faith in these new-fangled contraptions. His father had never used one.

So Sos was detailed to prepare an airstrip. Six aircraft of No. 8 Squadron of the Royal Naval Air Service would be flying in, any time within the next few hours.[19]

Thousands of natives were immediately employed clearing the scrub and bush, while others built a hangar of reeds and wattle. The dimensions of the landing ground were some three hundred yards by two hundred yards. It was within easy range of the enemy guns. Nevertheless it was complete and ready when the flight of B.E.2C's and Voisins arrived a few hours later.[20]

Sos watched them come in, one by one, rocking a little as they 'lobbed down', and bouncing like ping-pong balls. It was a very remarkable spectacle to see these two-seater biplanes come out of the sky at a great height and land so neatly, when they had been flying well over 60 miles an hour. It reminded him of his previous experience when 'Admiral' Weston had taken him up and he'd twice reached twenty-five feet in five straight furlongs. He felt there was something very attractive about this business in the air. A week later the commander of the flight called for volunteers.

The flight had come out in a hurry under establishment and were short of observers. Sos volunteered at once, and found

---

[19] The R.A.F. had not yet been formed. Air support was divided between the R.F.C. and the R.N.A.S.

[20] One of the more spectacular exploits in the Second World War was the laying of landing-strips which made the construction of a complete advance aerodrome possible within forty-eight hours. But while readily admitting that the size and landing-speed of the R.N.A.S. aircraft was vastly less than modern aircraft, nevertheless, this completion of the Kondoa Irangi aerodrome, in relation to the difficulties, seems remarkable.

himself seconded to the R.N.A.S. He thought it might prove an entertaining and novel adventure. He found himself caught up in an enterprise which at times seemed beyond the realms of fantasy.

It was only with the greatest difficulty that the aircraft were even reasonably serviced and maintained, chiefly owing to the lack of spare parts and the incessant attention of the earwigs, which developed a passion for invading the engines as they were being re-assembled in the open air after a stripping-down.

The main difficulties encountered by pilots were engine failure and bad weather, rather than enemy opposition. Some of the logbook items of Sos's first pilot[21] make interesting reading.

Date & Time: 11/6/16, 6.10 a.m.
Machine: Voisin 1705
Observer: Lt. Cohen
Course: Kondoa Irangi to Champala and back (About 90 miles.) Time: 2hrs. 15 min.
Remarks: Took 1 hour to climb to 3000ft. Engine missed twice en route. Machine would not climb above 3000. Revs. dropped when flying over Champala so made for home at once. Managed to crawl into aerodrome at 1000 ft. after going past some thick mist.

Date & Time: 12/6/16, 5.45 a.m.
Machine: Voisin 8705
Observer: Lt. Cohen, 1st S.A.H.
Course: Aerodrome circuits. Time: 35 mins.
Remarks: Tried to proceed to Handeni but view obscured by heavy bank of cloud. Returned to aerodrome to save petrol as ordered.

---

[21] Now Air Vice-Marshal Sir Leslie O. Brown, K.C.B., C.B.E., D.S.C., A.F.C.

Date & Time: 12/6/16, 6.30 a.m.
Machine: Voisin 8705
Observer: Lt. Cohen, 1ˢᵗ S.A.H.
Course: Kondoa Irangi to point 15 miles along Handeni Road. Time: 1 hour.
Remarks: Second attempt to get to Handeni. Clouds still very thick so returned after proceeding 15 miles along road.

Date & Time: 8/9/16, 9.30 a.m.
Machine: Voisin 8705
Observer: Lt. Cohen
Course: Attempt to fly to Ruaha River. Time: 5 mins.
Remarks: Engine cut out 4 or 5 times. Revs. dropped to 900. Force landed in field and crashed tail unit.

Date & Time: 8/9/16, 3.11 p.m.
Machine: Voisin 8705
Observer: Lt. Cohen
Course: Kilossato Ruaha and back. Time: 2 hrs. 10 mins.
Remarks: Very bumpy. Fired on a maxims; 3 wires broken. Voisins struck off war service. A damn good job too!

But Sos was interested. The task of the flight was reconnaissance, and this new method of scouting appealed to him. It was exhilarating to fly low and loop the loop over the enemy lines, in order to tempt him to disclose his position by opening fire, but the act of re-fuelling was slightly nauseating. The range of a B.E.2C, in which he frequently flew, was some three hours, but it was prolonged by the simple method of carrying spare tins of petrol and re-filling the tank beneath the observer's seat. All that Sos had to do was to open the tin, unscrew the cap of the tank and pour in petrol. The tropical sun and heat did the rest. He was, at times, nearly gassed.

It was a life of infinite variety. Flying in a B.E.2C, near Kilossa, engine-trouble developed. The aircraft at once lost height, and though they were comparatively near base it became quite apparent that they would have to force-land. And beneath them was a sisal plantation.

The sisal plant grows to six feet high and is armed with sharp points; in particular an especial poniard adorns its apex. The plantation beneath them was uncut, and to have landed in it would have ripped both plane and crew to ribbons. As it was they only just brushed over the top of the sisal and landed, quite inelegantly, in a cotton field.

But flying did not occupy all the time of an operational officer in the R.N.A.S. Aerodromes had to be constructed and often enough they were sited actually in advance of the infantry column of the advancing Brigade, as was the case at Aneti.

There was no defence of aerodromes and they were often under fire. A further extract from the log of Flight Sub-Lieutenant L. O. Brown, with whom Sos was flying at the time, illustrates the point very well. It is reproduced verbatim.

Date & Time: 12/6/16, 4.35 p.m.
Machine: Voisin 8705
Observer: Lt. Cohen, 1st S.A.H.
Course: Kondoa to Handeni. Time: 1 hr. 40 mins.
Remarks: Machine climbed very badly. 1 hr. 5 mins, to climb to 2,600 ft. Very bumpy and hard work. Had to return because light failed; 3 shells exploded in middle of aerodrome between 6.15 and 6.17 p.tn., making total of 53 in vicinity of aerodrome to date. The 3 shells burst in my wheel tracks, almost did us in. Taxied machine under lee of hill out of sight of Huns. Good shooting.

The selection of landing-ground sites was made from the air, and then it was necessary to rediscover the position by ground and organize native labour on the spot. At Dodoma Sos travelled in a Ford lorry, with four Askaris and a sergeant, over country which was completely trackless and, for all he knew, hostile. He was again well in advance of the main body and encountered on his journey over hills and through dongas, through the scrub and bush, several parties of the enemy Askaris. But in every instance they surrendered without firing a shot, supposing the British now to be in the ascendant with the Germans retreating, they themselves running true to form in siding unconditionally with the winning party. It reminded Sos of those witnesses who had been so tragically suborned at his court-martial in Chibuto, those many years before.

At Mpwapwa, he was instructed to prepare a landing ground at a few hours' notice. It was a nightmare of an aerodrome when completed, with a hill on one side which it was just possible to avoid when coming in to land, and a prickly pear hedge on the far side to greet anybody who was rash enough to over-shoot.

During the construction of the site, and working against time all through the night, Sos came across a ridge of rock which had to be levelled. The only possible method, in the short time at his disposal, was to blast the reef with a series of explosions. The infantry who were in the vicinity were immediately turned out as the enemy were presumed to be attacking.

Once at Iringa he crashed on the escarpment near the aerodrome in a B.E.2C, carrying two 25-lb. bombs. The machine was wrecked, but neither of the bombs exploded. The only injury received was a bruise on the observer's leg.

At times it was necessary for Sos to plead the cause of the aviator with Van Deventer. The Boer General, magnificent campaigner though he was, had little knowledge of the air arm, and was constantly urging the R.N.A.S. Flight to advance in conjunction with his troops. It was difficult to impress upon him that aeroplanes could be more profitably employed operating from a comparatively safe base in the rear of the column. For hours Sos would endeavour to explain the delicacy and fragility of the machine that flew. But with General Northey's final occupation of Iringa, the activities of the R.N.A.S. rapidly dwindled, and the flight was recalled to Egypt.

Von Lettow, who by now was in the process of being run out of German East Africa, was falling back on to Portuguese East.

Sos, who left the Flight on its new posting, *ipso facto* left the R.N.A.S. and joined the British Field Intelligence Force, forming up the unit which was to become eventually known as 'Co-Force'.

'Co-Force', formed and organized by Sos, consisted in the first instance of himself and one other white officer, Lieutenant St. Quinton, and some forty Askaris, including many Ruga-Rugas, ex-German Askaris who had surrendered and changed sides. Valuable undercover support was also given by the natives of the British University mission station.

The Force was, in fact, an armed intelligence unit in the field, operating in the rear of Von Lettow who was retreating to the Ruvuma River, which marked the border of Portuguese East Africa. It was no difficult matter to pass information through to the advancing British forces coming down from the north, by native runner, because even large bodies of men could pass unnoticed by each other in the thick bush and one single man accustomed to the country had very little trouble in getting through. Moreover, the native element, again influenced by the apparently approaching defeat of the Germans together with their hatred of them because of their harsh treatment, were only too ready to give information as to enemy movements.

'Co-Force', moreover, was to engage the enemy on all possible occasions, attacking small posts and camps and engaging in general 'mopping-up' operations. At the same time, the Portuguese, who were now actively in the war, would co-operate.

Von Lettow was still north of the Ruvuma with a column under Colonel Tafel on his flank. At the same time General Northey was pressing forward from the west. In Von Lettow's immediate rear and covering it were partially isolated sections of the German forces, many of them now in considerable distress with lack of proper rations and with the loss of equipment. It was these sections with which 'Co-Force' was to deal.

Sos landed at Mazimbwa, just south of the Ruvuma. He was to cross the river with his small command, in conjunction with the Portuguese, who would support him on either flank.

While Sos had some idea of the position of the German sentries on the left bank, no information had come through as to the strength or the position of Von Lettow's main body. Therefore to move into his area involved Sos in placing himself and his unit in a position which at any time could become precarious. Though the river at this particular juncture was comparatively narrow, it was rising with the heavy rains up-country. Knowing the rapidity with which an African river could swell into flood at full spate, he resolved to make his crossing at the earliest possible moment. The Portuguese, in the circumstances, were not immediately able to support him, so he gave orders for rafts to be lashed together without further delay.

They crossed at night. It was pitch dark, and the rising waters of the Ruvuma swirled past their crazy craft. They were ungainly vessels, carrying only some four men with their equipment at a time. Now and again they rocked precariously as they were paddled across. No one was allowed to speak and the only sound under the moonless sky was the steady threshing of the water along the reeds and high elephant grass of the banks or the occasional faint splash of a paddle.

But the faintest of splashes would be enough. Somewhere facing him, Sos knew, were the German Askari sentries, and their trained ear could pick up a sound inaudible to a European. The slightest error of judgment, and a warning shot would be fired. What might follow was beyond conjecture.

Sos accompanied the first party across. The raft swung clumsily in mid-stream, the men staggered together, and Sos cursed under his breath because this was a pretty mad adventure and he was just beginning to realize it. He was going through with it, but he didn't mind admitting he was worried by the dark night on the menacing river and with the unknown awaiting him. Then they were lurching through the reeds of the north bank and the men were scrambling off into the shallow water and wading up to where the tall grass grew on the brink. It had been a nerve-racking journey, short though it was.

Half a dozen or more similar passages were needed to transfer the whole of the company, complete with its two Lewis guns. Sos supervised all the journeys, and by midnight the operation was complete.

Wet through, unsupported on either flank and with no knowledge of the enemy strength awaiting them, the little force, so far unscathed and undiscovered, huddled together in the elephant grass, while their commanding officer made his plans.

The sky, which had been overcast, began to clear and the stars came out, and as the visibility increased Sos decided to strike northwards away from the river. Enemy patrols would be more likely to be working the river bank, with the possibility of observing any movement across the water, than further inland where the bush began, and there he could find cover. Accordingly an hour before dawn they set off in single file with Sos in the lead.

It was an eerie business threading their way through the shoulder-high grass, the shape of the man ahead but a darker shade in the darkness, while above the great vault of the sky glittered with starlight. Now and again from the bush an animal call would echo and once something brushed and fluttered across Sos's face. Not a word was spoken as they passed like ghosts.

As the heavy outline of trees came in sight Sos became aware that there was a movement immediately ahead of him. He stopped short in his tracks, bringing the long file of men, one by one, to a halt behind him.

The enemy was ahead.

Now against the gradually paling night, which very soon would drown in the sudden dawn, he could see the figure of a man, and even as he watched he thought he saw the glint of a bayonet.

A sentry was standing by a bush. Sos could see him distinctly now. He was moving his head from side to side in a strangely animal-like fashion as if he were turning his ear to a sound that had startled him. Then behind him Sos saw the *banda*.

It was the usual type of native-built hut with reeds interlaced and a thatched roof, and was square in shape and low to the ground. It could hold about twenty men. Sos had discovered an enemy post.

He motioned his sergeant to his side and pointed. The sergeant understood immediately. He beckoned and two men joined him. Sos waved them on. Then he drew his revolver and cocked it.

The undergrowth reached to the enemy sentry's waist. It was apparent that he was disturbed now, because he was turning completely round every few seconds in an uncertain manner. There was no sign of the sergeant nor of his companions. In the purple darkness of the night there was already a hint of grey.

Then the sentry went down. There was no movement around him but he sank into the high grass, as a sack might subside. There was a sudden coughing which died as abruptly as it had begun. Three figures rose where the sentry had stood. Sos motioned his men on.

They trailed along in his wake. He gave his orders by signs; a forefinger pointing in the direction of the *banda*, an encircling sweep of his arm, an indication to the Lewis gunners where to take up position. Within a couple of minutes the hut was completely surrounded, and every rifle trained on it. Sos himself took cover behind a tree. Dawn was breaking.

'Come out of there!' said Sos in a loud voice, and levelled his revolver at the door. It was the first words that had been spoken above a whisper since they'd left the south bank of the Ruvuma.

'Come out of there,' said Sos. 'One at a time, and your hands on your heads.'

There was a sudden chattering of voices. Then a voice shouting in German. The door of the hut flew open. A man in tattered trousers and a soiled shirt stood in the doorway an automatic in his hand. Sos could see his beard, dark against his white face.

'Drop that gun, you're surrounded,' said Sos. 'And come out of there, all of you.'

The automatic dropped from the German's hands. He muttered over his shoulder and then stumbled forward.

Twenty-five of them came out, two white officers and twenty-three Askaris, half dressed and some nearly naked. Their clothes were tattered and some of them were in rags. There wasn't an ounce of fight left in any of them.

The Askari sergeant went into the hut and collected their weapons and piled them in a heap. The ring of men around the *banda* had disclosed themselves by now, some standing, others kneeling. They looked very formidable in that small space. Behind the *banda* the tall trees of the bush loomed dark and brooding in the first light.

Sos went forward with his revolver in his hand. A second German officer stood beside his superior. He too was bearded, with a growth of pale hair to match his blonde head. Sos judged him to be little more than twenty. He was clearly frightened beyond measure, for he kept looking around him like a cornered wild thing at the grim circle of men. Then quite suddenly he was across the intervening space and sprawled before Sos with his arms around Sos's legs.

'Don't let them get me!' he said. He spoke very fair English.

'Get up, you fool,' said Sos. 'What's the matter with you?'

'I didn't beat them,' said the young German. '*Gott im Himmel*, I never touched them! It was the others that did it. I wasn't there.'

'Get up,' said Sos. 'My Askaris won't touch you, whatever you've done to their friends. Get up or I'll put a bullet in your brain.'

He marshalled his prisoners together then and sent them packing under an escort, which he could ill afford. He sent them off through the bush with a message as to their origin, in the direction of Colonel Rose's column which was advancing down the coast towards Lindi. He felt reasonably pleased with his first night's bag. It augured well for the future.

And still the waters of the Ruvuma steadily rose. It was no question now as to whether the Portuguese would cross or not. They had no choice. The heavy stream became a turbulent flood that swept yellow and foaming between the shrunken banks. Before and around Sos was the enemy, behind him the roaring torrent.

But that, he told himself, should in no way interfere with the original purpose of 'Co-Force'. It had set out to scout and pass information and to do as much damage behind the enemy lines as it could. Nothing should deter it and if in the end it should, by ill chance, encounter an opposition too large and too powerful, then it would go down fighting. There was nothing more simple.

He set off through the bush and some twelve miles further on came to untracked and open terrain.

They lived on the country. As once before against the Boers, in the self-same Portuguese possession, he drank the native beer and ate the native mealies. The population were well inclined towards the British. They had had enough of German treatment. They had, moreover, some excellent sources of information. As soon as the German Commander, Colonel Tafel, left Tabora with the intention of moving down towards the Ruvuma to cross into Portuguese East Africa, the news got round.

Immediately Sos heard of it he knew what to expect. Colonel Tafel, in conjunction with Colonels Otto and Aumann, commanded the German Northern Force and it was their intention to join up with Von Lettow before the crossing of the river. While the main purpose of the operation was naturally obscure to Sos, he knew what any movement on a large scale could mean to a force the size of his own. He would be swallowed up, as once Lobengula had threatened to 'eat' the Salisbury column.

So he built a strongpost. He had no intention of returning across the Ruvuma as yet, though he couldn't hope for any reinforcements. But he could still fight a delaying action, if trouble came his way, though it might mean the end of 'Co-Force'.

He selected a small kopje. It commanded a strategical position in the direct line of Tafel's expected advance. Around it the country provided very fair cover.

On the top of his kopje he built a dummy block-house. It was properly reinforced with rubble on its outer walls and suitably loopholed. From half a mile away, viewed from the scrub below, it looked quite formidable. He built another one. Then he built two more. He had only sufficient personnel to man one of them, but there was nobody to tell the Germans that story.

Along the slopes of his hill he dug dummy trenches, constructing a very plausible representation of an elaborate defence system. Then he sat down to wait.

The first sign of the enemy advance came some days after the completion of the defences. A look-out called Sos and it seemed to him that, peering through his glasses, he could see a faint trail of rising dust very far away on the ragged outline of the horizon.

He watched for half an hour or more. Sometimes the dust-cloud rose in a little haze; at other times it disappeared altogether. It seemed apparent that a body of men were on the move. An hour later, he thought he caught a glimpse of a fleeting sunstart in the scrub, near his kopje. He ordered a general 'stand-to' immediately.

He manned the front-line trenches, leaving the block-houses empty. They would serve their purpose in drawing the enemy's fire. He stood-to all the rest of the afternoon and all that evening. He felt pretty sure that the enemy had sighted his position.

Any delaying action that he made would, he felt, be a contribution to the campaign. Colonel Rose was still coming on down his right flank and if the Ruvuma dropped to a reasonable level, the Portuguese could cross over.

On the other hand, the whole affair turned on a matter of numbers. Neither side, in the dense country, had very much idea of the opposing strength. A little bluff could go a long way. He wondered if his would be called.

It was called the next morning. A shell whistled over his trenches and landed on the side of the hill. Then another fell and another. Sos waited for the enemy to disclose his strength more fully.

There was now movement in the neighbouring scrub, and Sos could see with the naked eye the movement of enemy Askaris. They were advancing steadily forward.

He opened fire with his two Lewis guns and with sectional rifle fire. For a little time the advance was halted and then it came on again.

Concentrated fire on Sos's part once more stemmed the advance, and he realized that he had pinned his opponents down in the open ground in his immediate field of fire. It very much looked as if the enemy infantry were not present in sufficient numbers to consolidate their attack. Possibly, then, Sos was engaging the 'point' of the vanguard only, as opposed to anything as formidable as the main body. Nevertheless, it was only a matter of time before the latter came up and sent reinforcements to reduce the position completely before the whole force moved on. The answer to that, then, was not to give anybody time to make such calculations. He must take a chance, and the devil seize the hindmost.

'Fix bayonets,' said Sos.

The order went down the line, the bayonets clicked into their holders and then Sos blew his whistle and he and his Askaris went over the top.

They went over in one wave and Sos carried a rifle and bayonet as well as his revolver. They scrambled down the short slope and tore across the open ground like forty demons. Sos thought he might just as well have been back on the Bembesi River a hundred years ago or whatever it had been, when he'd last used a bayonet.

He led his Askaris into the scrub and the enemy were so surprised at such a piece of impudence that they were too astonished to open any kind of effective fire. Sos drove his bayonet into a man's back and all around him his sweating, swearing comrades plied their weapons and men screamed and shouted.

The Askaris of 'Co-Force' didn't make much noise because they were too busy, and they pressed on panting and stabbing. Then the enemy broke and ran.

Sos retired then to his defences. All that day his little force stood-to, but no further shells burst on the kopje and only once did he see the merest suggestion of a dust-cloud receding. During the night he still kept his men fully marshalled at the alert, but after the following dawn, when there had been no signs of any impending attacks, he put one half of them in reserve. And thereafter, for some little time, no one came his way.

He continued to develop his offensive reconnaissance. He attacked and captured isolated posts and kept a continual stream of information passing through. He was the first in at Newala after Von Lettow had abandoned the town, being forced to leave his sick and wounded behind. The latter were in a wretched condition, their staple diet being a soup of elephant-meat extract.

Learning on a later occasion that one of the *Königsberg*'s famous 4.7 guns was in the vicinity of Masasi, he asked permission of his commander-in-chief to attack the site. He was told that his job was Intelligence and that his force was non-combatant!

He replied by asking, pointedly, if his command were non-combatant, why had they been supplied from the start with arms and ammunition? Mentioning at the same time, with all due respect, that to the best of his knowledge 'Co-Force' had been responsible for the capture of more prisoners than anyone else operating in that area. No denial was made of the claim, and permission was granted for Sos to attack. Unfortunately, owing to the delay, another British unit arrived there first.

He recrossed the Ruvuma then, linking up with the Portuguese forces on the southern side, working westwards in the tracks of the enemy, but once again Von Lettow managed to escape.

Sos's main task now was to establish posts along the river towards the direction of General Northey's advance. He crossed the Lujenda, a tributary of the Ruvuma, where a German attack was suspected. He had orders from British headquarters to instruct the Portuguese who were acting in conjunction with him to dig in. The Major in command of the Portuguese detachment refused.

'Dig in! Only cowards dig in.'

He was not to be moved. Sos pleaded with him in vain.

The enemy attack was developed. The Portuguese Major led his men out in battle array, as if they were on a drill parade. The Germans crossed the Lujenda, unmolested, in broad daylight and then set up their machine-guns and mowed the Portuguese down. The Major was killed instantly — a very gallant officer with a fine body of men, who were unfortunately not accustomed to anything more lethal than native warfare.

Sos, hearing of the incident later, like that other must admit that it wasn't war, but it was not a little magnificent — which hardly justified in his opinion the subsequent offer of the German General to exchange fifty Portuguese officer prisoners-of-war for food!

Towards the end of 1917 'Co-Force' was disbanded and Sos was appointed Liaison officer to Portuguese Headquarters at Chomba, in Portuguese East Africa, moving to Quelimane, on the coast.

Some twenty miles up the neighbouring Nyamakura River Colonel Gore-Brown of the K.A.R. was awaiting an enemy attack in strength. His force was indeed the only serious obstacle between the Germans and the Portuguese headquarters at Quelimane. There was considerable perturbation on the part of the Portuguese commander, who had little relish for a fight. He had already moved his own quarters to the Port Captain's pier, with a vessel under constant steam should he need to make a hurried retreat.

Up the Nyamakura, Gore-Brown was already in difficulties. He was rapidly growing short of ammunition. The news very naturally came through to Sos in the earliest instance. He was alarmed and immediately asked for co-operation from his allies.

'We've got to get ammunition to him right away,' he said. 'He's used a lot on these last enemy sorties, but the main attack hasn't developed yet. It's imminent.'

'No one', was the answer, 'can reach your English Colonel.'

'He's on the river,' said Sos.

'No doubt. But where are the enemy?'

'I don't know.'

'They are everywhere and anywhere. Nobody knows. It would be sheer suicide for anyone to venture up the Nyamakura, with either bank and possibly both occupied by the German forces. Not for a moment could anyone get through undetected.'

'That's unfortunate for Colonel Gore-Brown,' said Sos. 'I'll do the job myself.'

He took his Sudanese sergeant, who had been with him in 'CoForce', and they selected a launch by the quayside. It was crewed by a native helmsman and a 'boy' at the two-stroke engine. A working party loaded up the launch with boxes of ammunition. The little relief party set off at dusk.

The sunset came down on the river and the water went blood-red, then changed to purple while the night flooded in. The little engine of the launch chug-chugged in a cheerful way, advertising its prowess as it steadily steamed upstream. It seemed to Sos that everybody in Africa, let alone Portuguese East, must be hearing their progress.

The stars came out and a sickle moon swam into the sky, and still the little engine chattered along merrily and the wake of the launch sent a wave continually rustling along the reeds of the banks.

Beyond, the grass grew as always shoulder-high, and beyond again lay the scrub and bush, dark, mysterious and sinister.

There was no sense in preparing for any attack nor evolving a plan. If at any time there was an enemy patrol on the bank, nothing could be done to take any kind of evasive action. One volley and it would all be over. The crocodiles could complete the job.

At the end of the first ten miles, when they were now deep into enemy territory, both the helmsman and the engineer showed signs of panic.

A wild beast of some kind, floundering on a mud bank and struggling through the reeds and grass, provided the only sound the crew of the launch had heard for the last two hours. The effect was instantaneous. The native engineer whipped round, his eyes goggling and his hands at the gunwale; the helmsman dropped his tiller.

Sos grabbed the tiller and swung the launch back on her course, and with his other hand snatched out his revolver and thrust its muzzle into the helmsman's ribs before he could decide to jump overboard. The Sudanese sergeant waved the engine-boy back to his post with his rifle and then stood over him. In such a manner they continued on their way.

Now and again Sos had to change the hand that held his threatening weapon, because he knew that it must be levelled all the time, and after a little while his wrist began to ache. Not only the humid night caused his shirt to become drenched and stick to his ribs.

Towards ten o'clock the night seemed to become murmurous with all manner of suspicious sounds. How many of these were imaginary he had no means of telling. He could only feel that all the world was alert and aware of him, and in the darkness darker forces were at work, planning his destruction. Then, on a sudden, he was challenged and he knew his destination was reached.

They were ready waiting for him on a small improvised jetty — a young British subaltern and his N.C.O. They told him that they had received the message of his proposed attempt to run the gauntlet, but had very much doubted if he would get through. The enemy were in considerable force in the neighbourhood, but their precise position was unknown. Then they set a working party unloading the precious cargo and Sos went to report to Gore-Brown.

The Colonel was young for his rank and Sos thought he was a fine fellow. Possibly the Colonel thought the same of Sos, because he merely thanked him as if he had passed a cup of tea over the table. Sos wanted to stay with him.

'I've no authority to hold you here,' said Gore-Brown. 'Besides, you'd be more use back at your own base. It's a key job, you know.'

Then Sos and the young Colonel said goodbye and wished each other good luck. They shook hands and Sos went back to the launch, where the native crew of two were cowering in the sternsheets with the Sudanese sergeant mounting guard over them. Sos ordered the engineer to start up the engine, and though he protested, Sos had his way with him, saying that he would find himself in the middle of a battle if he delayed much longer.

The return journey, though they travelled faster downstream and were unloaded, was no less a nightmare, since they must needs race against the dawn. Moreover, the sound of their upstream passage might by now have been reported to the German authorities and pickets have been sent out to watch the river. Halfway back the engine began to splutter and Sos thought the end had come, since they could only drift hopelessly till daylight brought discovery, but the engine picked up again and before first light they were moored once more by the quayside at Quelimane. There had been no sign whatsoever of the enemy.

On the following morning, Colonel Tafel's force attacked Colonel Gore-Brown's detachment and completely destroyed it. The British Colonel was killed. The main cause of the disaster was panic among the civilian population.

A conference was immediately called at headquarters, by the Portuguese Commander. The debacle up the Nyamakura opened up the way to Quelimane. Sos in the natural course of his duty attended the conference, having first observed that the ship by the Port Captain's pier had steam up. He thought of the long dark hours of the night before, with their terror and suspense. Then he thought of young Colonel Gore-Brown only so short a time ago shaking him by the hand and murmuring his gratitude. Now Gore-Brown lay dead.

The General was a member of the Vermigo Branco party, and had perhaps allowed his left-wing political views to tinge his valour. He came into the conference looking very self-important, if a little agitated. All his staff officers sat round the conference table and the General addressed them.

He referred by chapter and verse to the Hague Convention rulings as concerned open and undefended towns. His argument was quite logical and delightfully simple. Quelimane, if undefended, would be an open town. If Quelimane were an open town it would not be attacked. Therefore evacuate Quelimane and the Germans would not make a battleground of it. And that was what he proposed to do.

Sos wondered if an earthquake would have been felt at that moment by anyone present, so completely amazed were they. The General looked from one to another of the blank faces before him and demanded in a loud voice if he had been understood. A Portuguese staff Colonel moistened his lips and was heard to mutter his disapproval. Several officers of an equal rank squirmed a little uncomfortably in their chairs. Sos sat, frozen with horror that any man could disclose his cowardice in such a manner before his fellow men. He almost thought he heard the steam whistle of the vessel by the Port Captain's pier, blowing the warning blast for departure.

Then, at the far end of the table, a young Portuguese naval officer rose. He looked very white and shaken and there was a little trickle of perspiration running down his temple, as if he were under the stress of some great emotion.

'Sir,' he said, 'I can only speak for myself, though I feel sure that there are others who will feel with me. I think there are some of us, sir, who, if the policy of deserting Quelimane without firing a shot is persisted in, would be glad to place themselves and their services not under the Portuguese authority, but under that of the senior British officer.'

The General had no time to reply. A dozen chairs were pushed back and a dozen other officers were on their feet in support of the Portuguese naval officer. But the General flung his papers, including the Directorate of the Hague Convention, on to the table and said if that was what they thought about it he supposed that they would have to do something about it. Then he waddled out of the room with as much dignity as he could muster.

The Portuguese did the best they could to put up some kind of defence preparations around Quelimane, but Colonel Tafel never advanced to the attack, being turned before he reached the town.

A little dispirited with staff work, Sos applied for a posting to more active operations in Europe, but the Armistice of

November 1918 found him in the Adriatic without seeing any further action.

At the German surrender at Abercorn on 25th November 1918, a characteristic and not unpleasing gesture was made. While the African troops, the Askaris, were ordered to lay down their arms, General Von Lettow-Vorbeck, his officers and all Europeans under his command were allowed to retain their own weapons in recognition of the gallant fight they had put up.[22]

For his activities in the 1914-1918 war Sos was awarded the Distinguished Service Order and the Military Cross.

---

[22] In December, 1929, a reunion dinner was held at the Holborn Restaurant for all forces engaged in the German East African campaign. General Smuts was in the chair. The guest of honour was — General Von Lettow-Vorbeck.

CHAPTER TWELVE: ELDORADO

In August 1920, the Portuguese Government granted to the Companhia Mineira de Mozambique a concession to prospect for gold, diamonds, coal, iron, tin and other base metals over an area of 29,300 square miles extending from a coastline on the Indian Ocean, stretching from a point adjacent to the Island of Mozambique in the north, to Mutiba on the Licungo River in the south. There were many navigable rivers and ports within the concession.

It was virgin territory, but the existence of vast natural resources had been suspected for many years, and in 1900 gold mines were discovered by the celebrated Portuguese engineer Palo de Almeida, who led an expedition into the interior, sank shafts and worked on the auriferous reefs. The venture came to an untimely end. Hostile natives attacked the prospectors and massacred them.

During the First World War, British forces had penetrated into Mozambique and Lieutenant C. J. Lewis of the 1/3 King's African Rifles progressed as far as Calipo. There his sergeant, an old-time prospector, went searching for water and while so occupied discovered the 'blue-ground', in which diamonds are found. Other operations over the same territory disclosed, through the information given by various engineers and mining experts attached to the forces, that there was every likelihood of gold being found in very considerable quantities. The Portuguese Minister for Marine could foresee 'important results for commencing and guaranteeing exploration on a large scale with sufficient capital'. Doctor Domingos Pepulim of Lourenço Marques was assured by 2nd Lieutenant Sebastiao

F. C. Ruivo that 'he had no hesitation in asserting the existence of petroleum by the oily signs appearing in certain parts'. A highly qualified English geologist reported on 6th September 1920, '.... in my opinion the Company has secured a very valuable Concession with great possibilities.'

At the end of August 1920 the Concession was taken over by the Mozambique Oil and Mineral Concessions, Ltd., with a capital of £200,000 divided into 800,000 shares of 5s. each, of which 240,000 shares of 5s. were reserved for working capital and the general purposes of the Company, and with a registered office in Southampton Row, London.

The Managing Director was Captain L. Cohen, D.S.O., M.C., late Managing Director of the *Rand Daily Mail* and Geldenhuis Main Reef Gold Mining Co., Ltd. He lived at Clarence Gate Gardens, N.W.1, should anyone have been curious.

Sos had returned to England and to his wife and family after the war and had joined a firm of stockbrokers in the City. He had done very well for himself. He was making money and saving it during the years of 1920-1921. He was forty-six and was thinking of settling down in earnest. That is to say at times he suppressed the desire to claw the stiff collar from his neck, consign the inevitable carnation in his buttonhole to the gutter and catch the next boat back to the wilderness which he had grown to understand and love.

Maybe the Promoter suspected something of these rascally and ill-conceived longings within the bosom of Sos when he approached him. Perhaps he felt an adventurous soul was losing the savour of its salt in the clammy atmosphere of the very society which Joseph of the great moustaches, in the Aldersgate warehouse of so long ago, would have worshipped. Or maybe he wasn't feeling in the least concerned with anybody's soul but merely, being a promoter, wanted to find a man of ability and energy to open up, manage, administer and direct the activities of a new Company which he had just promoted: namely, the Mozambique Oil and Mineral Concessions, Ltd.

He explained to Sos that the opportunity of a very great adventure, with the prospects of dazzling rewards, was open to the right man. He told Sos all about the reports of gold and diamonds and base metals. He also added that somebody had remarked that there were the hell of a lot of lions in the district, but he supposed Sos could shoot.

Sos assured the Promoter that he was a pretty fair shot and that he'd rather be at his end of his rifle than any damn lion at the other because he'd blow its brains out and pass the decanter, there's a good chap.

Then he realized that by such an. assertion he had practically committed himself to the proposition and he was as good as in Africa already.

He went to Africa. It was inevitable. He tried to excuse himself with such inept tags as 'if you've 'eard the East a-callin' you won't never 'eed naught else', but they didn't reassure him. The situation was painfully clear. The Promoter had dangled the luscious and maybe forbidden fruit of astounding adventure under the nose of his victim, a married man with children, a gentleman of the City of London aged forty-six, and the poor wretch had fallen.

He had fallen with glee. Like everybody else concerned with the Mozambique Oil and Mineral Concessions Company, he fully believed in its prospects. Here at last might be the very goal which he had always sought. One step more forward, the best and the last.

He arrived in Johannesburg six weeks later. Here, so many years ago, he had worked in the Elephant Trading Company's store while Uncle Harry Freeman had pegged out claims from his tin shanty. Here, he had returned to days of prosperity and happiness, with a splendid city rising where once the hutments had baked in the red dust. From here, he had departed, disgraced and ruined, with his name no longer on the books of the Stock Exchange. And now he was back again. Eldorado! Eldorado!

His first business was to organize a band of prospectors and allocate areas within the concession's territory, but before that, he had another small piece of business to transact. He made his headquarters in the Rand Club.

He had already, with his profit of the last few years in London, paid his creditors to the last penny. To no one on the Johannesburg Exchange did he owe anything at all from his former collapse. Together with the documentary proof of his clearance, he had found two sponsors to nominate and back him in the recognized manner. He stood again as an applicant for full membership of the Johannesburg Stock Exchange.

He was accepted. He went before the Committee and by noon of that day his name was once again on the members' list. It gave him very great pleasure to think it was there once more.

It gave him even greater pleasure to write to the Secretary of the Johannesburg Stock Exchange, that very same evening, a note couched in the most courteous of tones, resigning his membership.

He found his prospectors, all ten of them. They were a mixed lot, and only seemed to have one taste in common, which was whisky. He had to ration them, and one of them, an old-timer who was dissatisfied with his ration, distilled his own gin from mandioca, a plant from which starch and tapioca are manufactured. He carried his equipment with him, wherever he went. It consisted of an enormous native-made clay pot and the barrel of an old brass blunderbuss, with which he contrived to erect a still.

Sos went first to Delagoa Bay and then made his headquarters at Angoche. He distributed his pioneers over the territory and set to work.

He toured the districts in turn, by car and *mechila*. Communications were good, a proportion of the roads having been constructed during the war. But in every other respect the country was wild enough and infested with lions. It was essential for every working party to have at least one armed guard and every prospector carried his rifle.

Sos was in high spirits. All over the concession his men were working their Banca drills, boring down at selected places in the river to the depth of twenty feet, searching for gold and testing the bauxite for aluminium. Often he pored over his map with the area overlaid with the tokens 'Gold', 'Tin', 'Diamonds', 'Oil', 'Copper', 'Coal'. It was like standing on the roof of an Aladdin's Cave. It only needed the correct key for the 'Open Sesame'.

The key took a great deal of finding. Alluvial gold was discovered and great was the rejoicing. Then it was found that the quantity brought to light was insufficient to justify the working. A supposed tin deposit eventually only produced tourmalines, a semiprecious stone of very little value. Later a supposed ruby alluvial gravel only brought forth garnets. It was heart-breaking.

Yet still he could dream of his precious concession, within which, so legend had it, lay buried the Queen of Sheba's treasure. But the lions persisted.

He went up-country because of a lion. He had organized a gang under two of his prospectors to work what he hoped might transpire to be a reef, worth exploiting. The native labour lived in a compound, and among the lions in the nearby bush was a man-eater. The latrines were outside the compound and three natives had already lost their lives when visiting the latrines during the night. On each occasion it was suspected that it was the same lion. Sos was sent for, and arrived complete with his rifle and camp-kit. Several of the natives had already deserted.

He sized up the situation and gave orders for a stockade to be built. It was not a stockade in the customary sense of the word. Rather it was a wooden pylon, some fifteen feet high, with a platform on the top. On the platform he arranged his camp bed. At sundown he climbed his eyrie, rifle in hand. From this position of vantage, he could command the exit of the compound and the entrance to the latrines.

The lion appeared just after midnight. Sos was asleep. He was awakened by a shrill cry and a hideous growling. He rolled out of bed, seized his rifle and switched on the torch.

Beneath him was a horrible melee. He could see the great cat-like creature below, worrying the struggling figure of one of his men. Inside the compound was pandemonium. The whole camp was awake. In the uncertain light he dared not risk a shot for fear of killing his workman. But the torch and the tumult drove the lion off. The victim, terribly mauled, was carried back into the kraal. He died the following day.

This was very bad business. The Managing Director had been called upon for help and he had immediately complied with the request. He had constructed a very cunning contrivance to outwit the enemy and had himself been outwitted. Two more natives deserted.

Sos gave orders for new latrines to be constructed within the compound. It was an admission of defeat but he couldn't take a chance on further casualties. Moreover, the morale of the camp was becoming very low. He knew besides that, accustomed to a routine of killing, the lion would persist in its marauding.

There was no sign of the beast on the second night, but on the third Sos awoke to its movements and was again too late for a shot. The state of his own prestige was becoming critical. Then he conceived his grand idea.

It was impossible to stay awake night after night on the off-chance of a shot, but it was quite conceivable to organize a watch in relays by the men within the compound. A loophole was made in the wall of the kraal, overlooking the latrines. Half a dozen men were detailed in watches through the night. It was now a question of solving the difficulty of passing the information of the enemy's presence to the occupant of the platform on the pylon. It needed scarcely a minute's thought.

A length of strong cord was the answer. One end was to be held by the sentry at the loophole down below, the other end was to be tied round Sos's big toe. When the lion appeared, one sharp tug would rouse the sleeper. There could be nothing simpler, nothing more effective. Sos climbed aloft that night confident of success.

The moon was at the full and no lantern would be necessary. The watch below had been drilled in their duties. Nothing could go wrong. He adjusted the cord, turned in his blankets and under the moonlight went to sleep.

He awoke with an agonizing pain in his right big toe. His foot seemed to have found its way out of the blankets and his leg was outstretched to its limit.

At once he knew that the moment for action had come. He picked up his rifle where it lay by his camp-bed and rose cautiously to his feet. Beneath him he could hear the sinister prowling of the killer. In the full light of the moon he peered over the edge of the platform. The lion was beneath him. As he raised his rifle a second tug on his toe intimated that the sentry below was doing his job most conscientiously.

But it was not a warning tug on the cord, nor a mere jerk. It was a mighty hauling induced no doubt by the panic of the watchers within the camp. The rifle went flying from Sos's hand, his right leg went up, his left foot lost its grip. He fell over the edge of the platform.

As he fell he grasped the edge of the wooden planking and held there perilously for fully half a minute. Beneath him was an ominous snuffling. Then he lost his hold and fell.

He fell on his feet. The compound gate was fast locked. He was face to face with his enemy.

He could see the lion perfectly clearly. It was not half a dozen feet away from him. He could see the gleam of its yellow eyes and the smell of the beast was a stench.

'Get to hell out of this!' roared Sos.

He was extremely angry, because his toe was an agony with the constricting knot, because his plan had ignominiously failed and because he was being made to look a very considerable fool. Added to this, he was indubitably about to pass from this life into the next. So he shouted again.

The lion turned on its tail and disappeared.

It turned and faded into the scrub, and where it had stood in its dreaded strength was now only moonlight. Sos darted towards his stockade and re-climbed it. It took nearly half an hour to untie the knot around his toe, which was badly swollen. For the rest of the night he kept watch. There was no sign of the lion. It never returned again. The Managing Director's reputation was vindicated. The camp settled down to a regular and peaceful routine. The deserters returned, but nobody found any more gold.

Sos found another lion. They seemed to come his way, though his reputation was now established as a mighty hunter.

He had gone further north on the usual tour of inspection and had taken quarters at a chieftain's kraal near the prospecting camp. On the early morning of the day of his arrival he set out on a mule to the mining site, which was a couple of miles away. He had borrowed a carrier, who followed in his wake on foot with Sos's rifle slung over his shoulder. It was a fine morning with a little ground mist.

Their way led through the scrub and Sos let the mule have its head as it ambled along, aware that the animal knew its way better than he did and that the porter at his flank could guide them both. The reins lay loose on the mule's neck and Sos's feet swung loosely in the stirrups.

Then, sensing impending peril of some kind, the mule flung up its head and snorted. Sos could feel it begin to quiver beneath his knees. Then it was on its hind legs, wildly pawing the air with its forelegs and half falling back on its haunches in sudden terror.

Sos was flung over its near wither, sailing not ungracefully through the air till he landed with a crash on the ground just to the right of a high thorn bush. The ground gave way beneath him, being but a covering of branches and brushwood over a deep cavity. He had been flung into a 'game-pit'.[23]

He wasn't alone. There was a lioness in the pit with three cubs.

It was a poorly constructed game-pit, being too shallow for its purpose and with its sides too much on the slope. If the

---

[23] A cavity in the ground covered with brushwood etc., to trap wild animals.

lioness had shown any initiative she could have got out of her trap before. Sos provided the initiative.

He landed fair and squarely on her back. He clung there because he didn't know where he was and what he was doing. With a snarl of terror the lioness leapt from the pit and Sos went with her. They parted company as a second spring brought her to the edge of the bush. It had all happened, including the change of mounts, within a matter of seconds.

There was no sign of the lioness. His mule had bolted and the carrier had fled with his gun. Somewhere near by the lioness might be still possibly on the prowl. He set off for camp as fast as he could on foot.

The carrier was waiting by his hut for him, the rifle was safe and the mule had been caught. Therefore they all set out again with the minimum of delay. There was a day's work ahead.

It was not possible to leave immediately. The news of the episode had gone round the kraal. The chief's eldest son, sent by his father, craved an interview with the hunter. Sos asked him what he wanted. He felt he'd been made to look a fool and he could only blame his own carelessness for the whole affair. He had certainly not cut a very dashing and dignified figure.

'My father has sent me to you, Bwana. Your porter came back before you and he has told us the story of how you plunged into the pit and flung the great lioness out of it. He could bear to watch so great a feat no longer. Such strength and valour Bwana, is unknown in these parts.'

'Who do you take me for?' said Sos. 'Samson?'

'I do not understand those words, Bwana, but you are a great hunter and my father honours you and would make a request of you!'

'What's he want?'

'He wishes you to return to the pit and bring back the cubs.'

At the end of the year Sos was recalled to London to make a report in person to the Board of the Mozambique Oil and Mineral Concessions.

He went before the Board and told them all that he knew. It was a record of disappointment. If the Queen of Sheba had passed that way she hadn't left much behind her.

The Promoter, himself an explorer and prospector, felt he should take the opportunity of presenting the Managing Director as the man on the spot to the shareholders. Sos felt rather like a rabbit that might be taken out of a hat.

The Promoter became quite eloquent at the meeting, presenting Sos, who sat beside him on the platform, as a combination of crusader, saint and pilgrim with possibly a dash of the brigand thrown in to add a slightly piquant flavour.

'Mr Chairman, Ladies and Gentlemen, here sits your Managing Director, Captain Lionel Cohen, who has travelled all the way from our vast and promising territory in Mozambique to tell you how near to prosperity we may be. To be sure, the yields to date, of precious stones, gold and other rare minerals have not come up to expectations. But we are a young concern and our hopes run high. Would it not be churlish to a degree to look askance at the endeavours of our Managing Director and chief prospector?... Mr Chairman, Ladies and Gentlemen, cast your imagination into the gaunt wilderness which, for all our sakes, Captain Cohen has chosen for his domain. What daily dangers does he face? What terrors has he not encountered, nay, is still ready, on our behalf, to encounter? The appalling menace of fever and disease. The threat of extinction by hunger and thirst. The burning tropical sun that can boil a man's brains in his head and the lambent moon that can drive him lunatic.'

The Promoter was warming up very nicely.

'.... the wild beasts of the jungle —' he continued.

'Bush,' said Sos, *sotto voce*.

'I repeat, the ravenous, wild beasts of the jungle, that keep men ever on the watch, the venomous snakes, the barbed-toothed ants, the rivers infested with man-eating sharks —'

'Hey?' said Sos, amazed.

'Shut up.... The man-eating sharks in the jungle, I mean in the bush — what more should we ask of such a man? I ask you, Mr Chairman, Ladies and Gentlemen, what more *can we* ask?'

The figure that rose at the back of the hall had a scarf around his neck and a hat pulled down well over the forehead. A very pink nose peered out over a drooping white moustache.

'Yes, sir,' cried the Promoter. 'I challenge you. What is it you would ask?'

'It's no' a great matter maybe,' said the shareholder. 'And your eloquence is remarkable. But what about the dividends?'

Sos returned to Mozambique and took up the reins again. He was promised a geologist, of some considerable reputation. It would make all the difference.

It did.

There was treasure in Mozambique — maybe there still is — and Professor Goodchild was the man to diagnose the prospectors' findings, with an accuracy and foresight which would prove the case.

Professor Goodchild arrived and Sos made him as comfortable as he could, under canvas in a territory in which the lions still abounded. Professor Goodchild, who was a delightful person, didn't mind in the least about the lions, because he couldn't hear them on their nightly sorties, any more than he could hear Sos. Professor Goodchild was deaf. This affliction added slightly to the difficulties, but possibly a greater one was the thirst that the employed prospectors had developed in the Managing Director's absence.

Professor Goodchild was a religious man. Time and again, on their tours of inspection, he would expound upon the subject. It didn't interest Sos very much, because it all seemed a matter of philosophical speculation, quite unrelated to reality.

And then one night he had a practical experience of the Professor's idiosyncrasies.

It was a very dark night. Both men were sharing a tent in desolate country. Both turned in at the usual time. Professor Goodchild, who had been in the country some months by now, had enlarged once more upon the theory of the Transfiguration. It had all been a little beyond Sos. He was tired and glad to doss down. He awoke suddenly.

After all his years of campaigning and his many vicissitudes in the bush and scrub, he had become accustomed to sudden eventualities. Though the tent was in darkness, there was a light outside. It couldn't be the moon, because the hour was too early. Professor Goodchild's bed was empty. It might, therefore, be Professor Goodchild.

It was.

Sos found him standing in his night clothes outside the tent. He was swinging a hurricane lamp and there was a rapt expression upon his face.

Sos said: 'What the heck?'

But the geologist still kept swinging his light and waved Sos aside.

'For Heaven's sake, come to bed,' said Sos. 'You'll get a chill. And then fever.'

'For what's sake?' said Professor Goodchild, still swinging.

'I said for Heaven's sake —'

'Blasphemy,' said Professor Goodchild, hearing his companion for once. 'Can't you hear the bells?'

'What bells?' said Sos. 'Because you can't hear a thing.'

'The bells of the Infinite,' said Professor Goodchild. 'I am in tune with the Infinite.'

'You're cracked,' said Sos.

'I'm what?'

'You're off your onion.'

'I'm off my what?'

'You're barmy.'

'Did you suggest I am not right in the head?'

'Absolutely,' said Sos. 'You're mad.'

Professor Goodchild lowered the lantern to the ground.

'The only sensible thing', he said, 'which I've ever heard you say.'

Two days later he was an inmate of the hospital of the Scotch Mission near Malema.

Within the year the Mozambique Oil and Mineral Concessions Company was wound up.

Sos stayed in Mozambique and started cotton-planting at Sangage, near Angoche. He did very well and was, moreover, appointed British Vice-Consul in Angoche. Then the bottom fell out of the cotton market. He thought it was time to go home.

He left Africa for England in 1926. He returned for a brief visit in 1945, when he received on the 8th of November of that year the Freedom of the City of Bulawayo. As the *Athlone Castle* approached Durban, she ran up, above the ensign which she had been flying, the blue Rhodesian ensign together with the Union Castle flag, in honour of her distinguished passenger. It was probably the first time the Rhodesian flag had ever been flown at sea.

The house on the hill, at Slinfold in Sussex, was aptly enough called 'Hill'. It wasn't at all like Tankerville House, which was gaunt, or that other at Highgate, which was unfamiliar. To begin with it was Sos's own house and quite beautiful. He had his wife and two children with him. The years from 1927 onwards were happy and prosperous.

He joined a firm on the London Stock Exchange, in the capacity of a *remercier*. He owned at 'Hill' a herd of pedigree Guernsey cows, bred pigs, and entertained his friends. He also owned a string of race-horses.

It was all very pleasant. The house stood on a sharp little hill, overlooking a wooded valley with a stream at the bottom of it. The people in the village were kindly country people, and the church lay back, sleeping in an angle of the lane that led to the private road to 'Hill'.

Slinfold had been like this for all the turbulent centuries, and it was delightful after the turmoil of the City to walk in the fields that belonged to him, to inspect the cattle and listen to what the foreman had to say; to hear in the winter months the sound of the horn and the music of hounds; to be home again. So — after all these years — Eldorado?

Not yet, perhaps.

There was trouble in Europe. It had been boiling up for years. People wouldn't recognize it, because they didn't want to.

Munich!

Chamberlain waving a fatuous bit of paper on an airfield, and a hysterical House of Commons cheering because there wouldn't be any war. Anyway hadn't the Germans only got tanks made of cardboard? Any fool who'd seen them march into Czechoslovakia knew that!

Nineteen thirty-nine. That year of grace. 'Their finest hour.'

But they couldn't keep Sos out of the Royal Air Force, because he'd already contrived a commission through the Volunteer Reserve which he had helped to form.

So — *au revoir* to 'Hill'! A little time away, just once again. What was it to be sixty-four years of age, when the evergreen of youth still thrived within the mind?

1944: FINALE

Henry must at last have decided to come in, because he had just given his instructions:

'Straps on. I'm coming in to land. Take stations for crash-landing.'

Sos had taken station and fastened his strap. They had been circling away from the aerodrome at two thousand feet for the last half-hour in order to reduce their fuel as far as possible. Nevertheless, there would still be enough in the tanks to burn them.

What a beastly death! There was something obscene about it. It was agonizing and hideous and what was left was loathsome to look upon, and burning men smelt of roast pork. Sometimes, though, God was merciful and a man was suffocated and gassed before the torment began.

God was merciful. What on earth — or Heaven? — did he know about God, except that there was Something There? It was just the same half-conceived theories as Joseph of the magnificent moustaches had tried to implant in him about the Successful Man, or poor old Noakes with his philosophy of Square-Pushing and Booze, or half a hundred of the other half-baked conceits of the knowledgeable man of the world about the Ones that Do, and the Ones that Don't. What on earth — or Heaven? — did it all amount to? In a very few minutes one way or another it would be all over.

Down below everything would be in readiness for them. The flare-path would be on and the Chance Light ready. The fire-engine would be at the edge of tarmac engines running and the crew in their places. Beside it the 'blood-wagon' would be started up with the driver in his seat and the duty Medical Officer already beside him. In the Watch Office, the Flying Control Officer would probably find the Station Commander beside him, having heard as he passed through Operations Room that there was a 'flap on'.

And Sos thought that God had given him life, and now, after sixty-nine years, God might take it away from him. From a comparative stranger then, Praise be to God! Praise for all things! Praise for sixty-nine years of crowded life and the many paths of life he had trodden; for the burning tropic skies and the starry nights; for galloping hoofs in the scrub and the golden gleam of the campside fire; for the virgin bush and the teeming reef; for the calm and sun-kissed waters of the bay and the crash of the surf on the bar; for Sussex meadows and the lowing kine; for good men and bad men, little men and men of great heart; for all comrades; for women who kissed and ran away and for that other that remained for always, an image in the heart; for joy and disaster, for sorrow and high laughter; for the Eldorado, found at last in Henry's soul and all young men of his kind; for everything that was good, and bad, and indifferent, in all the glorious total of life. Praise be to God for His unspeakable gifts!

The sudden pressure of the safety belt as it took his weight nearly winded him. Then quite suddenly everything was most astonishingly quiet. There wasn't a sound at all. Then the croaking, crackling voice of the 'inter-com' came again, asking if everyone was all right and to get out quick.

Sos got out. The ambulance was there and the fire-crew were ready and a dispersal lorry was 'revving up' nearby. The night wind was cold on his face, biting fresh and very sweet. Sweet, he thought, as life itself.

He went with his crew to the Operations Room and they made their 'quick report'. Then they went across to the mess.

The fried eggs were extremely good. He supposed that they would have been just as good to anyone else, if he hadn't been there to eat them.

Some of the chaps must have been out in the neighbouring town, because there were now several of them coming down the corridor to the mess-room. The Engineer Officer and the Station Adjutant and several others.

They joined Sos and Henry at their table. The Adjutant was in a convivial mood.

He said to Sos: 'Been out with the Plumber. He drinks like a fish. In point of fact the fishes are now saying that they drink like a Plumber. Did you have a good trip?'

'So-so,' said Sos.

'No accidents?'

'Nothing to speak of.'

'Good,' said the Station Adjutant. 'Now you'll have a little drink with me and I'll tell you why. If you tell anybody else what I'm going to say to you, I shall get the sack, so keep your old trap shut. But the powers that be seem to take a good view of you. Maybe because you're like a cat with nine lives.'

'I was once bitten by a green mamba,' said Sos.

'I,' said the Station Adjutant darkly, 'was once bitten by a barmaid, so that's nothing. But what I wanted to say is that your D.F.C. has come through tonight and I want to be the first to congratulate you.'

A NOTE TO THE READER

If you have enjoyed this book enough to leave a review on **Amazon** and **Goodreads**, then we would be truly grateful.
The Estate of Anthony Richardson

Sapere Books is an exciting new publisher of brilliant fiction and popular history.

To find out more about our latest releases and our monthly bargain books visit our website: **saperebooks.com**

Printed in Great Britain
by Amazon

39424981R00169